Paddy Kelly

AMERICAN RHETORIC

FICTION4ALL

A FICTION4ALL PAPERBACK

© Copyright 2017
Paddy Kelly

The right of Paddy Kelly to be identified as author of this work has been asserted by him in accordance with the Copyright, Designs and Patents Act 1988

All Rights Reserved

No reproduction, copy or transmission of the publication may be made without written permission. No paragraph of this publication may be reproduced, copied or transmitted save with the written permission of the publisher, or in accordance.with the provisions of the Copyright Act 1956 (as amended).

Any person who does any unauthorised act in relation to this publication may be liable to criminal prosecution and civil claims for damages.

ISBN 978-1-78695-114-4

Cover Designed by:
Paddy Kelly

Edited by:
Katherine Mary Kennedy, B.A.

This Edition Published 2017
Fiction4All
www.fiction4all.com

Acknowledgments

First and foremost I must thank CNN, CBS, NBC, ABC and Fox News, all members of what we now call the 'Mainstream media', for exercising their rights under the First Amendment to continually broadcast 'news' stories so distorted from actual fact that they have easily kept pace with the wild and fantastical tales of the Trump administration.

When that awful practical joke of a poorly rehearsed, traveling road show of a circus known as the RNC, came to town back in 2016, many believed it to be a low point in the history of American politics.

However when it was then followed up in July of that same year by the ultimate prank played on the U.S. electorate to date, the other circus headlined as the DNC, the near universal impression became; how much lower can we sink?

Combined with both political parties neglect in treating the electoral process with the seriousness and dignity it requires, the system has devolved into a joke.

The joke? What do you get when you cross a sociopathic repeat felon with a Reality TV show clown?

We are seeing the punch line played out.

Without the concerted efforts of these two entities, the mainstream press and the two U.S. parties, and their headlong pursuit to play one-upmanship with the truth, the material in this book would never have been possible.

Dedication

This work is dedicated to those most adversely affected by the wreckage of the broken political system in the U.S. – the American electorate.

AMERICAN RHETORIC

AMERICAN RHETORIC

Based on true events which are yet to occur

"In the federal government we have a two party system. The Democratic Party, which is a party of no ideas. And the Republican Party, which is a party of bad ideas. By the federal government I mean republicans and democrats working together. And the only thing dumber than a republican or a democrat is when these pricks work together!"

Louis Black

IF 'PRO' IS THE OPPOSITE OF 'CON', THEN WHAT'S THE OPPOSITE OF PROGRESS?

THE CURRENT STATE OF AFFAIRS

**11:26, Friday, August 11.
The not too distant future.**

CHAPTER ONE

Ж

AMERICAN society had shifted in the intervening years since, having her prison record expunged by presidential decree, Helen Cliton had been appointed Secretary of State and Ronald Lump the Third, Great-Great Grandson of the New York real-estate baron, had, after changing the law, won his fourth consecutive White House term.

The last of the law suits following the mass suicide fad which had swept the nation after Helen's Great-Great Aunt Hillary had lost the election had finally been settled.

Lump, on the other hand, had managed to finally tackle the fact that 3% of Americans owned or directly controlled 97% of the wealth of that country.

Through sheer dint of effort, plenty of hard work, tireless campaigning efforts and unprecedented cooperation in both the House and the Senate, he was able to whittle that 3% down to 1%.

Legislation was in the pipeline to tackle that annoying little 1% as soon as Congress could raise the funds to clean up the miles and miles of unused bricks, mortar and scaffolding littering the highways, roads and prairie land along the U.S.-Mexican border.

Cruising overhead in one of the new multi-billion dollar hovercrafts, (which cost just under $125,000 to build) and which reduced the trans-continental voyage from New New York to Lost Angeles, no longer part of the 60th state, from three and a half hours to three hours and eleven minutes, President Lump could see that much of the landscape was still dotted with two story split levels, ranch homes and tasteless prefabricated houses like the kind seen all over Texas, Louisiana and most of the Bible Belt. But factories more or less dominated the land mass of most of America. All of course except for Arkansas, after all no one wanted to live there before the ECOLI, why would anyone go there now?

In a radically changing world it was comforting to know some traditions remained.

The overall map of the country had changed as well. Several of the northern states had been sold to Canada to raise revenue for the Twelfth Annual Congressional Bailout while the Hawaiian Islands now belonged to the Chinese having been traded for a treaty where-by the Chinese government agreed to stop hacking U.S. technology, stealing America's industrial plans and selling them to the largest country in the world the Ukraino-Russia Federation. Some found an odd poetic justice in this seeing as it was primarily Asian and Eastern European engineers who, although hired by the Americans, actually designed and built most of that technology.

This massive sell-off of real estate was generally accepted as part of the cause of what people now referred to as the Great Economic Collapse of Industry.

ECOLI for short.

To maintain the status quo and allow the random but steady price inflation the western world had come to rely on to motivate its economy, the citizens of the U.S. and now most of the rest of the world, had come also to depend on artificially manufactured food stuffs produced by multi-international conglomerates such as Consolidated Refined Agricultural Products which boasted over 500 facilities nation-wide processing, manufacturing and distributing CRAP products throughout the world.

SPAM Plus was one of their biggest money makers.

There were other changes too.

For example various social sub-orders had arisen and were branded with certain names, names propagated largely by the pop press through NewsCorps. These names became a convenient way to refer to the few remaining groups of people with political opinions, people who had not completely given up on the political system altogether. A political system which had grown like a mold on six month old Gouda as it crept across the land.

Collectively these people were known as the Logics.

The smallest of the Logics was the group who based their political viewpoints and opinions on logic, reasoning and established knowledge.

They were legally banned from public speaking when, one year when a Logical speaker, a physics professor, tried to explain gravity at a famous university. His explanation was dismissed as patriarchal ad riots broke out.

This Logical group was sarcastically labelled by the press as 'The Knowitalls'. They were so small a group that more people had claimed to have seen Bigfoot then to have actually met a Logical.

NewsCorps was the consolidated news wire service, which controlled and was the sole nation-wide supplier of info-tainment. What people used to call the 'news'.

T.V. execs found that ratings tripled when they mixed reality T.V. with news broadcasts and so info-tainment was born.

The president and corporate CEO of NewsCorps, Lush Limburger, Ph.D., (an honorary award), through his broadcasts had coined and there-by sanctioned most of the monikers now in common use.

'NewsCorps; Lush with the slush!' Could be heard dozens of times a day on radios, televisions and monitors across the nation.

Skilled at broadcasting in only two emotions, anger and indignation, combined with his 'clever' labelling of opposing political groups was considered the primary reason Limburger was consistently voted *News Man of the Year* by the United Associated Press International or the UAPI.

The UAPI, an organization which maintained their name despite the fact the title, *News Man of the Year*, could only be awarded to a member of the American press who was an active member of the UAPI, were the primary fundraisers for the Lush Limburger Program.

All foreign generated news was highly restricted and could only be accessed if an American was out of the country or on vacation in exotic places like Toronto or Detroit, which now belonged to Canada which meant one needed a passport to go there which in turn meant that few Americans went there.

Subsisting largely on hate rhetoric and creating discontent in those of lower mentality, Limburger's eight hour daily show focused largely on casting aspersions at the likes of *Doctors Without Borders*, (who he branded as 'bleeding heart socialists'), teachers, ('liberal morons'), and Planned Parenthood, ('condoms are the root of all the problems in our education system!') He particularly railed against Planned Parenthood because he argued, due to the fact they encouraged young people to use condoms they were the primary propagators of unsafe sex. Bumper stickers proclaiming: "CONDOMS CILL!!" could be had free of charge from Limburger's radio studios.

Limburger had his favorites too, like the Blinders.

These were the ones in the country who were shackled with the philosophy that the U.S., without reservation, was the greatest country in the world, despite the fact it was fourth in economic production behind China, Russia and Brazil, 26th on the U.N's *Safest Places to Live* list and 47th overall in education.

When cornered as to the flaws in the 'America is the greatest country' approach, the Blinder's comeback was, 'Maybe it's not a perfect system but it's the best imperfect system in the world.' Finally when confronted by the facts of their government's broken legal and judicial system, their homerun swing was, 'It's not a perfect system, but it's the best we got.'

As the democrats spent more and more money on gun control and the republicans more and more on fire arms promotion, there were dwindling amounts for less important social programs such as education and medicine.

As a result, the failing I.Q.'s of the nation's students was more than just an international embarrassment, it had become a real social problem compounded by the fact that 68% tested couldn't point out the U.S. on a standard map, (half even when it was labelled).

However, it was the teachers who suffered the most.

When the teacher's mandatory, unpaid five month Summer holidays became law, and their wages were reduced accordingly, some quit or were forced to take second jobs such as sanitation technicians in the factories. Those with higher degrees could find work as waste disposal collection engineers for the food service or housekeeping industries.

Parents and relatives did what they could to help the teachers by going down to the Federal Unified Collection points and donating canned food, old bits of clothing and slightly used body armor or bullet resistant clothing. These latter items had become popular when school shootings had been elevated to a national past time by the popular reality game show *Classroom Body Count*. However, despite such irresistible perks such as free body armor, the attrition rates of the teachers back to the factories and other industries had reached an all-time high.

Another side effect of the dilapidated education system was the gradual deterioration of the language itself.

Wiked-Period, the online ensikloopedea, had come to be the last word in academic reference, despite the fact there were no redundant checks on the information posted and anybody could pretty much write and post anything they wanted. Even though most of those who wrote on-line information sites could no longer write very well, especially after the highly publicized Wong Case.

Michelle Wong, an undergraduate student at Cal Tech, submitted her undergrad thesis entirely in text speak. When the department chair failed her, she resorted to that most American of cure-alls, she sued. In separate but equal law suits she sued the state, sued the university, the college, the department, the department chair, her professor and the librarian for referring her to a volume entitled, *A Hndbk For Txt Abrvs*.

As U.S. law is predicated primarily on *stare decisis*, or precedent, after she won the first case she won all the other cases. On the seven figure settlement she abandoned her studies in English Literature and her goal to teach English at Harvard and retired to the former Hawaiian island of Oahu, now New Beijing, where she sits in the sun sipping Mai Tais and texting her 600 cousins.

As most of the computer programmers who worked in the industry had little or no English, this made things difficult for the less than 37,000 native speakers of English, who were still left in the U.S., mostly sprinkled around the central states.

These events had in turn impacted so heavily on the nation that not only had the language itself suffered, but it was impossible to get a ham sandwich, a hot dog or a cup of coffee anywhere in the United States if all you spoke was Standard American English, as Spanglish was now the official national language.

The demise of the English language was not sudden but gradual over a period of several generations with changes thought to be too small or insignificant to matter. For example, as there were only three grammatical articles in the language, these were the first casualties of the undeclared war.

The Brits had long ago ceased using 'the' for most things uttering phrases such as, "Me mother's in 'ospital, again! Costin' me arm in a leg so it is! Inconsiderate bitch!"

If you could get over the fact that they spoke as if they had stones in their mouths and lived in deathly fear of dropping one and you could hack your way through any of the thousands of their cryptic dialects, you would find they were a fairly intelligible people. However Americans, being enamored, (enamored), with the British accent soon followed suit and communication suffered further.

The Aussies, Kiwis and South Africans hadn't fared much better in terms of preserving English. Having been isolated so long from the rest of civilization they had developed what they mistakenly believed to be their own form of 'proper' English.

What with 'roo' for kangaroo, 'bottling his bloods worth' to mean someone who was very helpful and 'G'day' for hello with 'Hooroo' for good-bye, people in the civilized countries were generally dumbfounded at how, beyond sex and eating, people below the equator communicated at all.

Except for the persistent inability to pronounce the word 'out', or any derivation with the vowel combination of O and U, the Canadians remained relatively unaffected as, not wanting to cause trouble, they were game to go along with anything everybody else said.

Prepositions were the next to be infected with the communicative cancer which insidiously metastasized until nearly all of these linking words had been eaten away save for a few such as 'to', now spelled exclusively 'too', too include the number, too.

Fifteen after eight, for example became just "fifteen eight". The confusion caused by fifteen before or until eight as opposed to after eight was eliminated by saying, "It is forty-five minutes seven." Which in turn, of course, meant that times like seven twenty had to be said to be forty minutes six.

All this, predictably, wreaked havoc on daylight savings time which, due to the economy, people only had to work a three to four hour work day anyway, and so was simply eliminated.

The U. S. GNP hit rock bottom.

So, much like the Celtic peoples who, thousands of years ago had been split into several nations, lost contact with one another and quickly fell into a situation whereby, even though they all spoke the Celtic language, they were completely unable to communicate with one another giving us the Welsh, Scots and Irish, the people who came to temporarily occupy Nurtheren Urop and the Amerikas, the English speaking, Anglo peoples drifted further apart.

Ж

Every school student of course knows about these events. You get all this when you take Chemercology in high school. Chemistry, Biology and American History combined, a course favored by most school districts to save money by hiring only one teacher in lieu of three.

Also since no one could pass high school chemistry

or biology and history was eliminated as a serious area of study and struck from the curriculum during the Olson Twins Administration. few now know of the bleak back story of how the country of The United States of America arrived at the situation in which it currently found itself. Allow me to elucidate.

(For members of the G.O.P. or D.N.C., that means: to explain.)

THE BB STACKERS

CHAPTER TWO

※

Middleville, Ohio could, in reality, be called an average American town. Some would label it middle of the road, run of the mill or politically centrist. It was all of these. At least by average standards.

People went to work, paid their mortgages, medical bills and grocery bills. They took out second mortgages to pay for the school tuitions for their kids so that they too could graduate college. Graduate college and get jobs, buy houses, pay their mortgages and in turn have kids they could send off to school, be disappointed in and who would grow up to resent them.

All this, of course, was done on credit.

Ever since the onset of the Economic Collapse of Industry, ECOLI for short, the good citizens of Middleville dutifully supported American industry by buying Japanese and German cars so folks like the United Auto Workers could still get their government mandated subsidy payments to keep the U.S. economy afloat and prevent it from collapsing altogether.

The subsidy was needed so that the United Auto Workers rank and file could still show up at the near empty factories, turn on the lights, oil the rusting machinery, rearrange the office furniture and sweep and mop the floors before closing up for the afternoon. This of course only took the massive work force a few hours each day but following the complete collapse of negotiations between the government appointed negotiators and the UAW union reps, under President

Oboomboom, fifteen hours a week was all the time the factory workers were willing to put in.

Other industries hadn't fared as well.

The farmers, for instance, who now in spite of only comprising 1.3% of the population but thanks to scientific advancements, were producing 100% of all the food for the country with an annual surplus of between 35 to 37%. Said scientific advancements however, had been largely mishandled by the former Paris Hilton administration, the first female president of the United States.

Though she had been legally elected on the imaginary 'Glass Ceiling' platform and served her full term, Helen Cliton had been disqualified as the first female president by *The Guinness Book of World Records* on the grounds that her actual gender could never be officially confirmed. Even when her brigade of lawyers argued that gender was a patriarchal construct.

The nation's farmers, thanks to negotiations led by the Republican controlled People Who Plant Things in the Ground for a Living Union, were paid to destroy all their excess crops.

Donating the millions of tons of excess wheat, barley and flax to the starving of the third world nations was voted down in Congress on the premise that it was a step towards socialism which, as everybody knew was the first step on the road to communism. Consequently, the logic went, those poor unfortunates of the Third World would only come to depend on the unlimited generosity of the good people of the U.S. of A. and therefore would never be motivated enough to develop their own, independent farming industries.

Burning the crops and letting a few foreign populations starve to death was, logically speaking, for their own good.

In fairness Congress had however, passed an appropriations bill where-by said, starving third world countries could purchase their own farm and factory equipment from the U.S. on a kind of lend-lease arrangement. After all such a scheme had worked before.

The generosity of the Congress even extended so far as to offer to offset the multi-trillion dollar price tag for the equipment by extending the lease over a 500 year period so as to make the payments smaller.

Ж

It was here in Central Middleville there resided a humble factory worker, Thaddeus Enoch Pervers.

Pervers was a tall man, so tall that in all the years since finishing the eighth grade no house he ever inhabited had seen or owned a stepladder. In fact when his public school, pubescent peers had all found part time employment with delivery jobs or paper routes, young Thaddeus earned his weekend movie money by changing light bulbs in neighbor's houses or retrieving stranded cats from low hanging tree branches.

'Stilts', 'Tall Boy' and 'Ichabod Crane' were but a few of the derogatory insults suffered by young Pervers as a school boy. His mother thought of him as more of an Abraham Lincoln. His father, unfamiliar with B. F. Skinner's theoretical concepts of child encouragement and himself of average height, didn't involve himself much in the young boy's school affairs.

Thaddeus' seventeen inch shoes had to be handmade and since all the trades in America had died off years ago, replaced by imported goods, it was only by the skilled cobblers in Mexico that he was able to buy footwear. As a consequence his bedroom closet was always stocked with no less than fourteen pairs of shoes. Shoes for all occasions. Informal, formal, semi-formal. School, casual, and recreational. Recreations such as basketball, a sport in which he eventually found it impossible to find opponents to play against.

He nearly never ate large full meals but took his food as nature and natural selection had intended for all mammals, eating multiple small feedings throughout the day. His constant but innocuous munching annoyed some, but all-in-all was the only manner in which he could derive any culinary pleasure, that is from small but frequent meals.

His wife, in contrast, a short stout woman, grazed constantly throughout the day.

This contrast in morphology caused Thaddeus to quietly keep the framed picture of his tall slender self and his short, plump wife in his nightstand drawer rather than on display. Standing side-by-side one was reminded of the Italian first person singular or the fourth moon of Jupiter, Io.

Thaddeus worked as a Steenberger micro heating unit calibrator for the Brubaker Ball Bearing Corporation, in Brubaker, Ohio. The Brubaker Manufacturing, one of the country's dozen corporations which owned the thousands of factories that now crowded the American landscape, had the world-wide contract to manufacture the ball bearings for the failsafe mechanisms in automobile safety belts.

It was Thaddeus's job to carefully regulate the temperature in the micro oven of the von Rollen machine which produced the calcium carbonate necessary to produce the mineral Arsonol which was needed to polish the seatbelt bearings to within the .0001 mm required so that they could fall into the little slots in the slotted locking mechanism which, on the car's impact, would lock the belt in place and save the driver and/or passenger's life.

Due to the new laser activated anti-collision sensors and the improved air bags installed in every car that now rolled off the automated lines, a mechanism which shut down and diverted any vehicle on a collision course with anything, the ball bearing mechanisms at Brubaker had become redundant and no longer served any purpose. They were as useful as a leaky boat in a storm. Tits on a bull. A democrat and a republican trying to agree on a congressional bill.

Useless.

But because Brubaker was the nephew of an uncle twice removed of the district Republican representative, he was allowed to keep his factories. For an annual contribution to the appropriate political cause of course.

Thaddeus was neither political nor apolitical. He wasn't a liberal nor was he a conservative. He was never sure what a NeoCon was so he had no interest in being one of those. Back in high school he had read how Communists, although they had devised a secret way to breed their children without the horns and forked tails most Americans had heard about, they in fact did used to have them at one time. Mostly back in the Nineteen Fifties.

He had no blood relations in the Republican Party that he knew of, and so couldn't engage in sexual relations with them to earn his party card in the GOP. Therefore the certified incest requirement to become a member of the Republican Party was an iron clad barrier.

He had also read up on Democrats and how they were always speechin' about 'the people' and 'helping the people' and 'doing things for the people' which sounded a lot like watered down communism to Thaddeus. Due to this and the fact that he read somewhere most of the money the Dems collected in taxes to help other people was unaccounted for, he decided not to grow up to be a Democrat.

Thus, back during his secondary education, when exploring political parties as possibilities in which to spend his parenthood once he reached the age of procreation, he came across nothing that attracted him. So he moved on to other pursuits content in the knowledge that he hadn't completely wasted those thirty-seven minutes that afternoon in the school library and still had time to go home and play a couple of hours of GTA.

He was particularly excited that day because version, 87 had just been released by CRAP Games Inc.

Thus Thaddeus had grown up with no strong political feelings, leanings or inclinations in any real direction which his friends or family could ever discern. To this day he didn't read either of the national newspapers, listen to the national radio station and only passively followed any of the major league games of football or baseball.

He had no interest in cars, as many young boys do, but he learned to drive just as SUV's were no longer practical and fell from their place of prestige in the middle class as the American soccer craze died down. After all, soccer was a European sport which they called football, and football without using your hands had always been considered a little suspicious to many Americans. Too socialist by their reckoning which was borderline communist c.

Thaddeus' wife, Prudence and he had a seventeen year old son. Due to the fact that tangerine flavored Jell-O was Prudence's favorite food, they named their son Taranjello. Had he been born a girl she would have been named Orangejello for his father's favorite food.

Taranjello was a good kid but his incessant bumbling was lovingly mistaken by his parents for hidden potential. Like the time he accidently overheard his father complaining about the skyrocketing cost of gasoline and so decided to help out by filling the gas tank with water. To save on buying more gas. So his dad could get to work.

This bumbling at times was costly but his hidden genius, his parents fervently believed, would no doubt manifest itself when the time was right. After all it was probably only a mere 15 to 16 year phase he was going through.

Now married and having made the Potential Future Homeowner's List in the government's Office of Residence Registry, the Pervers would have a place of their own soon. Just as soon as someone died and a home came open so they could have their name entered in the annual lottery. They currently awaited word for an interview but as the main office of the O.R.R. in Middleville had been shut down due to lack of available rental space, there was still no word.

Even though funding had run out for the Republican sponsored San Diego to Houston barrier wall project and Americans were flooding over the border into the Free Republic of Mexico, housing was still scarce.

This good news about the potential to win the lottery provided some comfort to the Pervers because with the allotted 1.5 children, the one room apartment they shared was getting more and more crowded. The .5 meant the Pervers had also made the waiting list to have a second child should the first born prove too intelligent, too productive, or threaten to make a meaningful contribution to society without proper government approval.

However, it was decided, after Taranjello's last school IQ evaluation, there would probably not be a second child.

Overall Thaddeus Enoch Pervers led a normal, Middleville existence. Thaddeus's life was abnormally normal to the point people would comment at parties and functions about the Pervers.

"I hope we never become that normal!" They would remark. To which the person they were with would usually reply, "Yeah, that's abnormal! I'm glad we're just normally normal!"

Except for his Friday night double American cheese-food burger with a side order of American

Freedom fries and a Diet Coke Extra Lite, at the local Bowl-A-Rama where his team, The BB Stackers, would practice for the thrice yearly, bi-annual Bowl Off, life was almost painfully normal.

The BB Stackers, Thaddeus, Joe, Bob and Fred were all sons of former assembly line workers back when the factories were still operational. They came by their jobs, in this time of record unemployment, through adherence of the hard hat mentality passed down to them by their grandfathers through their fathers and which they would in turn faithfully pass on to their children. Tradition was still held as a sacred value by these simple folk and therefore not subject to violation by influx of so called 'progressive' ideas.

"200 proud years of tradition unaffected by change or progress!" was the proud motto of the Beaver Lodge, proud sponsors of The BB Stackers, Thaddeus, Joe, Bob and Fred's proud bowling team. And to prove it a huge beaver was proudly spread wide across the backs of their baby blue and gold, silk bowling shirts.

They were some proud beavers.

It was just past half past eight one Friday evening down at the Bowl-O-Rama and Joe had just bowled his fifth consecutive strike which boosted his score to 150 and put him even with Thaddeus, Bob and Fred. Feeling a bit thirsty, and in an unusual deviation from the norm, Thaddeus decided on a second Diet Coke Extra Lite.

He excused himself from the bench where he sat next to Fred, across from where Joe sat next to Bob, where they always sat, and meandered up to the snack bar next door in the Greek Diner.

He was compelled to stand in line as several members of the Youth for Change in America were ahead of him. The YFCA were having their monthly mixer.

They were a non-political youth organization designed to inform young people of how the American political system worked. Essentially the group encouraged the youngsters not to waste their youth trying to change things that couldn't be changed. That could be done later by somebody else.

"Old age and treachery will always overcome youth and enthusiasm!" read the motto on the backs of their jackets.

As he stood in line he overheard a couple of Blinders in the booth next to him discussing the latest NewsCorp broadcast emanating from the big screen, vapor T.V. hovering above the door to the men's toilet.

Although most of the country was occupied watching one of the popular reality or game shows at that hour, some like those in the El Greco Greek Diner which occupied the east half of the Bowl-A-Rama, were watching the Eight O'clock NewsCorps Info-tainment Show. The smartly appointed studio set, from where the show was being broadcast, featured a well groomed, well lighted and well quaffed, perfectly postured digital announcer with just a touch of grey to add respectability. With a Walter Cronkite -like staccato voice he was announcing an announcement.

The twelfth consecutive twenty-five year ban on the findings of the Warren Commission have finally expired and the results were today given to a senate sub-committee which has released its findings.

CUT TO: Massachusetts Senator Edward Kennedy the 17th standing at a dais in the Senate. He spoke with a thick Bostonian dialect.

On closer examination of theCIA's enhancement of the Zapruder film and accompanying testimony it has been determined that the JFK assassination mystery has been solved!

It has been determined that President John F. Kennedy actually shot himself!

The tragic accident occurred while the president was apparently mishandling a side arm which belonged to one of his Secret Service body guards. This conclusion is based on the evidence that the bullet entered the president's head from the front, exited the back and made a measurable bullet-sized hole, in the head.

The Zapruder film clearly shows, at the moment he is shot, the Glock 9mm being thrown from the president's hand and that is when, through quick, split second thinking and cat-like reflexes, Jackie Kennedy, the President's alleged, espoused wife, climbed out and onto the back of the limousine to retrieve the weapon.

RETURN TO STUDIO:

There you have it! Conclusive evidence indeed that the wrong man, Lee Harvey Oswald was unjustly executed by Jack Ruby, no doubt a government agent hired by the CIA, for the murder of our thirty-fifth president, John Fitzgerald Kennedy.

"I knew it, I knew, I knew!" A Dweeble Head yelled through a mouth full of Freedom Fries and cheese burger from the back of the diner, "Didn't I tell you it was suicide all along, Bert?!" He elbowed the diner next to him who nodded several times in quick succession.

"You told us it was suicide all along Marv! Yeah ya did, you told us!" Bert in turn elbowed the slightly drunk guy next to him in the booth. "He told us it was suicide all along didn't he Herb?" Herb, in a drunken stupor, just grunted and fell over on his side.

Dweeble Heads were an experimental bunch who had accidentally escaped the genetics labs of the

GenCorp company, a division of Consolidated Refined Agricultural Products, who at the time were attempting to find a cure for Anti-evolutionism. This disease, according to researchers is characterised by a limited ability to think for one's self, score above a six year old level in any sort of logic based exam or contribute to society in any meaningful way. Through years of research this disorder had eventually been traced to the affected individual's inner conscious which apparently develops a capacity to deeply and emotionally believe the most ridiculous, far-fetched shit anyone can dream up.

Anti-evolutionism had its roots in Supremeism, a cult founded by a former Scientologist who started out as a talentless movie star who soon discovered he could attract a larger audience through the Dweeble Heads with his far-fetched action movies, most of which were sequels of re-makes. These people, for example, believed that Amelia Earhart was actually a secret agent working for the U.S. government when she crashed and was captured by the Japanese, brain washed, turned into a man and later returned to the U.S. after the war as Richard Simmons, the illegitimate father of Lady GaGa.

Anti-evolutionism was now characterized as a psychological disorder brought on by Supremeism, an apparently genetic disease suffered by individuals who possessed the 'R' gene and who were related to or descendants of those who were previously, but politely, referred to as being 'religious'.

The 'R' word was no longer used in polite company.

Research at the labs continued unabated in other areas.

Since research costs money, reason dictated it was only logical the scientists concentrate their efforts on the areas people were most willing to pay the big bucks for. So over the years the most urgent of mankind's problems such as safer and larger breast implants, the correction of erectile dysfunction and penis enlargement had become the biggest areas of concentrated study.

With a degree in Breastology or Penis and Vaginal Studies one was guaranteed steady work for a lifetime at top dollar. Scientists, with advanced degrees in Sexology, proved very good at their job and as a consequence *The Guinness Book of World Records* currently listed the largest penis, which now belonged to a Jewish accountant by the name of Hershel Hirshbaum from Hoboken, New Jersey at thirty-seven and one half inches, flaccid.

Of course this rendered Mr. Hirshbaum unable to walk, get around on his own or engage in sexual intercourse, (at least with a human). So by way of compensation the government had granted Mr. Hirshbaum tax free status on the $20 fee he charged visitors and tourists to view the "Hershel & The Beanstalk." at a small tent set up in his back yard.

For an additional ten dollars one could have an autographed photo inscribed 'May you live Long and prosper'.

No accurate measurement had been recorded for the largest, artificially enhanced breasts as the subjects keep dying. Usually in their sleep, of suffocation.

On return to the his bowling lane with his drink Thaddeus thought about telling the rest of his friends about the discovery that President Kennedy had actually killed himself, but by the time he reached his seat at the lane where the other BB Stackers were, it had slipped his mind.

A TYPICAL WORK DAY

CHAPTER THREE

Ж

That Monday morning Thaddeus sat at his factory station doing what he was paid to do which today was nothing. That is nothing for the most of his 3.752 hour shift.

However, thirty minutes later, as he peered down the 350 yard long factory floor, (The U.S. had still failed to be able to adopt to the metric system), to the loading docks and saw a large dump truck backing into Bay Seventeen, he knew a new shipment of recycled but unused ball bearings had just came in and it would only take about twenty minutes until they were re-melted down and liquefied, re-purified and fed along the line to where he sat.

He patiently waited as the truck driver dumped his load into chute number 17 adjacent to Bay Seventeen, retracted the big box-like, holder thingy on the back of the truck and pulled away.

He listened and waited as the melter thingy under the floor commenced doing what a melter thingy does, namely melting things, and then waited a little bit more until the melter thingy gurgled its load into the feeder thingy which connected to the raise-it-up what's-ya-ma-call-it and fed the load into the hoses which led to his precisely calibrated, laser guided, computer programmed Steenberger micro heating unit mounted on the German, precision engineered von Rollen machine.

Thaddeus didn't know the names of the machines which preceded his, nor did he know the names or functions of the machines which followed his. Everyone at Brubaker Industries only knew one job and so only one machine. Their own. It was never deemed necessary by management to cross train anyone or for anybody to know anyone else's job. Also it was considered a health and safety risk by the unions. If everyone knew everyone else's job, that would allow management to use any worker to fill in if someone were suspended or fired. From the union's standpoint that was dangerous.

A green light flashed on his control panel and it was time for Thaddeus to do his job carefully regulating the temperature in the micro oven of the von Rollen machine by adjusting the thermostatic controls on the heads-up display in front of him to generate the calcium carbonate necessary to produce the mineral Arsonol which was needed to polish the new, carbon steel, soon-to-be-recycled seatbelt ball bearings to within the .0001 mm required so that they could fall into the little slots in the slotted locking mechanism which, on the car's impact, would lock the belt in place and save the driver and/or passenger's life.

This despite the fact that these mechanisms, due to the new laser activated anti-collision sensors installed in every car which now rolled off the automated line, which shut down and diverted any vehicle on a collision course with virtually anything, had become redundant and no longer served any purpose.

But Brubaker had a cousin who had an uncle twice removed in the district who was a Republican representative and so was allowed to keep his factories.

For an annual contribution to the party of course.

The folks at this particular Brubaker factory were discouraged from mentioning the fact that the ball bearings they produced were useless. It was bad for morale and had been proven to instigate unacceptable behavior. Like the time Floyd Kapinski, fed up with the fact that the ball bearings they didn't work so hard to produce, were useless after they produced them and there by extension so were they. Floyd ate three large beef and bean burritos for breakfast, drank a bottle of liquid Ex-Lax on his coffee break and took the mother of all shits down the ball bearing chute adjacent to Bay number twelve just after a load of recycled ball bearings had been delivered.

It made no difference to production, didn't even slow it down. But it did cost the company nearly $12,762.37 in union fees to retrain the new guy they hired to produce more useless ball bearings and keep the flow going after firing Floyd.

Thereafter the workers never talked about the stunt. They just referred to a shitty day at the factory as a 'Floyd Day'.

Owing to the utter tedium they endured each day, while still having to devote twenty-five to thirty years of their lives to the Brubaker Corporation, the members of the BB Stackers, Joe, Bob, Fred and Thaddeus along with the occasional hangers-on, would congregate in the employee lounge at break times to engage in energetically charged but pointless political discussions on every issue which had been broadcast by Lush Limburger on the NewsCorp station that morning.

Although they were never conscious of it, Joe, Bob, Fred and Thaddeus routinely entered into these only partially informed, politically charged but intellectually bankrupt discussions as a means of catharsis.

"Well if they hadn't taken America off the copper standard we'd'a never seen hide nor hair of that there ECOLI economic collapse! That's all I'm sayin'!" Fred responded to Bob's comment that the economy would one day pick back up again,

"Well it don't make no sense that them there people down in Washedupton P.C. wouldn't want the economy to pick back up again! I mean, we do better, they do better, ain't that right?!" Bill interjected.

"It's a good God damned thing that we ain't livin' in Pakistan, Afghanistan or India! You know, one'a them countries what's got the whatch'a'ma call it system!"

"Castjagated! The castjagated system!" Fred added.

"What the hell's that?" Thaddeus asked.

"That there is a system whereby you gotta stay in the caste you was born into and thereby the class that your daddy was in! You can't never move up or down. You gotta stay at the same work your daddy did. I mean, there ain't no advancement in life in them countries!"

"All I know is our fathers got their jobs because their fathers had jobs in this factory, and we got our jobs from our fathers, in this factory and I'm damn sure gonna see to it that my boys get a job in this factory when they's old enough!"

"You said it Fred!" Bill reinforced.

"God bless America! That's all I gotta say!" Bill played it down but in his heart, he was a diehard Blinder.

With the announcement over the PA system that the next shipment of ball bearings had been delayed due to a twelve hovercraft pile-up on the I-2001, there was no rush to get back to their stations. The topic of conversation that morning switched to the world's first zillionaire, Ronald Lump III, who also happened to be the Republican party's front running candidate at the moment for the upcoming November elections.

Like all the other candidates, he had used his fortune to buy his place in the Republican party, kick start his campaign and then suck off corporate America who could then claim their unlimited contributions as tax deductible.

Although while on the bowling lanes they were tight as a Wall Street commodities broker and the CEO's of Bank of America, MasterCard, Chase Manhattan and the head of the Securities and Exchange Commission, the BB Stackers differed tremendously on politics. Which of course left the apolitical Thaddeus pretty much out in the cold and sitting in silence.

"He's just another of the 1% whose entire campaign and candidacy is just a PR platform for his investments." Joe declared.

"How much is a zillion anyways?" Bill queried.

"Well you got twenty-six letters in the alphabet, so it must be twenty-six more than a million! What's a matter, didn't you go to school, stupid?" Fred scolded.

"Yeah, I went to school, stupid!" He snapped back mocking the question. "And I came out the same way."

"I heard he wants to buy Spain." Joe added.

"I heard it was Greece."

"Naw! That there was the Chinese wanted to buy Greece, but they ain't doin' so good there. The whole investment was based on their restaurant industry. Turns out soy sauce ain't no good on kebabs and souvlaki which already comes with one chop stick."

"Lump said he'll buy Michigan back from the Canadians if he's re-elected."

"Lump's a moron! What the hell we gonna do with Michigan?!"

"I don't think he's so bad. Half the lies his opponents are telling about him ain't true!"

"Bill, you get your car to the mechanics?" Thaddeus wedged himself into the conversation.

"Yeah, but he couldn't fix my brakes. Couldn't get the part."

"So what'a you gonna do?"

"I ain't worried . . . he made the horn louder."

"Read where the first transgender, cross species, transsexual, full body operation was a success." Thaddeus again attempted to involve himself in the pointless banter.

"Oh yeah? Where'd they do that?" Bill casually asked.

"Someplace in Orange County, California. They cross bred a young boy with his favorite pet Shih Tzu."

"How's he gonna get married and have a family when he grows up?" Bill asked.

"It's okay, the boy's mother went to court for to protect his civil rights under the new Universal Equality Law. You know, where any two species can co-habitate and its still tax deductible. He can get married, have kids, eh . . . pups, vote and own property. Long as he lives in California. But he ain't allowed in restaurants. You know, on account 'a the health laws."

"Least ways his rights is protected!" Fred declared.

"Makes sense to me."

"Me too."

"Equality is important." Thaddeus profoundly declared.

"Equally as important." Agreed Joe.

Ж

It was early February and Thaddeus, as well as all the other workers at Brubaker's Industries, had been given time off for Black President's Day, an annual four day weekend which came into law during the Olson Twins administration after they had signed a secret but lucrative deal with the Hallmark Greeting Card Company.

The greeting card scam was eventually uncovered by the infotainment stations but was over shadowed in the press when it was discovered that the twins, in all the thousands of photos taken of them, weren't really leaning on each other. They had actually been born Siamese Twins who hadn't been fully separated at birth. Congress was forced to convene an emergency session to deal with the scandal and decide whether or not they had one president or two, but in the end decided that they were separate issues.

Black President's weekend was a natural off shoot of Black History month which came from Black History week which evolved out of Martin Luther King Day.

Despite the millions spent by the government on promotion, parades and media promos most blacks boycotted the holiday with protests and refused to celebrate because they claimed they were being singled out.

So as the Thaddeus' 20th wedding anniversary was only two and half months away, he and his wife decided to use the time off to travel to where California used to be and visit the place where they had been conjoined in holy matrimony.

It was the place, aside from a drive-through liquor store and the local methadone clinic, that was the happiest place on earth; New Disneyland.

Ever since the Las Vegas City Council had legalized free Heroin in the casinos, (free booze wasn't bringing in the numbers like it used to), the amount of couples wishing to get betrothed there declined dramatically. Shooting heroin apparently had become preferable to marriage as a way to lose all your money. Because of this shift in bad habits Disneyland in Anaheim, California had become the marriage capital of America.

Coincidently the University of California's esteemed College of Sexology & Hydroponic Farming was located directly across the road from the country's most famous amusement park which was where Thaddeus and his wife had also spent their honeymoon.

They were married on Space Mountain and spent their first night together in the Goofy Suit of the Mickey Mouse Inn located in the *It's A Small World* portion of the park. It's a resort where all the staff were Disney characters. Not people in outlandish costumes and masks but actual people who had volunteered for elective reconstructive surgery to look like their favorite Disney characters.

Such was the dilapidated state of the job market in America that the government footed half the bill for the surgery reasoning that the surgically enhanced cartoon characters, Mickey, Minnie, Donald and Goofy, could later be hired to do political promo ads on television after a survey found they were more believable then most of the actual candidates.

Now, twenty years later, Thaddeus and Prudence stood holding hands in front of the Matterhorn watching the fake bobsleds flying down the artificial snow banks and gently pretending to crash into the man-made, chemically produced snow banks at the foot of the plastered over, wire armature of the mountain and gazed in wonderment.

"Ja remember all those years ago Prudence, how excitin' it wuz to skooch down that there mountain?"

"I surely do Thaddeus, I surely do." They sighed in unison. "It was the most excitin' time of the entire three days of our honeymoon!" The slightly overweight spouse reminisced.

"That and the time we went to Wrestlemania!" He conceded.

In the background a multi-car studio tour tram driven by Donald Duck slowly crept by as the tour guide spoke into his head set. The monotone drone of his duck-like voice wafted through the air enhancing the romantic ambience of the moment.

Thaddeus and Prudence were moved to put their arms around one another and embrace.

The driver stopped the five car tram, turned and faced the passengers as he indicated the Disney film studio building to his left.

"Ladies and gentlemen you are now looking at the actual location used by the famous director Oliver Stone who filmed the famous moon landing in 1969 which was broadcast around the world."

Some passengers in the rear car snapped some photos of a bronze plaque on the corner of the studio building which read:

One small step for man of a kind, one giant leap for a man.

"There's an interesting story," Mr. Duck teased the tourists as he continued. ". . . the actor who played Neil Armstrong nearly twisted an ankle as he leapt from the fake Lunar Excursion Module to the moon set because the invisible bungee cord he was suspended from was a tad too long. But he was okay. Fortunately, Houston did not have a problem!" He forcefully chortled. All the sun glass, micro-camera laden passengers in floral print shirts laughed.

Thaddeus and Prudence wandered over to the pavilion area where they took a picture of each other by the replica statue of Walt Disney. The studio heads were compelled to fabricate a replica of his cryogenically preserved corpse when it melted and eventually rotted during the big blackout a few years back.

The Pervers then bought a couple of tickets to the Cyklone Rollercoaster and as they meandered back to their hotel room to await the phone call which would alert them that the 3/4 mile long line had died down and they should start back to the park to enjoy their ride, Thaddeus spat out the idea he had been wrestling with for the last few weeks.

"Prudence?"

"Yes Thaddeus?"

"I believe a thought has taken seed in my head and as such has begun to sprout into a full fledged idear."

Having been warned about the dangers of free thought, thinking for one's self and the all too hazardous concept of 'idears' by the Federal Thought Control Bureau advertisements on TV, Prudence felt a cold chill run down her slightly slouched spine at what was to come.

"What . . . kind'a . . . idear Thaddeus?"

"The kind that comes into a man's head but once or less in a lifetime Prudence." He proudly proclaimed knowing that were he to be struck dead by a lightning bolt from the god he doubted existed at that moment or were squashed by a mis-directed hover craft landing in the wrong place he would have thrown off his mortal coil fulfilled in the knowledge that he had lived his life to the fullest.

He would have died having had an idear.

He proceeded with his explanation.

"The idear that Thomas Jefferson, Abraham Lincoln and all them fellas-."

"What about'em?" She apprehensively pushed.

"They was all presidents but simple folks like, wasn't they?" He queried with the innocence of a child.

"Well, I ain't never met none of 'em, up close and personal like, so's to speak, but that's what it says in all them there history books the government gives us."

"Well, we's simple folk. Too. Ain't we?"

"Well, I suppose."

"Well then . . . I reckon I could be involved in politics."

Like a suddenly short circuited analogue computer the words flashed through her mind at over 19 miles per hour until they eventually arrived at the deepest recesses of the shallow, convcluted folds of the grey matter of her encephalon. At that moment Prudence was left with no option but to do her best impression of a young Helen Keller. Before she had learned sign language.

"You mean . . . the president of these here United States!" Taken aback by his wife's confidence in him as well as the lunacy of such a suggestion, he was compelled to laugh to relieve the tension.

"NO WOMAN! You think I'm crazy?! President of the United States! I'm talkin' about president of the Mayor's Clean Neighborhood Program! Ain't you seen the posters? They's askin' for all citizens to do they duty!" Prudence breathed a sigh of relief.

"Well, how many people's on this here Clean Neighborhood Council?"

"Well if I volunteer, two."

There was a long silence before she spoke.

"I ain't sure about that idear." She confessed.

As the 21st Century infection of PC culture still existed it was on that last night of their 20th anniversary, in their honeymoon suite they were serviced by Snow Caucasian and the Seven Persons of Slight Stature, formally known as Ms White and the Seven Homunculi.

Prudence, Thaddeus's betrothed, chose this floor of the hotel so as to not make Thaddeus feel too self-conscious about his manhood.

THE SCREW-UP
12:27, Friday, October 31st

CHAPTER FOUR

※

Working to pay their mortgages, grocery bills, and school tuitions for their kids so that they could grow up, get jobs, buy houses, pay their mortgages and in turn have kids they could send off to school was not all the good folks of Middleville, Ohio did. They also voted.

One early November morning, as he was about to step through the front door, Thaddeus was gently reminded by his wife to renew the car insurance.

"DON'T FERGET TO PAY THE DAMNED CAR INSURANCE!" She screeched from the bedroom as she manned the TV remote and simultaneously lifted another chocolate to her cavernous mouth as if the large box of bon bons besides her on the night stand might suddenly have concocted an escape plan.

Thaddeus dutifully returned, made his way to the kitchen drawer where all the household records were kept and excavated the envelope labeled, "Car Insurance", stuck it into the breast pocket of his jacket and made another dash for the door.

Downtown, a short time later, he pushed through the front door of the office of *You're in Good Hands Insurance Agency* on the corner of Big Street and Wide Avenue and approached the front desk.

"Hi and welcome to the *You're in Good Hands Insurance Agency*. My name is Zelda. How may I attend to your insurance needs today?" The perky little bleached blond greeted.

"I'm here to see Mr. Lester Forbes."

"Do you have an appointment?"

"No ma'am, I don't."

"My I ask what it's pertaining to?"

"Yes ma'am, you surely can." Following the exchange there ensued a brief staring contest. A full minute later there didn't appear to be a clear winner so the receptionist took it on herself to reboot the conversation.

"Hello. Welcome to the *You're in Good Hands Insurance Agency*. My name is Zelda. How may I attend to your insurance needs today?"

"I'm here to see Mr. Lester Forbes."

"Is he expecting you?" Once burned, twice shy, Zelda realized.

"I don't think so, no."

"Are you here to see Lester the agent, or Lester the District Manager?"

"I don't know no Lester who's a district manager, so I suspect I'm here to see the other Lester."

"It's a good thing you're not here to see Lester the District Manager."

"Why's that ma'am?"

"Because he's gone to vote."

"Okay then I'm surely here to see the other Lester."

"Is he expecting you?"

"No ma'am, I suspect not."

"Well, that's okay. You can't see him neither."

"Why's that ma'am?"

"He's gone off to the voting polls. To ahhhh . . . help out."

"But the polls don't open for voting until after lunch, that's another three hours!"

"He's gone a little early to stand in line account'a he's a deathly a feared of the rappers coming to kill him. You know, under the vote or die law."

"I see."

When the voting abstention fad swept across the country following the 2040 elections, Paris Sheraton, Lady Goo Goo and other minor celebs whose public images had begun to sag were recruited by politicians to promote the idea 'to get out and vote'. This too failed to boost turnout numbers, so the politicos hit on another approach.

In an attempt to counter the negative perceptions of the country's two party electoral system, the V.O.D. Act, Vote Or Die Act was created.

"I can refer you to Lester's assistant." She offered.

"Well. I have to pay my car insurance. Can he do that for me?"

"Oh my yes! That's just a small little bit of paper work. He'll take your debit card, your blood sample for your DNA verification form then stamp and sign your papers and you'll be all set."

"Why thank you ma'am." Zelda couldn't help but notice that Thaddeus made no effort to move from in front of her desk but stood there as if waiting for a bus.

"Will there be something else sir?"

"Where can I find this assistant fella?"

"Shane. His name is Shane."

"Shane?"

"Yes, his assistant's name is Shane."

"Shane, like the old cowboy movie?"

"Yes, Shane, like the old cowboy movie. He's down at the Saint Hilary Clinton Middle School at the polling station where he's doing community service for embezzlement. He has some payment papers with him, be there until three o'clock." She said to him with the self-assurance of a senior Democrat about to buy a traunch of votes.

"Thank you ma'am."

Thaddeus found his way down to the school and located Shane, a dusty blond haired twenty-something patiently sitting at a table in the middle of the empty basketball court seated behind a long folding table playing a video game on his I-Phone 3000.

"Voting or paying insurance?" He didn't bother to look up from the phone as he addressed Thad.

"But I thought the polls didn't open for another few hours?" Pervers inquired.

"New hours for schools and churches. Supposed to reduce the crowds, so they say. Besides, this is just pre-registration. You still gotta use the machine to actually cast your vote." Shane grumbled.

"Okay then, paying and voting and registering to vote too!" Pleased by his tax dollars at work Thaddeus smiled.

Without speaking Shane saved his work on his I-Phone, set the phone aside and hefted a brown brief case up onto the table, opened it and shuffled through a thick stack of papers, folders and some forms. He pulled a few from the case and set them off to the side.

He then folded his hands in front of him, looked up, smiled and made eye contact.

"Welcome to the *You're in Good Hands Insurance Agency*. My name is Shane. How may I attend to your insurance needs today?"

"I'm Thaddeus Pervers and I'm here to pay my monthly car insurance premium. And I'd like to vote also. And register. Also."

Shane took Thaddeus's premium form and debit card from him, removed a form from the brown briefcase and copied the personal info onto the form in triplicate, then did the same with three more forms. Shane then produced a glass pipette, a pin and some alcohol and took a blood sample from Thad's finger.

He handed back the debit card and reached to the floor for a second black, briefcase which he set on the table after sliding the brown one to the side.

After opening the black one, he repeated the first process of shuffling papers and from this case he extracted a red folder from which he pulled a Form 1-80-A13-V or Voter Registration-Application for Dog License-Intention to Run For Office-Donate Your Body to the State application. Thad perused the voting portion of the form on page 16.

There were two large boxes at the top of the form, one for Democrats and one for Republicans, and one teeny tiny box way down at the bottom labeled 'Other' just opposite the place for his signature and citizen registration number.

He did as required and handed the form back.

"Nice of you to volunteer and help out at the polling center, Shane." Thaddeus cordially commented. "I read where all the old folks who used to work here for free passed away."

"Not here by choice really." Shane answered as he began to write. "Didn't exactly volunteer." His dejected response caused Thaddeus's face to contort, but only slightly.

"How do you mean?" He asked as Shane scribbled away.

"Got caught littering on Main Street, now got'a do community service."

"Why'd you go and do a fool thing like that for? Litterin' on Main Street I mean."

"'Cause, didn't realize there was a donut shop across the street!" They exchanged glances then Shane forced a sarcastic smile. "Now I got'a do community service." He made no attempt to hide his anger this time. He passed the partially filled form to Thaddeus. "I filled in the important parts, this one just needs your citizen registration number and signature on the bottom line." Thaddeus slid the form around and took the pen from Shane.

"How long you got'a do community service for?"

"Judge says 300 hours."

"I understand ever since that new *One Time Loser*

law come in, they's really crackin' down." Thaddeus thought it prudent to show empathy as he signed and slid the form back over to the insurance assistant.

Shane stamped it with the proper rubber stamp and placed it in the brown brief case then stamped the other form several times in the right places and slipped it into the black case before closing them both up and setting them back on the floor to resume his miniature video game.

Seventeen and a half minutes after he had arrived, Thaddeus Pervers, secure in the knowledge that he had served his community doing his duty to the community, state and country, exited the polling center to get a cup of coffee before the voting stations opened.

Shane, with the name like in the old cowboy movie, still flustered by having been caught for littering by the five cops in the donut shop and having to do 300 hours of community service, and so would never discover, until it was too late, that in his agitated state he had gotten Thaddeus's insurance premium and the Form 1-80-A13-V or Voter Registration-Application for Dog License-Intention to Run For Office-Donate Your Body to the State application mixed up.

Ж

Thaddeus entered the Vote-O-Matic 3000 voting booth, locked the steel plated, terrorist proof door, activated the perimeter laser warning beam designed to make the voter feel safer and took his seat. While the built-in lie detector monitored his ass for honesty, he placed his chin into the chin stirrup and looked into the peep hole as required to present his eye implant identification chip.

Welcome Thaddeus Enoch Pervers. Citizen registration number 27-C-06

The pleasant but androgynous voice greeted. Both voting knobs on the choice panel in front of him lit up and the voice continued.

To vote for corporate choice number one, please press the red button. For corporate choice number two, please press the blue button.

He fished through his trouser pocket and came up with a Curtis James Jackson commemorative 50 cent piece and flipped it in the air as he mumbled to himself.
"Heads I vote left knob, tails I vote right knob." Unfortunately he dropped the coin and had to bend over to search for it along the floor. As his ass lifted from the seat the lie detector activated an alarm and a red light on the ceiling began to flash.
WHA-WHA, WHA-WHA! The alarm wailed loudly.
As he felt around the floor for his coin the Vote-O-Matic 3000 detected his hesitation in voting.

If you choose neither candidate or you are undecided please re-enter your name and citizen registration number by looking into the eye piece to schedule an interview with an officer of the D.A.V.P.

Thaddeus found his coin on heads and so righted himself and yanked hard on the left knob. The red light ceased flashing and the alarm died off.

Thank you for doing your patriotic duty by freely voting for the candidate of your choice!

The machine cordially thanked him.
Following the 2028 presidential election, as people began to realize that the two party system no longer worked as they had been led to believe, but they had

been too subjugated to do anything about it, the voter turnout reached a record low of 14.7%.

Democrats and Republicans. Of the 37 registered parties only two had representation in congress because they had the connections to raise the money and so buy their seats. As the two parties drifted closer and closer to one another in terms of policy, scandal and corruption, citizens became disenchanted and gave up on the system that only the elected politicians believed still worked. This dynamic, choosing between two candidates given them by party officials, just didn't seem right in the world's premier example of a supposedly democratic nation.

Something had to be done.

As more and more people became aware of this dynamic the government panicked and began to realize that maybe the public was catching on to their scam. So the two party Congress, which in reality was a one party Congress since there was always a majority and one party consistently refused to cooperate with the other, the one party congress was compelled to at least appear to be taking correctional measures.

As voting has little or no relation to crimes, one of the first measures was to reinstate felons the right to vote. A curious maneuver, taking away the 'right' to vote from anyone, given that the constitution doesn't guarantee the 'right' to vote to U.S. citizens anyway so Congress never really had the 'right' to take it away in addition to the fact that you can't take away 'a right'. Especially when the portion of the U.S. population of convicted felons had reached 19.5%.

Given that the majority were convicted of crimes they didn't commit or were handed down sentences far in excess of what their crimes called for, they bore no love for a system that was designed to convict who ever came in front of its courts. Primarily for its own financial gain. Crime was big business in more ways than one.

Re-instating convicts the right to vote didn't help alleviate the problem of low voter turnout to even a limited degree.

The next step to boost voter turnout, championed by a faction of Republican bankers, was to hold a lottery and award random voters a prize of first ten thousand dollars, then twenty until finally the much touted Votto as it came to be labeled, reached a maximum grand prize of $50,000.

The failure of that measure was attributed to the fact that of the 250 million eligible voters your chances of winning your state, local, county or school lotto were calculated to be 76% better than winning at the government Votto.

When the lottery scheme didn't seem to make a dent, a scheme which had been previously rejected was revisited. The allocation of money to establish the *D.A.V.P.,* or Democratic Association of Voter Police. This didn't work out so well either.

In an effort to counter this sudden epidemic of reality of failures, emergency sessions of Congress were called to deal with the persistent problem.

The Supreme Court was consulted and, ever ready to counter the well-known fact that they only deal with less than 1% of all the decisions brought before them, the Justices beamed at their new found power.

Coincidentally, that very next Autumn in a presidential election, a dispute arose when candidate's brother, who was a governor, was caught cheating by striking thousands of voters off the records in his home state.

Feeling duty bound to relieve the government, (not to mention the public), of the torturous burden of public servant selection, the Supreme Court settled the dispute by 'appointing' a president, which they reasoned only seemed fair in that they themselves had been appointed by a president to the most powerful court in the land without the messy process of being elected. The Justices saw it as a, 'what's good for the goose' situation. So they appointed the next president.

In the aftermath of this national crisis, the legislation that came out of the latest emergency session was dubbed the V.O.D. Act of 2040. The Vote or Die Act, where-by anyone refusing to vote for two consecutive elections was, as a deterrent, subject to a penalty.

Various penalties were considered. Extreme fines, confiscation of property, extended prison sentence or being forced to listen to boy band music for 36 hours straight. These were all rejected including the later after being declared cruel and unusual punishment by the ACLU, the U.N. and the International court in De Hague.

In contrast to most government policies instituted for the public good, the one they settled on was guaranteed to work 100% of the time.

Execution.

However, another problem arose. The police forces had become too incompetent at shooting suspects and legislation was briefly considered to take their guns away.

For example, in one New York City shootout where an unarmed suspect was killed, three policemen had fired a total of seventeen rounds hitting fifteen bystanders and one black and white Schnauzer. The other round on target killed the suspect, who was not only unarmed but later identified as a lost tourist who had approached police to ask for directions. The perpetrator escaped unharmed.

In all fairness, not counting the dog, the police had a 94% hit ratio.

Consequently further alternatives to enforce the V.O.D. Act were sought. Following lengthy debates a solution was finally arrived at.

Due to their expertise at using handguns at close range it was decided that the job of executing those which had been deemed guilty by a non-jury of their peers of violating the V.O.D. Act, that is the "No-Vo's" or "Non-Voters", should fall to the rappers.

To date over 200 rappers had been killed or themselves had killed a like number of opponents, so their qualifications were beyond question.

An unpredicted positive side effect of this was, due to the ridiculously large sums paid the Rapper Squads, they no longer had to rely on the pointless and repetitious lyrics of rap music which had finally began to fade from the scene.

The rappers did such a good job, that voting numbers rose to pre-V.O.D. legislation levels. Additionally the rappers earned enough money to take music lessons, become literate at music and to play a variety of instruments.

As is a traditional approach in Western politics, the underlying cause of low voter turnout was never addressed; that is widespread political corruption and complete loss of trust in the partial elected leaders. The cleaning up of the politicians and bankers through tougher laws for them as opposed to tougher laws just for the people, followed by public prosecutions with actual prison terms in real prisons, was never considered.

So with voting returning to a near normal rate, the country could continue the ages old two party system it had enjoyed since the late Eighteenth Century when the Electoral College was set up to further restrict the people's power to control their government.

However, since then a precedent had been set by the Electoral College and up held by the Supreme Court. A precedent set back in the mid-Twenty-first Century where-by after the general population had voted, the Supreme Court reviewed the election results and if they agreed the good people of America had made the right decision, the vote would stand. If not, the Supreme Justices could select the next president of the United States and pass it onto the Electoral College for a co-signature.

This became known as 'do process' because no one could ever explain exactly where the Electoral College actually came from or what the hell they were supposed to do.

Ж

After casting his vote, Thaddeus met up with Mike from the BB Stackers, his bowling club. Thaddeus had been wanting to run his thoughts about throwing the hat he didn't have into the political arena he didn't know existed and the ensuing anxiety had begun to take its toll. So he asked Mike to meet up with him after he voted.

They decided to meet at a KFC on Michael Moore Mountain Boulevard and he considered, as he drove under the big neon and plastic sign which read: "Over 100 Billion served! 50 Billion eaten. 25 Million digested!", how to frame what he was going to say. Thaddeus was never any good at public speaking much less one-to-one, heart-to-heart chats but he had finally decided to share his decision with Mike and get his feedback.

Minutes later they were inside at the ordering station.

"Welcome to the Dr. Christian Bernard KFC! How may I help you?"

"Ahh, yeah. Can I get a Clinton lunch box special, a small basket of fries and a 72 ounce Diet Coke Extra Lite, please."

"Yes sir. Would you like to upgrade to a two pound basket of Multi-cultural fries for just ten dollars more?"

"Nah, no thank you. I'm on a diet. The small will do." He gently patted his slightly bulging belly as he courageously refused the fries. The one pound basket would have to do. Mike put in his order and they took a seat by the window with the artificial rolling landscape glued to the outside. Each window featured a different season. They chose early Autumn.

Thaddeus cleared his throat to speak. It was at that point that Mike knew something important was about to be said but before he could the loud speaker blared to life.

"Order number 6,127!" Once back up at the counter Thaddeus pressed his left thumb against the screen, was identified to be the right recipient of the order and was asked the standard personal question by the server technician to verify his identity. A question that only he would know but was readily accessible through the J. Edgar Bush Central Data Agency in Washedupton, P.C.

"Where did you and your wife spend your honeymoon and was it, A great, B good or C satisfactory?"

"Are we allowed to lie?" Thaddeus laughed.

"Not if you want your food sir, but that's a good one!" The forty-two year old counter boy conjured up a nearly convincing forced chuckle.

"Disneyland! Where the heck else? And it was A, great." Thaddeus lightly joked.

"Thank you sir! Here's your two small breasts, two large thighs and a left wing. Enjoy your Hilary meal sir!"

Back at the table, halfway through the meal, Thaddeus sought to elicit his best friend's opinion. Once again he cleared his throat.

"Mike, I been thinkin' on an idear."

Mike, not a big fan of idears and having been warned most of his adult life of the dangers of independent thought, just turned and stared out at the lightly, multi-colored oak and birch trees contrasting against the green and brown hills of the window stick-on scene as they pretended to undulate across the open fields.

"I'm your friend so I guess I got'a listen." Mike uttered as he slowly pushed the remnants of his reconstituted Multi-cultural fries to the side. "What's on your mind buddy boy?"

"If all them political leaders is just plain folks, like they keep tellin' us they is . . ." Mike braced himself against the table. "Then do you see any reason why one'a us can't be no politician like all them people in Washedupton P.C. always passin' laws and tellin' us what we can and can't do?"

Thaddeus Pervers talking about politics! Mike thought to himself. The words stuck in his head as if his mind had swallowed a chicken bone of an idear sideways. Even thinking about it hurt his head. Mike was temporarily struck with selective mutism as he very nearly underwent a hysterical conversion reaction.

"What all's got you thinkin' on politics!" Mike challenged. "You got a perfectly good position sittin' on your ass all day at the factory. You're good at your job, the boss likes you. Least ways he says he does. And with Brubaker's connections that factory ain't never gonna close!"

"I know all that. I just don't feel like I'm doing nuthin' with my life! A man ain't supposed ta not do nuthin' with his life, I mean that's right, ain't it?"

"Well . . . yeah but-"

"Well, I got a phone call, and they asked me to sit on this town council thing, only thing is . . . I don't know nuthin' about sittin' on no town council! I mean, what the hell is a town council anyways?"

In order to assume an air of superiority Mike sat back in his seat and threw his right arm over the back of the booth. The booth back proved too high for him to reach so rather than look stupid he just let his flab draped appendage hover for a while till he couldn't support it any more then let it drop back to the seat.

"Well, Thaddeus, that there is a council of folks that sits around a big table every so often up in the city hall building and councils other folks."

"Councils them about what?"

"About stuff they need councilin' about!"

"Sounds complicated. I reckon you need some kind'a dee-gree or somethin' to qualify to be on a town council?"

"Oh hell no you don't got'a have no qualifications! Matter-a-fact, I heard it's better if you don't know nuthin' about nuthin'! That way you can advance more quick like."

To indicate he was taking it all in Thaddeus hemmed without hawing. Mike continued the lesson.

"I seen a documentary on it. On MTV. There's only three things ya got'a do to qualify to get yerself on a town council! First ya got'a have money in like a business or savings, or an inheritance, something like that. Next ya got'a have opinions."

"Opinions?"

"Yeah opinions, lot's of em'! You know, like assholes. Everybody has one but some are bigger than others, but according to that guy on that documentary, they all usually stink."

"Okay."

"And finally, ya got'a have time on your hands."

"Time?"

"Well yeah, an account'a the meetings and all."

"I see."

Mike detected the reluctance in his friend's response.

"You'll do fine! Look, if you decide to go with this thing, you know the boys and me are behind ya, no matter what. So if you do come down on the side of politics . . ."

"I been thinkin' about that! What the heck does that mean anyways? 'Poli-tics'?" Mike beamed secure in the knowledge he didn't have about the definition that he didn't really know.

"That there's an old Greek word, comes from two words slapped together! Back in the old days Greeks done that a lot. It comes from poli meaning 'many' and 'tics' the small parasitic, blood-sucking leeches that live off of other animals."

Thaddeus sat back, digested Mike's explanation and nodded his approval, secure in the knowledge that he had friends who knew such things.

"And if you get in with the government and might one day need somebody to . . . you know, a friend who maybe one day might need a friend to help him out of a tight spot, like helping him with his heavy load of governmental duties that pays a good salary . . ."

"Thank you Mike. I do appreciate your consideration of the bigger issues."

"Don't mention it! How's Prudence these days?" Having exhausted nearly his entire storage of knowledge on all things political, Mike sought to change the subject.

"She's fatter."

"Oh." Mike sighed. He pushed his basket across the table. "You want som'a these here fries?"

THE POLITICAL PARTY

CHAPTER FIVE

Ж

United States Senator Sydney Ogden Snodgrass, (Ret), was a very rich, old school senator who belonged to a very small, very secret triumvirate.

He had amassed his fortune the old fashioned way, through kick-backs from judges, lawmakers and industrial lobbyists. He specialized in alcohol, tobacco and borderline illegal pharmaceuticals. But he was particularly admired by his colleagues for earning millions playing the NRA lobbyists against the Coalition for Gun Control, Mothers Against Drunk Drivers against the Alcohol lobby and The Coalition of Clergy against the 719 registered Gay Rights Organizations as well as a host of other similar 'pansy-assed, left wing liberal' organizations, as he referred to them behind closed doors.

Early on in his career he accepted the fact that no one trusted a politician and, having read Sun Tzu, determined to use this reality to his favor. He learned to appease the people and the Press by dividing them into sects and carefully wooing them one at a time by eating pierogies with the Poles, spuds with the Irish and pasta with the Italians. Rice and beans with the Hispanics, rice and chicken with the blacks and rice and moo shu pork with the Chinese.

Behind closed doors he drank moonshine with them all.

Senator Snodgrass didn't look as though he was actually born of the human race as much as he stepped off the drawing board of a Gahan Wilson cartoon.

The few scraggly blades of white hair which desperately clung to the front ledge of his head only served to emphasize the blue road map of his bald pate. His one hundred and nine pound frame sometimes served as a distraction as he sat and spoke with others causing them to lean forward and surreptitiously peer around to look for the ventriloquist they were sure had a hand up his back operating Sydney's mouth, one twig-like leg dangling over the other gently waving in the non-existent breeze .

His ever-present gold plated walking stick, which he used to lean on when he sat forward to reinforce his point, served more as a prop than a third leg. Few could personally testify that they had ever seen him walk or arrive anywhere by foot. He always seemed to already be there when they arrived for meetings and such.

In his tenure as senator Sydney ruled his state as completely as Cetshwayo had dominated the Zulu tribes of his African territories.

After retiring from the U.S. Senate Sydney slid seamlessly into the lobbyist's game and did quite well there.

As part of his standard deal he got a piece of every copyrighted manual, machine or new tool the lobbyists or he himself represented for funding. Over a fifty-seven year career span that added up to dealing with a lot of tools.

The second member of the secret, ultra-low profile triumvirate was J. Pete Moss, Esq. formally of the firm Hardwood & Rattlebag. He started out in the family business, law. Working his way up to District Judge specializing in natural resource law, he was a wildly successful oil baron before he was forty years old. Moss came from a proud lineage as a direct descendent of the infamous 19th Century Robber Barons and had twice won the Environmental Man-of-the-Year award for having oil rich districts in Texas and Louisiana rezoned as commercial so that Exxon and BP could clear away all the pesky wildlife and drill thus allowing the people to enjoy the natural resources of their land.

But it wasn't a total environmental disaster. He was a man of many dimensions and so was smart enough to also get a piece of the financial action when the dead animals resulting from environmental contamination were sold off to biological supply companies to be used in school labs and biology classes.

The last triumvir was a former gun smith who made his money as a gun dealer and later, as an expert witness for congressional committees on gun laws particularly on sales of military weaponry to foreign militaries. Richard 'Rick' O'Shea was the youngest of the group and at 99 years of age, everyone reckoned he still had some mileage left in him.

His greatest claim to fame, the thing which made him a household name, was the U.A.D.

Back during the St. Anthony's school mass shooting in Upstate New York where over 100 lives were lost, and another 150 wounded it was Rick O'Shea who was credited with saving dozens of lives.

Just months before the massacre O'Shea was able to get regulations passed that restricted the use of the U.A.D. on standard home defence, automatic weapons such as the AK-47 and the M16, but allowed it for police and military use.

The Ultra Automatic Device was a mechanism which allowed the shooter, with the flick of a switch, to convert from full automatic fire to Ultra Automatic thus upgrading the standard AK-47 or the M16-A8 assault rifle from firing 600 or 700 rounds per minute to firing 1100 to 1300 rounds per minute.

Because the two disgruntled school boys who perpetrated the bloody massacre against the young students at St. Anthony's could only fire the normal 600-700 rounds per minute, it was reckoned that a lot of lives were saved that day when the S.W.A.T. teams showed up with their superior fire power complete with the new U.A.D.'s.

O'Shea had been called to testify before Congress multiple times due to his expertise on the U.A.D. because there was no better expert around. He invented it.

Following the massacre Rick was hailed as a hero and recommended for the Citizen's Medal which he modestly declined.

However, the story had a happy ending. O'Shea has since been hired as a private technical consultant for the producers of the reality T.V. series *Classroom Body Count*.

That Friday morning O'Shea entered the imitation 19th Century, faux granite building known as the Northside Gentlemen's Members Only Private Club and passed through the simulation brass revolving doors into the plush lobby. It was one of the oldest gentlemen's clubs in the city and sported a bar on each floor, gaming rooms with bet minimums higher than most working class annual incomes and as the ultimate sign of its exclusivity, women were still banned from full membership and not allowed above the ground floor.

However, back when the Supreme Court ruled that the club could not exclude anyone on the basis of race, the club's board members quickly responded by first paying for a week's worth of elocution lessons for the southern gentlemen members affected with the common speech defect characterized by use of the word 'ya'll' for the second person then drafting a clause into the by-laws which forbade the use of the word on the club premises. Blacks stopped applying for membership. The courts were once again proven impotent in the face of big money.

Rick nodded to the old man at the reception desk who waved back as he made his way around the circular, button tufted leather love seat and tall areca palms to the elevators and up to the seventh floor.

As he stepped out of the car a well-dressed, young messenger, barely in his eighties, stepped in. O'Shea thought nothing of it until he reached the executive smoking room down the hall.

Despite the fact that no one smoked any more the sprawling, antique festooned space was still referred to by its original name due to the fact that if you were a former smoker you could still ring for a page to bring you a nicotine button.

The button was applied to the forearm and seeped a nicotine-like substance which filtered into the blood stream through the skin at a controlled rate to fool the wearer's mind and body into believing they were actually smoking tobacco. These were good for up to 24 hours and had succeeded in completely eliminating lung cancer due to smoking from the population.

Other types of 'buttons' could be had as well such as anti-histamine, orgasm buttons and various muscle relaxants.

Former smokers were easily identified by the surgical scars on their forearms from where they had developed arm cancer. The marijuana button laws were still in debate by Congress largely because the Democrats and Republicans needed more time to invest their private fortunes in the marijuana farms throughout Mexico and Central America before passing legislation.

As he turned the corner and entered the well-appointed, red carpeted room the dozen or so occupants scattered around in their Queen Anne high backed chairs upholstered in rich oxblood leather had taken a break from their Wall Street Journals and John Grisham novels and were staring at a pair of paramedics attempting unsuccessfully to revive the 110 year old Professor Hilburton lying on the floor by a window.

After long continuous minutes of CPR, electro shock and a dozen injections of cardiac stimulants the paramedics pronounced the professor dead.

Rick, who knew Hilburton only in passing, stared down at the gurney as they carried him out.

"What happened to him?" He asked as he took a chair across from Snodgrass who had resumed his reading.

"Damn fool left an orgasm button on his arm for too long."

"Damn shame." O'Shea conceded.

"His own fault!" Snodgrass unapologetically grumbled. "Damn things come with a warning; Not to be applied longer than three minutes for persons over 100!" He returned to his book.

O'Shea glanced over but in place of Snodgrass' face spied the dust jacket of the two inch thick book held in front of it.

How to Fuck Your Business Partners and Make Them Like It! By Charles H. Keating the Sixth.

Rick listened as he overheard a partial conversation from some chairs closer to the soft red neon lights of the fake hearth.

"Good thing she was a lesbian when she was in office or we'd'a been inundated with her and Bill's YUPPIE larvae!" The unknown story teller's voice echoed.

Pete Moss was the last to arrive and the three now sat in their private alcove off to the side of the Gold Club Members Only smoking lounge.

Separately they pursued their own ends but when they came together they were like a married couple with Moss as the bastard child. Snodgrass fit the father roll with O'Shea as the perpetually pessimistic mother figure.

"What is it you wanted to meet about?" Rick snarled at Snodgrass. The super-centenarian leaned forward in his initialled Queen Anne chair propping himself up with his gold plated titanium cane.

"You seen this?" The senator tossed a copy of the *Brubaker Times* on the table between them. "Editor sent it over about half hour ago by special messenger."

There was a photo of a smiling politician and the headlines read:

President says: 'Teen Pregnancy Drops Significantly
After Girls Turn 20'

Rick perused it then passed it to Pete who took a bit longer to read it.

"I got another one for ya!" Rick unexpectedly threw out. "Friend of mine in the NRA says somebody in the Guns For Jesus Association of America heard it through the grape vine over at the Gethsemane Bar & Lounge that that fool's gone and got himself mixed up in a paternity suit with a fourteen year old down in Georgia!"

Snodgrass cursed under his breath.

"She from Georgia too?" Asked Pete.

"Yeah, why?"

"Well problem solved!" The old lawyer declared. "That's marrying age in Georgia!" They both stared at Pete.

"You need a lobotomy!" Snodgrass snapped. "I called you here for a reason. I come to a decision." Snodgrass announced.

"Uh huh?"

"After that last debacle that idiot great grandson of that other idiot Lump has little or no chance of getting his ass re-elected! I've made a decision, he's got'a go!" Sydney made no bones about how he now felt regarding the current president.

"First things first! We got'a figure a way out of this paternity thing before it hits the infotainment stations!" Rick argued.

"You think about things too much! Lighten up!" Sydney corrected.

"Yeah!" Moss added. "Not thinking too much is what made America great in the first place!"

"Give it to The Firm." Sydney commanded as if he were ordering a hit.

'The Firm' was Snodgrass' long time lawyers, the esteemed Sixth Avenue law firm of Due, Wee, Cheatem & Howe who, ever since the great election scandal of the last decade had been the go-to-people for any and all high profile law suits. DWC&H advised the Supreme Court on how they could circumvent the law and appoint the candidate of their choice for president, the man who had appointed half of them to the court.

"What'a you want me to tell 'em?" Pete meekly inquired.

"Tell them to put some kind of spin on it!"

"Like what?" Asked Pete.

"How the hell should I know?! You're the lawyer! Tell them . . . tell them to get a Republican hired at the clinic where the girl had the pregnancy test done then tell the press that the Republicans switched sperm samples. That's why the test came out positive."

"But Sydney, the President is a Republican!" Pete protested.

Sydney leaned on his cane and with a puzzled expression as he turned to Rick.

"I thought he was a Democrat?!"

"No that was the last one we put in office."

"Oh, sorry. God damned Alzheimer's! Well then get some Democrats working in that clinic."

"And if that doesn't work?"

"Then buy the God damned clinic or leak something to the press about illegal abortions or some such bullshit!

That'll tie them up in law suits and scandal for a year or so and by that time the press'll have moved onto something else. People in this country got the attention spans of a gnat and the memories of goldfish anyway."

The man they were discussing was President Ronald Lump the Fifth, the latest but currently not the only member of the Republican Party, who had been plagued by a plethora of scandals brought on partially by his own stupidity and naivety but also by his lack of knowledge about how to do business in the great district of P.C.

Between leaked sexts, alleged dalliances with female and male White House interns and a myriad of other scandals the seat of the Presidency had lost what little respect the remaining two or three Third World countries, as well as a significant sector of the U.S. population, had for it. Recently a good percentage of the people had taken to flying the flag upside down in protest to the state of the government.

"I'm not just talking about a new candidate." Snodgrass continued. "We need more than just somebody's been around the block a few times on the Hill and been in bed with all them Sena-tutes up there! I'm talkin' about a whole new attack. From a different angle!"

"I'm not readin' ya S.O.S.!" Pete Moss declared. O'Shea slid forward on his seat and made eye contact with Snodgrass.

"Gentlemen I propose we convene a formal meeting of the entire board!" O'Shea concluded.

"I second the motion." Sydney added.

"We do need to do something!" The 109 year old Pete Moss got up to go upstairs to the board room.

"Where the hell you goin'?" Barked Snodgrass.

"Upstairs, we get'a call the Board, get them up to the meeting room so we can get a consensus!"

"Sit down ya stupid, old goat! Since when do we use that dusty old room for anything but showing the press?!" Moss shuffled over and fell back into his imitation, naugahyde chair. "That room ain't been used since they put that first colored fella in the White House by mistake! Besides, **we are** the Board god damn it! **We make** the consensus!" Sydney admonished.

"Well, what's your solution then?!" Moss shot back. Snodgrass sat back, relaxed and assumed his lecture mode.

"There used to be a time when the people of the Third World, and by Third World I mean every place that's not America, used to look up to us. And by 'us' I mean Americans lead by us! They all wanted to be like us. Look at all the contributions to civilization we made! Why, take the automobile for instance. There wouldn't be any automobiles if it weren't for a great American, Henry Ford." Snodgrass patiently proposed.

"Actually Ford gets credit for the assembly line." O'Shea corrected. "You know, so he could get more work out of his factory workers but not pay them more. I think it was some German fella built the first practical car, a guy named Benz."

"Oh. You sure?" Sydney sought to confirm.

"Pretty sure Sydney."

"Well we wouldn't have the telephone if it hadn't been for another great American, Alexander Graham Bell. A New Yorker I believe."

"Actually Senator, Bell was from Edinburgh. That's in Scotland, I think it's somewhere near England." Moss contributed.

"Well, Benjamin Franklin invented electricity! Now God damn it don't go trying to tell me he wasn't an American!"

"I thought electricity was invented by Michael Faraday from England?" Moss questioned.

"Actually Moss, electricity was never invented. It is a naturally occurring phenomenon. Michael Faraday developed the first practical way to harness its power and apply it to good use. Franklin only showed that lightning was made of electricity."

"WELL GOD DAMN IT THEY DID IT ALL WITH AMEICAN MONEY, DIDN'T THEY?!"

"In point of fact Sydney, most of their start-up capital was largely family-"

"I DON'T GIVE A SHIT YOU NUMBSCULLS! YOU GET MY POINT!"

Moss and O'Shea temporarily withdrew from the conversation. Rick signalled the on duty valet for a round of drinks.

"Bottom line is Demon-o-crats and the Bumpublicans both ain't done **shit** in the last coupl'a decades except get us in debt, in wars and in scandals!" Snodgrass argued.

"Couldn't agree more!" O'Shea quickly said.

"That's exactly what I was thinkin'!" Pete demurely chimed in.

"I propose we start from scratch! Redesign the whole thing."

"You suggesting we form a new party?!" Rick sought to clarify.

"That idea is touchier then a Vatican sponsored Summer camp for boys!" Moss countered.

"Hear me out! The answer is yes, but first things first! We got to come up with a suitable name for this new party we gonna invent. Problem is there's been over 200! Every time one comes up through the ranks, the two big ones gang up on 'em and put 'em out'a business!" O'Shea argued.

"And how do they do that?" Sydney baited pointing a long, crocked finger No one bit. "MONEY! That's how!" He declared. "Only this time around we got the money! More money than you can shake a stick at!" Snodgrass waved his cane for emphasis, although he only got it a few inches off the floor he made his point. "So I called you here to start brainstorming names."

"Names? How about The Teabags?" Moss, wanting to impress, quickly threw out.

"Been done." Sydney countered.

They sat silently thinking some more until the drinks came.

"I got it!" O'Shea declared.

"Got what?" Sydney's Alzheimer's, although allowing him to always meet new people, was unpredictable in its occurrence.

"A name!"

"Oh. What is it?"

"The Dixiecrats!"

"This ain't no Rock n' Roll band we're naming damn it! We need a sturdy name, a political sounding name, a name so folks won't suspect what-we're-really-up-to kind'a name!"

"What about the Know Somethings? I mean there was the Know Nothings way back when, so what about the Know Somethings?" Pete tossed out.

"And what's our answer gonna be when some smart assed reporter asks us what'a we know that they don't?!" Snodgrass demanded.

"The Workers Party?"

"Too Socialistic!"

"You mean Communistic!"

"Same thing!"

"The Party of the Workers?"

The ensuing banter graduated to argument which escalated until it rivalled a gaggle of drag queens at a garage sale fighting over the last Lisa Minnelli CD. In time they all sat back and ordered a fifth round of Martinis.

"What about something relating to nature, like The Bucktails?"

"What about somethin' relatin' ta nature?" Snodgrass mocked. "Why not the Beavers or the Elks while you're at it?! You'll have us soundin' like a God damned men's, working class social club!"

"We are a men's social club! A very limited membership social club, but . . ."

"How's about the D. R.'s?" Rick tossed out.

"What in tarnation is a 'D-R?" Sydney challenged.

"The Doctors?! We ain't doctors." Pete Moss mumbled.

"Not doctors! D. R., Democratic-Republicans! You know, so's people think we are finally working together!"

"Never work!"

"Why not?!"

"Two parties working together?! Nobody will buy it! Regardless of what most people think, even the American public has limits to its gullibility!"

"THE FEDERAL UNIOINISTS BEHIND THE REPUBLIC OF AMERICA!! THAT'S IT!" Rick shouted.

Silence blanketed the room as the two and a half minds seriously considered the first palatable proposal in over an hour.

"Say it again!" Snodgrass asked.

"THE FEDERAL UNIOINISTS BEHIND THE REPUBLIC OF AMERICA!! THAT'S IT!" He reiterated.

"NO DAMN IT!! THE AMERICAN REPUBLIC! THE FEDERAL UNIOINISTS BEHIND THE REPUBLIC OF AMERICA!! THAT'S IT!" Snodgrass shouted.

"What about the Federal Unionists **Behind** the American Republic?" Rick proposed.

"I like the America's Republic party better than Republic of America!" Pete Moss added.

"Okay then! The Federal Unionists Behind the American Republic it is!"

They all nodded their approval, shook on it, sat back in their Queen Anne, high backed chairs and ordered a tenth round of Martinis.

And so it was at 19:27 in the p.m. that Friday evening that the first political party to seriously challenge the American two party system since 1912 was born.

The martinis arrived and the triumvirate toasted their achievement and the fact that they would forever be known as the FUBAR's.

Ж

To his shock and chagrin a week after The Brubaker Town Council received Thaddeus's unintentional application for membership in a council he knew nothing about which was about to have a vacancy none of the council could foresee, the application was reviewed and accepted.

The Council had unanimously voted to accept Thaddeus as a member even though he didn't own a restaurant or any other kind of business nor did he have a chunk of money in the bank or a university degree. What he did have however, besides time on his hands, was his abnormal normalcy.

The governmental shake-up, due to the lowest voting rate in history, had finally filtered down and reached the local level and so town councils state-wide who had been sucking off the government teat began to get nervous. It was then they reasoned that, as a pre-emptive strike, they would quietly slide people like Thaddeus Pervers, plain ordinary folk, (meaning individuals who had no chance to make a significant contribution and therefore posed no real threat to any of the sitting members), onto the council.

However, there was an even more important reason to allow Thaddeus onto the council. They needed a scapegoat. As any efficient political body knows, it's always good to have one in your back pocket. Any major fuck-ups could be attributed to the new guy and so no one was in danger of losing their very cushy job.

Thaddeus would essentially serve as, what is known in the political vernacular as a Meat Puppet. Someone in a position of relative authority whose ass you could stick your hand up and make do whatever you wanted. They had a vacancy to fill and what better way to fill it then with their very own dupe?

The vacancy on the council came about because Duncan, Duncan Donaught a local cop, had been killed in the line of duty.

Duncan was something of a hygiene fanatic who used aerosol deodorant at least three to four times a day spraying himself until he was immersed in a cloud of the stuff. Usually in a confined space.

One afternoon during lunch he went home took a shower, dried off then doused himself with Men's Right Guard, the blue label scented kind, all in the cramped bathroom of his small apartment.

The butane, triclosan, cyclomethicone and aluminium chlorhydrate in the deodorant had been accumulating in his system as well as in the air and that day, and just as he applied the last spritz of the aerosol can, his lungs sent a message to his brain saying: "ENOUGH!" and shut off the oxygen supply to his heart. He wasn't thinking too clearly just before he died. Just a as he lit his last cigarette.

DNA, dental records and blood type suggested that what was left on the ceiling and bathroom window was probably what was left of officer Donaught. It was that afternoon when his mother found his remains dripping from the overhead lighting fixture, and under the tub with the Right Guard aerosol can still clutched in his left hand.

The line of duty 'yes' on his official police death certificate, meaning his mother would get benefits for the rest of her life, was because he had just chased a purse snatcher three blocks down Main Street and was all sweaty. Which is why he went home to shower.

The press said it was a heart attack.

Ж

It was a Friday afternoon when Thaddeus showed up for his first town council meeting on the 17th floor of the City Building.

Argyle Greenpasture, Hiram Higgenbottom's 102 year old secretary, had just spent the better part of a half an hour reading the minutes of the last meeting to those gathered in the meagrely decorated, glass and aluminium room. The sole piece of art, a black canvas with a small white dot painted slightly off center, hung in a polished steel frame directly behind Higgenbottom's Mackintosh, Hill House, high backed chair at the head of the table.

The twenty-five foot long, fake mahogany table was surrounded by the forty-one city council members with the president at the head, the secretary off to his right. One empty chair stood at the far end of the table.

As there was no old business to conclude, (there rarely was), new business was called for and the subject of next month's budget renewal was brought up.

Thaddeus listened attentively as someone suggested emptying the litter bins on the town's streets three times a day instead of the current practice of twice per day.

"This way we use twice as many garbage bags and give the city street workers thirty extra minutes on their daily earnings!" The council member explained. Thaddeus nodded in agreement and dutifully scribbled on his yellow legal pad.

"That's a good start but we really got to get up to more than that. We got another $67,482.37 to spend." Higgenbottom insisted.

"What about if we lower the price on the Brubaker City hooded sweatshirts, tee shirts and ball caps for sale around the city to below wholesale so's we lose money and sell them at a loss each quarter?!" Someone suggested.

Thaddeus, unsure of himself, leaned over and quietly whispered to the woman next to him.

"Aren't we just wasting money? Why not save it and give it to the children's hospital, build a library or something?" Thaddeus quietly asked.

"That's not the way it works." She whispered back. "If we don't spend it all and show we need more money they'll give us less money next year and that would be a terrible waste! Disastrous!" She quietly explained. "Simply disastrous!"

"Ohh!" He nodded.

Thrilled that he was learning so much about the inner workings of government on his first day on the job, Thaddeus nodded and wrote some more notes on his legal pad.

THE EPIPHANY

CHAPTER SIX

Ж

Taranjello, Thaddeus's teenaged son, sat watching his favorite T.V. game show, *Classroom Body Count,* the weekly reality program was fashioned along the lines of the old *Big Brother* programs.

Each week the show featured several high school students with failing grades who had been picked by lottery and sent back to their respective schools with two automatic weapons of their choice and 1,000 rounds of ammunition. A time unknown to the school was picked by the home audience and phoned in, (calls cost only $25.00), and the contestants were then secretly driven back to the schools where they were allowed to attack them.

The contestant with the highest body count won that week's show.

The point system was fairly straight forward with the younger students that is under 10 years old, counting for a flat ten points. Students over ten were worth one point per year of their age with bagged teachers earning the contestant a full 25 points, 40 points if they were over 50 years old.

Wounded students were not counted unless they were crippled for life in which case they were worth half, 5 points, or unless they died within a twenty-four hour time limit. Then they were worth 7 1/2 points.

But the real jack pot was the big P! The principal! If a contestant was skilled enough to stalk and kill the school principal, on or off the school grounds, he or she earned a 100 point bonus plus a free, all-expense paid four day weekend at the NRA sponsored shooting camp of their choice!

Currently some ninth grader who competed in a middle school in Beaver Lick, Arkansas had just won. During the postgame interview the youngster expressed disappointment at only wounding the principle and therefore not earning the trip to the NRA shooting camp. Still his parents expressed how proud they were of him and were sure as heck grateful that they had been teaching him how to shoot since they bought him his first gun when he was three. It was a shame about that instructor he accidently shot and killed when he was five but, the parents reasoned, if people stopped dying for freedom they wouldn't ever be free anymore.

Taranjello had gone to make a sandwich and go to the toilet so Thaddeus, who had come into the room, picked up the remote and flipped the stations. He stopped on an interim news report.

The police Chief of near-by Smithville was addressing a microphone held in front of him. He was explaining to the perfectly quaffed female reporter, the one with the bouffant hairdo who looked like she had just stepped off the runway at a fashion show for near-middle-aged women with bad taste in clothes, how difficult it was being a police officer in that town.

In the background, one of his men was being given oxygen and escorted into the back of an ambulance by a paramedic. The source of the Sheriff's remorse as he spoke about the officer, who wasn't injured in any way, was that he had been traumatized by the fact that he had been compelled to kill a local homeowner. His fifth since he had joined the force at age eighteen.

"No matter how many times you have to do it never gets any easier."

The Sheriff explained with a forlorn face.

According to the report, the homeowner, due to losing his job, had just threatened to kill himself, which he hadn't done. It was only when he put a pistol to his head the distraught wife called the police. A squad car quickly arrived and it was determined that immediate action was required of the responding officers to prevent this terrible tragedy and stop this guy before it was too late.

Following his standing orders, which were to deal with anyone with a firearm swiftly and neutralize the danger, the officer felt duty bound to act with a sense of urgency and so took the most immediate course of action. He killed the homeowner before he could shoot himself and before the assailant could do harm to his family or others.

The Chief referred to the now emotionally scarred officer as a hero.

Sheriff Straightrod, why do you refer to the brave officer's action as a 'mercy killing'?" The reporter queried.

"Itn' it obvious?! If we took him alive, the pain that man's family would go through being dragged through the convoluted and also twisted court process which has many twists and turns, would have lasted five maybe ten years!"

"But Sheriff, what about the constitutional guarantee of the right to a speedy trial?!"

"SHIT MA'AM! You seen how long it takes to process the seven to ten thousand perpetrators we arrests each month? In this state alone! What we did was a speedy trial!"

Thaddeus flipped through the channels a little further and was attracted by an overhead shot of a crowd scene the police were trying to make their way through. The barely controlled melee was taking place in front of the Hilton Hotel in Palm Beach, Florida. The broadcast was in Spanish so there were Spanglish subtitles. Unfortunately the crawler at the bottom of the screen containing the subtitles went by at the normal speed at which Hispanics speak so they were just a blur, far too fast for Thaddeus to read what was going on.

From what he could gather the people were on the verge of rioting because the president's motorcade was getting in the way of anyone wanting to view or get of *One Erection*, the latest twelve year old boy band sensation to be fabricated and sent down the pipeline to the Pop starved masses by the Simoné Scowl Incorporated division of Merde Music Productions.

Secret Service Guys in tandem with the local police, who had reached their daily quota of arrests, struggled to clear a path to the door of the Hotel Hilton for President Lump and Mrs. President.

Thaddeus watched, fascinated, as the Secret Service guys ran from the car to hold the door open for the President. He was generally referred to as 'Mr. President' because few young citizens bothered to learn the name of the people in Washedupton P.C. anymore. Fewer still knew how to vote.

It was then, watching the S.S.G.'s that Thaddeus's mind accidently tripped over an epiphany.

If he could somehow get out of his dead end job and find a new one, perhaps became a S.S.G. door opener or a petty politician, he would never have to work again as long as he lived! His allotment of 1.5 children would be upgraded and he could have a mistress and keep his wife just like a normal politician.

There would always be food in the fridge, or at least someone to bring him food, there would always be plenty of ice cold beer and he could have new underwear and socks at least twice a year.

But most of all . . . he could afford his dream: a two room house. Maybe even one with an en suite toilet! It would have to be white of course, white was the only authorized color in his area of the country. Mrs. Pervers had her heart set on a ranch home with mauve, fake plastic aluminum siding, peach window frames to accent the lemon yellow kitchen and an artificial chimney to which they could wire an inflatable, plastic Santa Claus at Xmas time. But he was certain he could talk her into white .

His train of thought was disrupted by the flush of the toilet as Taranjello returned and had his dad flip back to the game show. Thaddeus forgot about improving his lot and quitting the factory, leaving the town council and seeking a new job.

The next teen contestant was introduced and part two of *Classroom Body Count* began.

Brubaker Town Council Chambers
Brubaker City Hall
15:28, Friday, December 11

All eyes stared vacantly while the sweep hand on the face of the 2027 antique, commemorative clock reached the numerals which read '10+2' at the top of the clock face.

Gasps of breath were accompanied by startled glances being exchanged and a deathly silence blanketed the council chamber as the entire town council minus Hiram Higgenbottom sat huddled around the massive genuine artificial oak table.

It was one Friday morning, about a month after Thaddeus joined the Brubaker Town Council in Brubaker, Ohio when the situation arose. Hiram Higgenbottom the council's long-time president hadn't shown up for the meeting.

"He's usually five minutes early!" Declared Candy Caine, a former stripper who owned a chain of pole dancing clubs across the state and who had, in the course of her career as a polefessional exotic dancer established many political connections.

"Ten minutes more like!" Corrected Gooden Small whose name origin generated much speculation. He was retired from an unknown profession but was known to be independently wealthy.

"You're both wrong! Never known the man to come less than fifteen minutes early. For anything!" Interjected Barbra Dwyer an abrasive woman who just seemed to rub people the wrong way. Very abrasive but she had a sharp wit and had been married to a wealthy factory owner who died under mysterious circumstances one day while they were on vacation in Punxsutawney, Pennsylvania. Her second such spousal mishap.

As the debate escalated, fuelled by fear and confusion which soon threatened to reach Israeli-Palestinian proportions, a steady rhythmic squeaking noise could be heard. The arguing stopped and the room again fell silent. All eyes turned to the far end of the brobdingnagian piece of furniture which must have been built at the cost of a small artificial forest somewhere in the north of what used to be Sweden.

Along the edge, peeking just above the top of the long surface of the meeting table bobbed a tuft of blue hair jaunting in rhythm with the squeaking. It slowly danced the entire distance along towards the other end of the table.

It was Hiram Higgenbottom's 110 year old secretary, Argyle Greenpasture who walked behind her alloy aluminium-titanium, walker around to the high backed chair at the head of the table.

With the aid of two council members and a nine and a half inch thick, Webster's Unabridged Dictionary to sit on, she made it up into the Art Deco President's chair. With someone holding her wrist she was able to hammer the gavel home three times to signal that the town meeting should begin. Silence still prevailed. Shocked with respect for their most senior colleague the members gradually complied, slowly took their seats and gathered themselves.

"As you are no doubt unaware," Her mousey voice resonated through the chamber without echo. "Mr. Higgenbottom's wife, Trudy, has been pregnant with triplets." Nods and mumbling, highlighted with an occasional 'harrumph', prevailed from around the work area. "It is my deep suspicion that she, Mrs. Higgenbottom that is, in all likelihood has entered into the delivery phase of the gestation cycle. That is to say she commenced giving birth and the good Mr. Higgenbottom has chosen to be at her side as she popped one out!" She paused for comments. None were expressed. "That being the case," Greenpasture continued, ". . . there is no way to know when to expect Chairman Higgenbottom will be disposed to return to his duties at the council."

Thaddeus shook his head in understanding.

Truth was that Higgenbottom, unknown to The Council, his wife being pregnant for seemingly so long, had accidently died when he O.D.'ed on a string of twelve orgasm buttons he had mistakenly taken for nicotine patches while he was nervously pacing outside the delivery room at St. Steve Job's Hospital over in Smithville. Doctors found the still convulsing body an hour later in the third floor men's toilet.

The press would report it as a heart attack.

"So what are we supposed to do in the meantime?!" A voice called out from the distant end of the table.

It was Hiram Cheaper, partial owner of a small but growing factory which manufactured safety signs for manufacturers and various factories which manufactured parts for other factories.

Repulsed by Cheaper's total disregard for Robert's *Rules of Order*, Ms. Greenpasture indignantly pushed on quoting the 417 page *Brubaker Town Council Handbook of Regulations* from memory.

"According to the *Brubaker City Ordinances*, Section Nine, Sub-section 7, Chapter 12, Paragraph 3, said council is required to follow the *Brubaker Town Council Handbook of Regulations*."

"Well what the hell does the *Brubaker Town Council Handbook of Regulations* say we gotta do?!" Snapped Melanie Meade, a cantankerous straight-shooter always ready with a cut-down for those who thought they were better than the rest and a staunch advocate of frontal lobotomies as a way to cull the shallow end of the gene pool.

"The *Brubaker Town Council Handbook of Regulations*, chapter on procedure states . . ."

Suddenly Argyle stopped speaking, her eyes closed over and she fell back into the chair. Puzzled and shocked faces glanced around at each other. Presently the super-centegenarian began to snore. The woman next to her leaned over and gently shook her shoulder.

"Argyle! ARGYLE!" Greenpasture snapped awake.

". . . that in this event we are required to select through either a vote by show of hands, or by mutual agreement, a suitable volunteer for the position in question. In this instance the position of President of the Town Council."

Apparently refreshed following her brief power nap, Greenpasture perused the room which had now assumed the air of a funeral parlor.

"Will someone please put forward the motion to select an interim president for the council." Greenpasture requested.

"I so motion." Said Jack Uzi a wealthy plumber who seemed never to be at work.

"I second!" Candy blurted out.

"Very good, then to save time I will proceed with the vote. Will everyone please take half a sheet of paper, write the name, clearly and legibly please, of your nominee on it, fold it in half once and pass it forward." Argyle instructed.

The membership obliged and ten minutes later, with the aid of Candy Caine, all votes were tallied. But there was a problem.

Every single member of the council received exactly one vote. Every person had voted for the person next to them.

With no clear winner they tried it again. And again. After three attempts, as proscribed by the regulations, there yielded no clear winner and they were back at square one.

What Thaddeus had no way of knowing was that everyone there wanted the job on the council, the wages and the benefits to include their own parking spot and the imagined prestige which accompanied a position on the town council but no one wanted any real responsibility, much less the responsibility of leadership.

Taking over as head of the Brubaker Town Council would entail massive responsibility with all its attendant efforts. Reports to higher ups, additional, higher up meetings, work production reports, ensuring organization, and worse of all, assuming that most dreaded facet of leadership which was not only alien but completely antithetical to American politics - assuming responsibility for anything.

No one in America could say precisely when 'the buck' had stopped stopping at a designated point, but it certainly had. It was considered political suicide to assume responsibility for anything. A handbook of P.O.D.'s, Phrases Of Denial, could even be had at any book store within one mile of any town, county or state capital. Featuring in said publication some of the most noted excuses which worked:

"I have no first-hand knowledge of such events." – Anonymous

"I don't recall." - Ronald Reagan on Iran-Contra

"I categorically deny I had sex with that woman." - Bill Clinton on the Paula Jones Affair

"I can't remember." - Ronald Reagan on the HUD scandal

"I categorically deny I had sex with that woman." - Bill Clinton on Monica Lewinski Affair

"I have no memory of those events." -Ronald Reagan whenever questioned about anything.

"I categorically deny I had sex with those women."
- Bill Clinton as AG & Governor of Arkansas, 1977-1997

A pregnant silence filled the council chambers.

Once again Greenpasture made a motion for nominees to fill Higgenbottom's position. Once again crickets could be heard in the back of the room.

"Why don't we dump it off on . . . I mean give the new guy a chance?!" Al Dente, owner of the famous Italian take out restaurant chain, *Mama Berlusconi's* whispered to Candy Caine who sat next to him.

"I nominate Mr. Pervers!" Candy blurted out. Everyone looked around the room, including Thaddeus.

How democratic! Thaddeus thought to himself with a smile. *Just when everybody wants such a prestigious job everyone is willing to selflessly give someone else a chance! Is this a great country or what?!* He mused with satisfaction

"I AGREE! WHAT A GREAT IDEA!" Yelled Uzi.

In quick succession everyone else was on board. In what has to be a political world's record, they all reaffirmed the nomination then voted for the new guy who had no experience what so ever and hadn't a clue what he was doing. The Meat Puppet Rule had been invoked. Thaddeus Pervers was the new President of the Brubaker Town Council.

"Well, congratulations Mr. President!" Greenpasture was the first to say. The words rang in his ear as if spoken from a distant city. A distant land, a distant planet even.

"Very well now, if there are no objections, as Mr. Thaddeus is new to the Council, I'll continue with the procedural portion of the meeting." There were no objections. Argyle proceeded. "Good. We'll take up the first order of business, the critical decision we must make on Proposition 19½!"

Thaddeus leaned over and whispered to old lady Crabtree sitting to his right. The 107 year old, life time permanent member turned up both of her hearing aids.

"How have the other towns in the mid-state areas voted on 19½?" Thaddeus quietly enquired.

"They ain't!" She emphatically whispered back. "We's the first council in Ohio to vote. Brubaker has always been the first town to vote. The rest of the folks in the county always stick behind us to get a reading of where we are. Like a thermometer. So does the rest of the mid-state districts."

Thaddeus nervously glanced around the large table. All eyes were on him seeming to ask: 'Well Mr. President?' Thaddeus cleared his throat.

"Well, I think . . . I mean, nineteen is past the age of consent, isn't it?" Thaddeus proposed to the group.

"Yeah but, what's that got to do with anything?!" Uzi challenged.

"Well . . . I believe once a woman reaches the age of consent she has the right to choose what kind'a work she wants to do! And if she wants to be a prostitute then that's her right!" Thaddeus spoke with the courage of his convictions.

"Acting President Thaddeus," Argyle Greenpasture interrupted, "Proposition 19½ deals with the state mandated increase of water taxes. If approved it will affect virtually every village, town and city in the state."

Thaddeus sat quietly not sure of how to react. "I knew that." He finally uttered.

Candy Caine suddenly spoke up.

"I agree that a girl should be able to do what she wants with her body! I mean for years society has been telling us what's right and what's wrong. What we can and can't do. I think it's time we took matters into or own hands!" She demanded with just the right amount of little girl pout.

"I just meant to say that this Proposition 19½," Thaddeus skilfully added in a half-hearted attempt at damage control. ". . . if it's gonna affect so many people, it should be taken real serious like. You know what I mean?" It worked. Harrumphs and chatter filled the room.

"WAIT!" Without warning, Barb Dwyer stood up and spoke. "Don't you see what he was doing here?! What he really meant?! He's sayin', 'so many people!', meaning everybody. All of us! And Candy's right too! The State legislature has been wielding their power over us since we've become a state way back in 18 . . . back in 18 . ."

"1816!" Argyle piped up from memory in her seat at the head of the table. "December 11th, 1816 at 10:21 in the a.m. when the population was announced to be 63,897, well above the requirement for statehood." She elucidated in her mousey and quivering voice.

"Thank you Argyle!" Barb interrupted.

"Although it was in 1812 that Jonathan Jennings first introduced the idea of statehood-"

"THANK YOU ARGYLE! WE GET IT!"

"And the Peony was first declared the state flower." She quickly managed to squeeze in.

"As I was sayin'," Barb continued. "If we don't stand up to them and stop the state legislature right here, right now! Then we give them carte blanche to run amuck! Next it'll be the age of consent. Then they'll be after our right to vote!"

"Barb is right ya'll!" Now Jack Uzi joined in the growing frenzy. "How long before they make us have to have permission to go abroad to California or . . . or to foreign countries like Hawaii?"

"Ohh! I've always dreamed of going to Hawaii!" Mused Argyle. "To eat poi, dance the luau and get laid!"

"It's called a 'lay' Argyle, it's not verbal in nature. And the dance is the hola." Hiram Cheaper pointed out.

"I say we get behind Thaddeus and vote NO! across the board on this Proposition 19½!" Greenpasture declared. "Show them State fellas that we mean business!" In an attempt to pound the table to reinforce her opinion, Argyle was only able to manage a slight tap. But her point was made.

With a newly instilled sense of power, purpose and poise the Brubaker Town Council carpe-ed the diem in a manner not seen since the great snow storm of '37 when Doris Huntsacker was attacked in her front yard by a gaggle of disoriented Canadian geese and beat them off with a broom.

The rejection of Proposition 19½ was unanimous and Walter the postmaster was immediately summoned and sworn to deliver the sealed rejection notice to the county seat before close of business that day so that it may reach the state capital of Columbus by next Friday without delay.

Once news of the unanimous rejection, the first unanimous decision ever rendered by the BTC, hit the press through the *Brubaker Times* the next day, they were touted as Middleville County's own heroes.

Like a large bull approaching a grazing cow the rest of the state quickly got behind Brubaker.

When later interviewed council members attributed their new unity to Thaddeus, now that they knew Higgenbottom was dead, their new dynamic PFL, Permanent-For-Life, council head.

In less than a week state-wide headlines read:

Elected by Unanimous Consent New Town Council Leader Gives Head Like No Other!!

Council member Argyle Greenpasture who had been with the town council longer than anyone, was quoted as saying: "I been with this council a long time, and he's the best head I've ever had!"

Finally a small town in the U.S. was on the map for something other than police shootings and civil unrest. Some journalists even speculated that it was widely perceived that states were once again on the road to self-government through self-control and unselfishly able to, partially at least, eject Federal control from state affairs.

The story was picked up by the national wire service and by default the national infotainment networks. Lush Limburger spoke for a full hour and a half, taking phone calls in between comments from house wives and the unemployed, on the topic of the rising movement to state's independence and the possible foreshadowing of a second Right of Secession movement in the mid-West.

Was this unexpected movement actually spawned by aliens from Planet 10 as seen on You Tube?

Could civil war be far behind? Limburger queried as he badgered his callers.

What next? Democrats marrying Republicans and spawning? What religion would they raise the kids?

Was this the beginning of the end?!

Stay tuned. We'll be right back after a word from our sponsors.

THE IDEAR

CHAPTER SEVEN

Ж

That Friday evening as Senator Snodgrass, (Ret.) sat on his double king-sized, circular bed and sipped his extra dry martini watching the day's market tallies on the *All Wall Street Station* something caught his attention.

Scans of well-designed modern, spacious, condo estates with immaculately groomed lawns and gardens filled the screen. These were followed by a 60 foot Chris Craft yacht slicing its way through an undulating green sea as voice over from a well-spoken announcer came in over the footage.

Are you tired of waiting around while your money sits in the bank earning somebody else interest?

Sydney sat the portfolio he had been perusing aside.

"Volume to eight." He ordered Siri Home, the in-house, I-servant system which ran throughout his home.

On the wide screen, vapor TV the well groomed, middle-aged guy manning the helm of the yacht flashed his perfectly white teeth as he smiled and looked up into the camera.

We have a solution!

A sparkling, platinum Leer jet did an overhead fly by. The V.O. continued.

Are you looking for the next great investment opportunity? Always thought prisons were only for criminals? Well think again!

The announcer suddenly appeared in a well-appointed studio.

Let me introduce you to the unbelievably profitable, great investment opportunities in the ballooning U.S. prison industry!
Think about this! The exponentially growing, non-diminishing profit returns are clearly evidenced by the high rate of recidivism! As soon as they're out, the system is automatically programmed to get them back in as soon as humanly possible!
And now with our courts 96.4% conviction rate set to rise next year by at least another 1to 2 percent . . .

Sydney's mind was gearing up to hatch a new plan of some sort which wasn't yet clear but like the Wicked Witch of the West the smoke was clearing and soon the black spectra of evil personified would stand tall.

Combine this with the low cost of maintaining the prisons and maintaining the prisoners at the low, low cost of $2.10 per day, guard salaries not included, with the utter absence of government supervision . . . unless too many of them die of course, (he emitted a forced giggle for levity). *But isn't that true of any of any commodity? Just take a look at these figures for the last quarter . . .*

Snodgrass did something he rarely if ever did, he smiled. Not just a smirk like when he realized how to screw somebody out of something he wanted but the kind of face-to-face grin which comes to you when you see your first born accomplish something laudable like perfectly execute his first multi-million dollar swindle.

But his temporarily instilled joy wasn't in response

to the possibility of being one step closer to his ultimate, perpetual goal - increasing his financial power base to be the largest in the world. It was because he had hit upon the perfect idea. The age old technique of advertising. The ultimate, efficient and effective form of propaganda which, best of all, was perfectly legal! Just the thing he needed to act as a base for his new assault on the capitol of Washedupton P.C.

And remember, we here at IncarCorps do all that is humanly possible to rehabilitate prisoners before helping them return to prison!
And now a word from the Michael Jackson Day Care Centers . . .

He looked closely at the credits as they ran at the end of the advert and noted the company which had produced the testimonial based infomercial. It was a group calling themselves F.O.U.O., For Office Use Only.

He switched off the TV set and reached for his portable intercom and buzzed his young P.A. Miss Stone.

"Yes Senator?"

"Rosetta, first thing in the morning get me somebody over at a place called FOUO! They're an Ad agency."

"Yes Senator." The young fifty year old assured.

Ж

Network news is like porn.

It's all over the internet, nobody wants to pay for it, but somewhere little men in cheap suits hunched over desks in a dark room are creating it. Probably with love lives flatter than a dead man's EKG.

But also like porn the money to broadcast the news has to come from somewhere and that somewhere is advertising. It follows then, some might suggest, that ad agencies are the prostitutes of the business world and like prostitutes there are ad agencies and then there are ad agencies.

Like street walkers you have your dodgier agencies, who wander the seedier parts of town looking to snag Johns where ever they can. Usually this class of ad agency can be found in lower rent districts, occupying questionable premises. You can usually find them via hand out fliers done up in loud colors, stuck under your windshield wiper following an afternoon of shopping at the mall or through late night television ads interspersed between low budget dramas featuring soft porn shown just before the infomercials kick in.

Sometimes you can find them in the phone book under an alias such as 'lawyers'.

Then there are your professionals who work out of specialized cat houses and brothels strategically called 'offices' or 'studios'. These are generally listed in the e-Yellow Pages.

Finally, like high priced call girls, you have your more expensive agencies which are essentially a mixture of both. They charge very high rates to have interaction, called 'meets', with clients, frequently attend high class parties on Madison Avenue and usually have a penthouse office somewhere in the city which sports an expensive leather couch where clients can engage in intercourse, verbal intercourse that is. Also there's usually a mini-bar to help ease into the negotiations and ashtrays for after the meeting on the expensive leather couch.

Boasting a plethora of national and international ad agency awards, the For Office Use Only Ad Agency was **The** Wall Street agency.

If you had a security firm, for example, FOUO could easily produce a thirty second ad featuring 10 reasons why the government was failing to protect you, the citizen, from . . . Blah, Blah Blochmed or Blahdum Hussein. The ad would be sponsored by your firm, the

Guardians of Freedom Personal Protection Agency for example, and they, the FPPA, would easily convince the Holy See, (alias John Q. Public), that you were the guys for the job.

For an extra $50,000 they could come up with 20 reasons why you need them and even arrange a relatively harmless terrorist attack at peak traffic time anywhere in the city guaranteed to make the six o'clock report on all the infotainment stations. You know, to boost your sales.

In advertising there were always 10 simple tricks to make your diet healthier brought to you by, for example, *Two-A-Day Multi-Vitamins* or 11 ways to turn your workout into a fun session brought to you by *Crunch Fitness Centers*. Or of course there were always the agency's very lucrative stand-by ads in the women's journals and magazine to explain *12 Ways to Know He's Cheating on You* or *15 Things To Do To Please Him in Bed*, or 25 *Things to Insure You Get Everything in the Divorce When You Catch Him Cheating*. Or even if he wasn't cheating. Especially since not pleasing him in bed was no longer grounds for divorce.

At least that's what they said in a follow-on article in *Feminist Magazine*: *Why It's Okay for You to Cheat if You Suspect Him of Spending Too Much Time at Work.*

The line defining journalistic integrity from pure tripe for manipulative purposes at one time was clear. Then, due to corporate sponsorship, it gradually became blurred. Now it was virtually non-existent.

With national politics simply a subsidiary of the corporate world, big ad agencies were ever on the prowl for the right people to create promos for the right political candidate with which they could, through any means possible, convince America of their high moral ground.

One of the things that made FUOU **the** agency, was that they knew this better than most. They realized that ads must be recipe-ed into 'news'. Kind of like you have to blend just the right amount of rat poison with heroin to get the job done.

Coincidentally, both of which have the same end effect on your brain.

FOUO were master chefs at the recipe. In fact there were those who claimed FOUO invented the recipe.

And so it came to pass that the FUBAR'S had decided to hand the PR wing of their new campaign to their soon-to-be reliable and dependable standbys, the For Office Use Only Ad agency.

Ж

The heels of his knee high, purple leather Gucci boots could be heard 30 yards down the hall as they slapped into the marble floor. Like a gay, Bloody Red Baron heading for the cockpit of his bright red tri-winged fighter, his four foot long, paisley printed silk scarf floated behind him while he sipped at the silver plated straw emanating from his limited edition Perrier Signature Edition water flask. The silver reflective Ray Bans hid all his eyes might accidently reveal.

Smothered in a transparent cloud of the latest fashionable men's cologne, the staff could tell what day it was as his scent approached.

"Hmm, *Boss for Men*! Must be Friday!" The intern at the water cooler quietly declared as P. R. and his small entourage breezed by her.

P. R. Bloodbank-Leech was the head honcho of the largest, most ruthless and therefore the most successful ad agency in what was left of the United States.

As CEO there was no end of speculation as to how he had brought FOUO Ads to the financial and popular pinnacle of Wall Street success, but he had. It seemed that before him all obstacles crumbled. Governmental freedom of speech restrictions, the 'it-can't-be-doners' and worker's rights all folded like a school girl's knees at a boy band concert featuring *Men2Boyz*.

No one could ever say for sure why he could so efficiently rally the troops, kick ass and take names or put the fear of God into his workers, but he could. He just demanded respect from everyone all the time.

He had succeeded and was able to do this presumably because he had the one trait that all Americans valued as a sign of intelligence and sophistication above all other traits physical or mental.

He had an English accent.

The JGE or Just-Gay-Enough, twinge no doubt added to his charisma but it was his use of the word 'shop' when he meant store, 'lorry' for truck and 'lift' for elevator which so dearly enamored him to that wealthier segment of the public who longed to have a family tree of some description of which they were not ashamed.

After all, the thing to be most proud of, in the minds of most Americans was where you came from. That is with the exception of how much money you were worth.

Turn over any coin or glance at the face of any note and you are instantly reminded of the new American national motto replacing the old and antiquated e pluribus unum:

'Pecunia non omnia. Suus tantum!'

'Money isn't everything. It's the only thing!'

Bloodbank-Leech entered the packed meeting room that morning and took his seat at the modified throne in the corner and set his Perrier water flask on the small, gold Coco-Baroque table to the left.

Without uttering a word the office supervisor at the head of the long mahogany table realized P. R. was ready for the Monday morning pitch meeting to begin. Starbucks coffee cups, Croissants, bagels and scones disappeared from the table faster than a factory full of illegals in Laredo, Texas during an immigration raid.

At the head of the table the forty-something supervisor made up to look like a thirty-something and dressed like a twenty-something stood. The perfectly quaffed, bleached blond in her $1800 red, Armani dress laid her Gucci bag on the table, stepped forward in her Prada heels and spoke.

"Alright who's up first?"

A lanky twenty-something in the back with an orange Page Boy, a white shirt, purple skirt, green high heels and an impeccably made up face stood up and without preamble dramatically launched into his pitch.

"Are you tired of having to wade through advertisements? Are they a major cause of headaches?!" He dramatically read. "Then let us give you 18 reasons you get headaches brought to you by Bayer aspirin."

"Target demographic?" The supervisor snapped.

"This is a spot for the Lush Limburger *Only Atheists Don't Believe in God Hour*." He paused for comment. Instead she frowned as she attempted but was unable to identify the brand of shirt he was wearing.

"Is that shirt draped on your sadly, sagging and slumping shoulders sourced from one of our clients?" She accused.

"No ma'am, actually it's an Izod."

"That will be all."

"But it's a limited, signature edition." He floundered.

"SIT! NEXT!" She barked.

A twenty-something female who had apparently seen *Annie Hall* one too many times reluctantly stood and addressed the gathering.

"I have a pitch for the American Psychiatric Association account. I call it the *My Mother Had Me Tested* approach to mental health. It features the old, gay icon character Beldon Cooper."

"It was Sheldon Cooper." The Sup corrected.

"Sheldon Cooper. Because of the upcoming vote -"

"The guy from the last century?!" Someone challenged.

"Yes but . . . a recent survey shows that over 47% of gays –"

The presentation evaporated into silence as a rhythmic tapping rose to dominate to room. All heads turned to His Most Serene Highness seated in the corner.

"GOD DAMN IT PEOPLE!" P. R. yelled from his throne. "The heads of the FUBAR's are due here in one week and you're givin' me Pablum!" He lightly pounded on the ornate arm of his chair to display his anger. "I've ordered the Full English breakfast and you're fuckin' settin' a bloody bowl of Cheerios in front of me! And not the fun flavored ones with all the pretty colors! The ugly plain ones the color of Ebenezer Scrooge's toe nail clippings!" The young female intern at the back of the room audibly gagged. P. R. paused and looked down for dramatic effect. "I mean my god! My grandmother has flushed better material down the loo!"

As part of his carefully rehearsed act he stepped down from the thrown to circulate.

"Are we not the people who single-handedly brought smoking back into vogue thereby saving R. J. Reynolds and the entire Carolina economy? The ones who convinced the Vegas hotel accounts that a little bit of heroin before hitting the craps tables increased your odds of winning and then went on to help the lobbyists to help the Senate to understand the economic logic of passing the necessary laws?! Nevada, the only narcotics friendly state in the country!" Grumbles, harrumphs and miscellaneous chatter ensued. "Are we not the very people that rescued Houston execs with our infamous 'Ten sea creatures that we can do without and were probably going to be extinct in a hundred years anyway!' campaign?' Thereby breathing new life into their oil rigs division?" He began to stroll across the floor.

"Reinforced by the fact that we have millions of species and new ones are popping up all the time!" Someone excitedly called out.

"Yes P. R.!" Another blurted.

"Certainly P.R.!" One of the copywriters at the back of the table unexpectedly chimed in.

"'And nobody will miss them!' That was for Exxon! I remember that one! I was a sophomore in college when that came out!" Spat out the latest member of Kiss Asses Anonymous.

"Made me want to go into journalism! Or advertising. Same thing really." Another across the table conceded. The Supervisor sat and yawned. P. R. continued his controlled rant.

"We need an angle so hard, so new so . . . so . . ."

"So obtuse!" The one with the magenta hair threw out.

"That's it! We need an obtuse angle!" The copywriter chimed in again.

"Now you're gettin' the idea!" P. R. encouraged now in the back of the room.

"Like, political candidate types like. Like who's campaigning and also at the same time like running for office like. Right like?" Magenta astutely observed.

"Yeah?!" Someone agreed.

"Well, running for office like means they are always building themselves up like and also saying like good things about themselves, like right?"

"Okay."

"That in turn like means they got'a say bad stuff about the other guy, like. Like right?"

"I know what you're sayin', like! Totally!" The dress concurred.

"Okay, so just like we pointed out that evolution was gonna get rid of those sea creatures for Exxon anyways, why can't we just say like the FUBAR's are gonna get rid of the other guys and say it's evolution like?!"

"**Good**! Don't forget to work the sponsor in there somewhere!" P. R. encouraged.

"Oh yeah! Brought to you by Exxon Oil."

"NO Justine! Our current client, The FUBAR's." The supervisor rejoined in the verbal safari.

"So let me get this straight! What we're suggesting for a tent pole campaign slogan is that we use, 'You Can't Help Stupid.'?" P. R. deduced.

"LIKE EXACTLY. LIKE!" Magenta hair screeched.

"How about if we add; 'But we can!'" The fifteen year old gay kid next to her said.

"Genius Jerami!" P. R. shouted. "You're someone the Queen would be proud of! If we still had a queen."

"You could have me!" The boy exclaimed.

"That's good! I like that! 'You can't help stupid! But we can!' Where'd you get it?"

"Heard it on a news broadcast." The boy told him.

"Can it be traced?"

"I doubt it. It was from some podunk town in the Midwest."

"Good! Then get it to legal, tell them to copyright it immediately, register it so we can sue anyone who uses it and we'll run with it!"

Ж

That Friday afternoon, as Thaddeus wasn't as smart or clever as most people, wasn't well respected or educated, had no political opinions and was only working in a factory and so wasn't particularly productive, he had been called for jury duty, which he couldn't get out of. In fact, Thaddeus Pervers didn't know you could get out of jury duty. He believed, like the near 100% conviction rate of the Texas court system, it was his duty to 'do' a jury, so he had to do it.

He was running late for registration so, driving in his sky-blue pink GE electro-matic, Twizy Urban Model 80, City Tour compact two door, Thaddeus decided to take the 407-311A by pass to the highway to get downtown a little faster.

Racing to the intersection just before the on ramp he didn't notice the green light had changed and so inadvertently shot through the amber. His timing was impeccable as the big, black, gas powered Lincoln Continental which ran the red light travelling on the east-west road, was in the perfect position in the middle of the intersection. At 55 miles per hour he T-boned the Lincoln.

The oncoming traffic swerved avoiding further disaster and the little traffic there was behind the big, black land yacht quickly changed lanes and drove on leaving the smoking wreck of his City Tour car jutting out of the side of the Lincoln like a large sky-blue middle finger to any low flying aircraft.

Thaddeus was appalled at the crumpled accordion-like condition of his destroyed car as he kicked open the door which popped off like the top of a coffee can lid and fell to the ground with a clang. But being the good Samaritan he was he immediately made for the other vehicle to check if everyone was okay.

Approaching the completely undamaged Lincoln he could see, besides the driver, the car contained a passenger and in the back seat there was a baby carrier complete with sleeping baby. Fortunately the industrial cargo straps holding the child carrier in had held, and the side airbags built into the Mattel Delux A-1 Model baby carrier had deployed so the tyke lay undisturbed.

The driver however, looked to be in a mild state of shock as he just sat, clung to the huge steering wheel and stared straight ahead without response. The pugnacious looking passenger on the other hand climbed out of the car and calmly approached the ruffled Thaddeus slowly shaking his head while looking down as if he just made a minor arithmetical error on a high school algebra test.

Thaddeus was partially relieved that no one appeared to be hurt and instantly reached for his wallet to produce his driver's license and prepare for the customary exchange of information.

The massive six foot four, strong arm-looking monster draped in a shin-length black leather coat stopped just inches from Thaddeus and looked first at the car door of the Lincoln then at Thaddeus. There was hardly a scratch on the apparently new Continental but Thaddeus was visibly shaken.

"I trust you are uninjured in your body parts or otherwise remain unhurted or traumatized?" The giant enquired in his somewhat circuitous lexicon.

"No . . . no, I'm okay. Thank you." Shocked and relieved that homicide wasn't already being visited upon him, Thaddeus relaxed somewhat. "Are you and your friend okay?"

They both glanced over at the small but clearly terrified driver who apparently had now mistaken the steering wheel for a life preserver and was doing his impersonation of Leonardo DeCappacino in the last scene of *Titanic*.

"Yes." Came the terse reply.

"I assure you I'll do the right thing and not to worry, the You're in Good Hands insurance company will -"

"Excuse me?"

"My agency, The You're in Good Hands Insurance Agency, they'll cover everything!"

The big man glanced at the thumb nail-sized scratch on the Lincoln's door then again at the crumpled, smoking, unsalvageable wreck of the electric car with the back seat where the front seat used to be and smiled.

He then reached for Thaddeus who flinched and smiled a nervous smile up at him. Big Man laid his massive paw on Pervers' shoulder and spoke.

"My nervous, newly found friend, while I have small reluctance regarding your hands insurance agency, which I am confident covers a plethora of everything, I have grave misgivings visa vie the damage caused by said mishap in which we now find ourselves entangled in, requires recompense of any sort. Not to mention reportage."

Like the ancient Rock n' Roll song of long ago, Thaddeus was dazed and confused by the response.

"You mean you don't want to file a report to your insurance company?"

"Leave us say that my particular insurance firm is located somewhat out of state as it were."

"But the law . . ." The obedient citizen in him insisted.

"Besides . . ." Big Man reached into his breast pocket and produced a wad of bills which would choke a Republican. He peeled off fifteen or twenty, one thousand dollar notes, folded them over and stuffed them into Thaddeus' jacket pocket. "You would be in an elevated state of happiness with a new automobile, would you not?"

Pervers looked at his bulging coat pocket then up at the stranger. The only reaction he could muster was a single nod.

Suddenly police sirens could be heard quickly closing in.

"SHIT!" The stranger loudly whispered. "Please forgive my profane use of impertinent language and allow me to take my leave. Have a nice day." The man cursed again and scurried faster than his huge frame would allow back around to the passenger side of the car. "GO, GO!" He yelled at the driver who had already restarted the car.

Unfortunately it was not quite fast enough for just as Big Man slammed the door closed a police hover-cruiser gently set down in front of the Lincoln supported by one in back effectively barricading the vehicle in.

Four heavily armed cops dressed in standard police battle gear, with four more assuming firing positions behind the cruisers as back-up, surrounded the car from all four corners. Armed with standard issue M16A-12's/203's equipped with grenade launchers and modified, banana ammo clips they initiated their standard procedure attack formation and riddled all four tires and wheels with the entire fifty round clips in their weapons which they immediately and expertly changed out and reloaded.

It was standard procedure.

Certain they were all going to die if he stayed in the car, Big Man pushed open the car door and climbed out. Petrified by the attack, Thaddeus scurried off to the side of the road abandoning his wreck.

With his right hand the Big Man reached into his breast pocket but before he could produce anything he was instantly transformed into a black leather coat of chopped meat by the four cops emptying their reloaded weapons into his convulsing body. A minute later, save for the tinkle of spent brass shells on the pavement, silence ensued.

Next to the Lincoln the decimated lump of goo that used to be the Big Man lay motionless as a single dime-sized air bubble rose to the top of the oozing lump and burst with a tiny 'pop'.

Trails of smoke wafted from each of the police weapons.

"SIR, PUT DOWN YOUR WEAPON AND STEP AWAY FROM THE VEHICLE!" One of the police loud speakers mounted on the rear hover craft loudly announced.

As they again reloaded one of the officers took the extra measure of producing a police issue, stainless steel cleaver from his belt and, walking over to the dead man, hacked off the mutilated corpse's hand to insure he couldn't use the gun he didn't have, just in case he had one.

It was standard procedure.

Thaddeus cowered dumfounded down in the berm, behind the guard rail.

The terrified driver was ordered out of the vehicle and taken into custody. After he was pried from the steering wheel by paramedics.

Another of the officers approached the crumpled City Tour car, scanned the rear license plate and, into his hand held scanner, punched in a sequence of numbers. Waiting for the beeps, buzzes and clicks to subside, he shook his head and walked over to Thaddeus.

"You Thaddeus Enoch Pervers, Citizen Registration # 27-CA-06?"

"Yes sir." He replied, the shock of events still lingering.

"We need to take you in."

"But I . . ."

"Somebody down town wants to talk to you in relation to the infant."

"Okay." Thaddeus' advanced state of confusion now advanced a little more. "Uh, what infant?"

"Take what you need from your car, we'll have the government sanitation engineers clean up the rest."

As they led Thaddeus to their hovercraft a third cop went into the back seat of the Lincoln produced a tiny little set of handcuffs, and gently handcuffed the still sleeping infant. Just in case, and quietly read her her rights.

It was standard procedure.

Up ahead on the highway, as the police hovercraft lifted off amidst the accumulating traffic jam, the screeching of tires followed by a tremendous crash and the honking of horns was heard off in the distance. The police immediately realized there had been another car crash. And, as they handcuffed and stuffed the driver/perpetrator into a black leather confiscation bag, sealed it up and carried their prey away, it was back near the previous exit that they saw a small mushroom cloud appeared. They all instantly realized what had happened.

It was the braking system on one of the new Toyota nuclear powered cars which hadn't yet been perfected.

Ж

Downtown in City Hall Thaddeus was escorted by two policemen upstairs to the Mayor's office leaving him at the door to the plush, spacious office. Thaddeus immediately observed he was alone in the room and so took a seat in front of the Mayor's desk in one of two ornate chairs standing next to each other.

A few minutes later a door to the left opened and two middle-aged, well dressed men entered. Pervers instantly recognized one as the Mayor but only partially had an idea about who the other was.

"Mr. Pervers! Thaddeus Enoch Pervers! My Man!" The Mayor approached brandishing a wide smile. In one hand was a glass of brandy while the other was extended and he greeted Thaddeus as if he were a long lost frat brother. "Mayor Dinkins Pervers! Damn glad to meet ya!" He announced. They shook hands vigorously.

Next to His Honor the Mayor of Brubaker stood someone Pervers had only seen in photos, paintings and on billboards. John Holcomb Brubaker the Third, owner and CEO of Brubaker industries.

"You know this gentleman, Mr. Pervers?"

"Please, call me Thaddeus your honor." He eked out as he stared like a flabbergasted schoolboy.

"Alright Thaddeus. You know this gentleman?"

"I think I might rec-"

"Well you ought to he's your damn boss!" The Mayor chuckled and slapped Thad on the back. "This is Mr. John Holcomb Brubaker the Third of-"

"Brubaker Industries! I'll be damned!" Thaddeus declared.

Pervers extended his hand but instead of shaking it Brubaker just stared. Thaddeus became unnerved. The man's eyes watered up and a tear rolled down his cheek as he produced a folded over sheet paper and passed it to Thaddeus. It was a typewritten note.

```
We have your kid! $10,000,000
 by midnight or the brat gets it!
```

"This is a ransom note!" Thaddeus realized out loud. The Mayor stepped between them.

"That's right! Turns out that baby you rescued was kidnapped! Mr. Brubaker's only grand kid!" Dinkins informed.

"Well, sir . . . I didn't exactly-"

Brubaker stepped forward and hugged Pervers so tightly he couldn't breathe and then broke into extended sobbing.

"You're a hero boy!" The Mayor declared and slapping Thaddeus on the back again he finished off his brandy. He then took Thaddeus by the arm and guided him back into the chair hastening to reach for the bottle on his desk. He poured himself another along with one for Thaddeus.

"You work in one of Mr. Brubaker's factories, that right boy?!" He shoved a cigar into Pervers gapping gob and took the seat next to him.

"Yes sir, I mean your honor. I operate a Steen-"

"No you don't boy, not no more you don't!" The mayor declared. Thaddeus stared. Brubaker cried. Dinkins continued talking. "We got a proposition for you boy! One I think you gonna like!"

Thaddeus sniffed the $200 brandy then sipped a bit.

"You see Thaddeus, alright if I call you Thaddeus? Good! You see Thaddeus, I'm in sort of a binding situation you might say, and you're in a unique position to help me out. You do wann'a help your mayor out, don't you Thaddeus?" Thaddeus nodded. "GOOD! That's good!" He poured Thaddeus more brandy even though he hadn't drunk any of the first drink. "I need you to take something off my hands."

"What's that Mayor?"

"My job boy, my job!"

The cigar fell from Pervers' mouth as it dropped open and he lowered the three quarters full brandy snifter to his lap and stared straight through Dinkins.

"But to make it look legitimate like, all of politics is about making things look legitimate know-what-I-mean?" Dinkins confided in Thaddeus. Pervers gave a single nod but didn't know what he meant. "I gotta step down in disgrace like. The thing is see, that we ain't got no time to orchestrate no emergency election, besides there'll be one come November any ways and by that time, with Brubaker's help here, you'll have endeared yourself to the people, there-by ensuring your legitimate election as their rightfully elected leader! Simple ain't it?!"

Thaddeus stared. "But I thought state regulations required a candidate to be in state politics at least a year before he was eligible for any office in that state? At least that's what my friends at the factory told me."

Dinkins turned to the factory czar.

"That sound right to you Brubaker? You ever heard such a thing before?" Brubaker shrugged and nodded in affirmation as he continued crying into his handkerchief like a baby. The mayor reached over to his desk and activated the laser operated intercom.

"Regina, get me Argyle Greenpasture on the line right away asks her about the state regs for being mayor!"

Yes mayor.

A minute later the intercom buzzed back.

Mayor, I have Ms. Greenpasture on line one.

"Put her through." He came around behind his desk and picked up the wireless transceiver. "Uh huh. Uh huh. You don't say? Uh huh. I see. Uh huh. You don't say? You mean . . . Uh huh. Okay. Thank you Argyle." He hung up.

"You was right boy! Regulations do say, 'in office', such as in the town council or some such nonsense 'for one year minimum'. But they also says that if said candidate garners 10,000 signatures in a petition to the election board of the county in which the office sought is located, he is automatically eligible! Providing the population of the jurisdictional area, the town that is, has a population **not to** exceed 100,000!" The Mayor was momentarily lost, shallow in thought. He re-manned the intercom. "Regina, get me Argyle Greenpasture on the line again!"

Yes mayor.

A minute later the intercom buzzed back.

Mayor, I have Ms. Greenpasture back on line one.

"Argyle, how many people we got officially listed living in Brubaker? 100,012?! Damn!" He thought again. "How many in that Vietnamese family just moved in last week over behind the rail yard? 13? Perfect! Have the sheriff draw up some papers and send a notice tellin' them they's been evicted!" There was a pause. "Hell woman, I don't know. Have him tell them we been getting' complaints about people's dogs been missin', again! . . . Well then say they's communists or something just have them outside the city limits by close of business tonight!" He hung up and turned back to Thaddeus.

"There we go, easy-peasy, Vietnam-easy! Population under 100,000! Now all we need is them 10,000 signatures and it's a done deal!"

"10,000 SIGNATURES!? I don't know ten people let alone 10,000!" Thaddeus declared.

"That's the beauty of it boy! You **do know** 10,000 people! You just don't know you know 10,000 people! Know what I mean?!" Dinkins declared. Pervers didn't know what he meant but he nodded anyway. The mayor jumped up and darted to the other side of his desk. From a drawer he produced a blank form and held it aloft.

"You're already head of the town council! This is just the next logical step."

"Well your honor, I ain't really head of the town council, that's just a temporary position until-"

"Johnny here can have those 10,000 signatures on this here petition in less than a day by offerin' his workers a $100 bonus each in their next pay slip, can't ya Johnny boy?!"

"Uh huh!" Brubaker loudly sobbed into his already soaked handkerchief and nodded with joy as he rung it out over the office trash can then resumed crying like a baby.

Dinkins had been trying to persuade Brubaker to help him to find and back a suitable candidate, someone to pass the office onto and to run come next election which wasn't until November. However, Dinkins wouldn't be around in November. In fact he was under tremendous pressure to take leave of his office by three p.m. next Wednesday. Which is when, he had been tipped off, the federal marshals were due to show up and take him into custody.

What the mayor and Brubaker knew that Thaddeus and the rest of the town didn't was that Dnkins, in the indomitable spirit of Warren G, Harding, Richard Nixon and George W. Bush, Dinkins had adhered to the timeless tradition of violating the public trust. In a big way.

He had been under investigation by the FBI for the last nine months and was on the verge of being arrested for embezzlement, gerrymandering and misappropriation of public funds. To the tune of seventeen and a half million dollars.

However, being the professional he was he had socked enough money away in a Swiss bank account to retire with to Cabo San Lucas in Mexico for the rest of his life.

If he could get out of Ohio in one piece.

From the moment he received the first police report that the little Brubaker baby had been found and rescued Dinkins' mind went into overdrive and fast forwarded to the hero's welcome for whoever had saved her would get from the humble people of Brubaker and the accolades said hero would receive as well as the high esteem in which he would be held. Just high enough for the people, with a little help from the right media spin, to accept him as their new mayor sans an election.

When he looked at Thaddeus Pervers Dinkins didn't see a dim witted factory worker, he saw a plane ticket to Cabo.

"But sir, I don't really know anything about politics! People go to school for years to learn about how to be politicians, negotiate and stop wars an all."

"And they all fail just as well as you will! Why do you think they use the term, 'gettin' to know your public'? It's because the secret to politics, all you got'a do to be a successful politician, is to talk to people just long enough to get them to tell you what they want, wait a few minutes while they explain it and then promise them that's what you'll do for 'em!"

"Sounds dishonest to me!" Thaddeus objected.

"What's honesty?" Dinkins moved forward and put an arm as high up as his short frame would allow around

Pervers' shoulder and switched into 'sincerity' mode. "Really, what is honesty? Honesty is doing what you're supposed to do, not making trouble. Doing what everybody else is doing! Besides, I can see by the way you carry yourself that you're an honest man! Me? I'm one'a the biggest sum bitches ever was! Ask anybody!" He again turned to Brubaker. "John Holcomb, ain't I the biggest sum bitch you ever seen?!"

"Uh huh!" Brubaker emphatically sobbed.

"So by doin' me this favor and favoring the good people of Brubaker, Ohio, you're replacin' a sum-bitch an puttin' an honest man in office! You'll actually be rightin' a wrong!"

"But your honor what about the Deputy Mayor? Shouldn't he be taking over?"

"Unfortunately boy, when this whole thing hits the infotainment networks people gonna wanna see somebody get spanked, know-what-I-mean?" Thaddeus shook his head. He sort'a knew what he meant.

"Well what about the City Manager?"

"Ain't got one! I abolished that office coupl'a months ago. Didn't wanna havt'a always be looking over my shoulder!"

Over in the corner Brubaker had temporarily toned it down to a steady sob.

Sensing he was losing Thaddeus, Dinkins sat back down and pulled his chair closer to Pervers. "At the end of the day it's just a job. A job where nobody believes you're gonna really do what you say you're gonna do! You're a politician! It's just like when you nod and say, 'yes dear' to your wife or, like all them damn fools who go to fortune tellin' gypsies. Minute they walk in the door she's sizin' 'em up, looking at how they're dressed, how they talk and walk. After a few minutes of sly observation, BAM!" Thaddeus jumped as Dinkins slapped his hands loudly together. "She's got them and their money soon follows." He stood again and went to his desk. "I'll get Greenpasture to sign off on it and Johnny here'll take care of the petition. It'll all be wrapped up by Monday close of business." He still detected residual reluctance in Thaddeus.

"What'a ya say we got a deal? Mr. Mayor?" Dinkins prodded. "I'll even throw in my two bedroom apartment!" Pervers' eyes lit up like a high school kid whose girlfriend just announced her parents were going to be away for the weekend and she was going to be home alone. "And about that honesty thing, don't worry too much about that. There's nothin' or no one in this country can't be bought, which means that's the standard which means as long as you don't go against it, you're being honest! You're doing what everybody else is doing, which means it ain't dishonest! Know-what-I-mean Pervers?"

Thaddeus knew what Dinkins meant, but he started to think about his friends, the BB Stackers and how he didn't deserve such a break. Then it hit him.

"I'll do it on the condition that all the folks at the factory get a raise!" Thaddeus declared. Dinkins' eyes narrowed and a Grinch-like grin crept across his jowly face. He had found Thaddeus' price.

Brubaker peeked over the top of his handkerchief.

"YOU SEE! It only comes down to price! You know, you wash my back I'll wash yours kind'a thing." Dinkins shook Thaddeus' hand and threw in a pat on the back for good measure. "Brubaker, okay to give them boys over to the factory a raise?!"

"Well, I'm not too sure-"

"GOOD!" Dinkins confirmed. "See what it is to have friends Pervers?!"

Brubaker howled as he broke into another fit of unrestrained sobbing.

Thaddeus and the soon-to-be-retired Mayor shook and the deal was sealed. Brubaker wiped his eyes with a clean hanky and forced a smile for the first time that afternoon.

Thaddeus headed home to tell Prudence the good news and Dinkins and Brubaker waited until he had left the office to stop smiling.

Dinkins' face fell serious as he grabbed his coat.

"Get one of your people to get over to the police station and check on the accident report!" Dinkins moved to gather his things. "Meanwhile, don't take any wooden nickels! I got a plane to catch!"

"What about the two thugs?" Dinkins inquired.

"One's dead the other's in jail." Dinkins paused in the doorway on his way out.

"Well, crime don't pay. I guess they found out the hard way!" Brubaker raced to the closing door as Dinkins waddled down the hall.

"When should I give the factory workers their raise?" He called after Dinkins who had just stepped into the elevator.

"Fuck 'em! They're factory workers!" The lift doors closed over and the car descended.

In less than a week Thaddeus Enoch Pervers would be able to quit his factory job, move into his new two bedroom apartment and step into his new role as Mayor of Brubaker, Ohio.

But more importantly he had discovered the secrets of big business. The principles which made the United States of America and her unique system of capitalism so successful thus propelling her to the top of the heap for the brief period from post-World War Two to the turn of the second millennium.

He discovered how to learn what the other side wants, gauge their weaknesses and apply blackmail.

THE FNG
14:29, Friday, March 12th

CHAPTER EIGHT

☆

Distraught that he missed jury duty registration and that his damaged sky-blue pink, GE electro-matic, Twizy Urban Model 80, City Tour compact car was taken to the nearest garage, it was after leaving the Mayor's office that Thaddeus hopped an electric taxi back home where, propped up in bed eating a second large bag of Fritos and washing it down with a gallon of Breyer's strawberry ice cream, his wife Prudence sat firmly planted watching her favorite soap opera, *As the Young and the Restless Doctors Turn*. He informed her of the events of his day.

She snapped at him to wait for the commercial when they could talk.

As he never got to register for jury duty Thaddeus was never called. But because he never registered and was never called, his name had gone forward to the New Office of Homeland Security & Personal Affairs where his citizen registration number was red flagged as a possible dissident and, therefore a future terroristic threat.

☆

Since so many citizens had opted out of jury duty over the years, following the confiscation of the *Jurors Handbook: How To Get Out of Jury Duty*, opting out of jury duty was no longer a legal option. Everybody was now required by law to serve. No excuses.

A reserved area had been set aside in each court room for the 'ambulatory challenged' so they could serve and if a selected juror was hospitalized a special Skype channel would be ordered set up at their bed side so they could still serve. During childbirth pregnant women were still required to follow the proceedings so they too could cast their votes at the end of the now abbreviated trial sessions.

They were deemed exempt during delivery.

Jurors were not allowed to ask questions or submit requests to the judges and had to watch the entire half hour proceedings, the time restriction had been imposed back in 2037 when the Judiciary decided that trials were taking too long and wasting tax payer dollars. Ergo jurors had to submit their verdicts, now referred to as 'votes', within ten minutes of the end of the trial. Besides the prosecutors had improved their batting average to a 99% conviction rate so, as the trials always ended the same, the new argument went, there was no point in dragging them out.

It had become a world where lawyers were the new priests, judges the new gods and court rooms the new temples complete with sacrificial alters called 'witness stands'.

The guilty, euphemistically called defendants, under the guise of 'the accused' but in reality were called 'the guilty', were marched into to the alter and paraded before the condemning eyes of 'The Court' to be put through the highly theatrical process. The only difference was the gods wore the robes, not the priests.

They wore expensive Armani suits.

"Run it by the judges." became the most common catch phrase whenever a politician was asked to write or vote for a new law. The actual merit or potential impact of any proposed new legislation was never really a factor, only whether or not the black robes would approve of it.

The utter lunacy of screaming for total equality while shouting for people to maintain their individualism never occurred to anyone. The idea of the two things being 'mutually exclusive' was not a concept.

In the new society everyone wanted to be considered and treated as equals while maintaining what they believed to be their personal individualism, and the jury system was touted as the quintessential demonstration of this, a system which hadn't undergone any real legal revision since its inception in ancient times during the Viking era.

Unfortunately, dodging jury duty was also touted as a trait associated with being clever. Logically therefore, the clever thing to do, was to show how clever you were by coming up with the most original excuse for not reporting for jury duty.

Additionally, the fact that 'jury of your peers' was increasingly becoming an out-dated concept and with convictions more and more routinely depending on circumstantial evidence, the presentation of 'facts' to juries had become more and more burdensome and so was deemed to take up too much of the court's time.

Finally a bill had been passed, at the behest of the courts, and signed by Presidential order, that juries had been done away with as the $13.50 a day each juror was being paid was seen as much too expensive and began to impinge on the financial support of the Federal Department of Prisons, the largest in the world, now burdened to pay €75,000 a year per prisoner to the respective private corporations that almost exclusively ran the prisons. This expense was expected to rise by 15% in the next year.

Despite having only 5% of the world's population the U.S. prison population had ballooned to 25% of the world's incarcerated. Plus judges, sheriffs' and police salaries were one of the few things holding the economy together in many areas.

The Presidential edict eliminating juries had been rescinded by the following administration, a Republican but re-instated four years later by the newly elected president, a Democrat. The following administration rescinded the rescind order and so the jury issue followed the common pattern of ping-ponging back and forth through the system continuing to serve as a prop for potential candidates needing to give the illusion of the 'C' word, Change, amidst their political promises.

This uncontrolled controllable vacillation was favored by most politicians as it also served to keep the people off guard and therefore just a little more confused as to exactly which law was in effect at any given time.

> In short, with questionable cases, retrials from an 85% appeal rate and backlogs, the courts were a mess.

Ж

Meanwhile, deep in the dark bowels of the FUBAR headquarters in the back of the back room of the exclusive Northside Gentlemen's Members Only Private Club, Senator Snodgrass and his two cohorts plotted and planned.

"Okay, everything's set up, now all we need is a meat puppet to use!" Snodgrass growled.

"What's a meat puppet?" Moss asked.

"It's a synonym for an FNG." O'Shea answered.

"What's an FNG?"

"A Fucking New Guy! Ain't you never had a proper job?"

"NO! I'm a lawyer!" Moss rebutted.

"Any ideas from the peanut gallery?" Sydney threw out to Moss and O'Shea sitting opposite.

"What about that retired governor from New Jersey?" Moss proposed.

"The one with the bridge traffic scandal?"

"No! The one that emptied the county treasury then got caught and denied it all from his $10 million mansion."

"Dead." Snodgrass snapped. "Heart attack last month."

"How about the one from Ohio who got nailed in that ABSCAM III sting by the FBI? He seems like a sure bet!"

"He's on the Funny Farm. Mentally committed after he found out his kid was a gay Scientologist!"

"There's straight Scientologists?!" O'Shea queried.

"Besides, he' ain't from Ohio. He's was from New Jersey."

"Well, what about the guy, the Democrat, who was nailed for embezzlement and misuse of government funds in New York?" Snodgrass queried.

"Had a stroke, so they made him a Republican. And he's from Jersey too." O'Shea informed.

"I seem to remember a fella who slid out from underneath a murder charge coupl'a years back. What was his name?" Pete Moss threw out.

"Kerns. Gerome Kerns, a mayor. Fixed the election."

"Sounds like a good candidate! What's his current status?" Moss encouraged. Snodgrass perked up.

"20 to life in the state pen for $50 mil in bank fraud." Rick said with equal disappointment. "And he wasn't from Florida, only had property there." O'Shea clarified.

"Where the hell **was** he from?!" Snodgrass demanded.

"Jersey!" Moss and responded in unison.

"Christ! Are all the criminals from New Jersey now days?" Sydney scoffed.

"Only the professional ones."

"So all the politicians from New Jersey are usually criminals?"

"It's a traditional state." Moss shrugged.

Frustrated by the conversation which was creeping moderately above his level and with his decreased attention span, Moss began to idly thumb through last month's issue of the *Harvard Political Review* which he had plucked from the coffee table. They ordered ore drinks and sat in further thought.

"Hey! Look at this!" Moss folded the magazine over to the open page and showed the other two the full spread, featured advertisement.

```
National Convention of Mayors
Boston-Kennedy Convention Center
       April 17th - 19th
   Sponsored by the AFL-CIO
          Free Beer!
```

O'Shea grabbed the magazine from Moss and Snodgrass grabbed it from O'Shea, scanned the ad and smiled.

"Fish in a barrel!" He mumbled with an evil smile.

"What? What are you talking about?" O'Shea queried.

"The National Mayor's Convention! It's the perfect cover to make us look legit!"

"Yeah, how?"

"Every year they give an Outstanding Mayor of the Year award, which gets national headlines. That's our way in!"

"Huh?" Moss grunted.

"We get him-"

"Him who?!" Moss, as always was playing catch up.

"OUR STOOGE! We get him this award, he's convinced he's capable of bigger and better things than just being a mayor!"

"Like maybe governor!" Moss had a rare moment of elucidation.

"Like maybe governor or better yet senator!" O'Shea jumped in.

"And BLAMMO! He's ours!" Snodgrass declared in rehearsed triumph. For the next few minutes they all sat, smiled and nodded in satisfaction at one another until Moss pointed out the obvious.

"One small problem Sydney. How we gonna ensure our man gets the award?"

"Are you shitting me? Tell me you never helped fix a contest or an election?" Snodgrass probed.

"Or seen The Emmys, The Tonys or The Oscars! When has the best picture **ever** won Best Picture!?" O'Shea added.

"Okay but that still leaves us short a stooge! Who we gonna get?" Moss persisted.

"Hey! Here's a story about a factory worker in Ohio rescued some kid from a bunch of nasty gangster types." O'Shea announced reading from the magazine.

"Is he popular?"

"Says here they made him mayor fer Christ's sake! They love him!"

"What happened to the old mayor?"

"Magnanimous guy, retired and stepped aside to make room for the hero then retired on a modest pension! So the papers said." Rick explained.

"Well then it must be true!" Moss concurred.

"Okay, he's a mayor but is he stupid enough? Can we pass him off as a politician?"

"He's a factory worker for cryin' out loud, how smart can he be?! Thaddeus somebody Pervers. Probably dumb as a box of rocks!"

"I make a movement we convince him to join the party." Moss proposed.

"If he's a pervert and such a fuckin' puppet why don't we just buy him outright? Add him to the collection."

"We can't buy him!" Rick challenged.

"Why not God damn it?! Ain't nobody can't be bought! This is still America ain't it?!" Snodgrass challenged.

"It's Pervers!" Rick pointed to the article small article at the bottom of the page.

"What?"

"It's PERVERS not Pervert that's why!"

"Well, says here he wanted to vote for prostitutes to be at least 19 years old " Moss argued.

"Oh, a humanist! That's good!" O'Shea approved.

"I miss prostitutes! Some'a my best friends was prostitutes." Moss mumbled out loud.

"Shut up Pete, you're confusing prostitutes with senatutes! We ain't talkin' about prostitutes, damn it!" Sydney admonished. "I heard about him too. But if he keeps makin' cracks about politicians doing the right thing he won't have a snowball's chance in hell of getting anywhere, not with talk like that! People'll think he's up to something."

"Alright, alright! At least we agree that Operation Bentwood is a go and-" Rick pushed on.

"Operation Bentwood?" Sydney questioned.

"Yeah, that's what I'm calling it, what about it? Besides, when's the last time you had any wood?!" Rick laughingly challenged Snodgrass.

"About the same time you did, fifty years ago when that Ronald Lump moron accidently fixed the economy! And mine was just as bent as yours!" Snodgrass snapped back. "Now, are we all agreed that we use this what's his name? This Pervers something with a T?"

Moss and O'Shea nodded in agreement.

"Okay, were gonna need money. How much is Arabian crude sellin' for now days?" Snodgrass barked to no one in particular as he lit a cigar.

"Yesterday closed at $700 a barrel." Rick reported.

"Well call Feruk, tell him to convene the United Arab Council we need it up another ten or so. Tell him make it close to twenty dollars by Friday. We're gonna need plenty of capital to launch this one."

"Will do S.S.!" Moss echoed.

"And get a hold of that private eye we used to cut my grandkids off of their inheritance, the one with one eye. Tell him I got a job for him."

"Will do S.S.!"

Ж

Now settled in to their new two room apartment in a better part of town, Taranjello had his own room, Prudence had a larger couch to accommodate her expanding girth as well as two T.V.'s, one in the living room and one in the bedroom, both with voice activated channel changers so she didn't have to get out of bed so often.

With the family satiated and safely tucked away Thaddeus could apply what little bit of an attention span he had to his new station in life down at the city hall. Working on the assembly line at Brubaker's for so long he had lost the ability to mentally focus and organize he started to develop years ago in high school. The question now haunted him, could he regain that skill and once again become task oriented?

Time would tell.

"What exactly are my duties around here Regina?" He asked as he sat behind the ornate, imitation oak desk.

The lanky, dark haired receptionist whose hair was not quite long enough to form a proper bun on her head and so presented as a small geyser of jet black water sprouting from the top of her oblong skull, busied herself with some filing.

"Well Mr. Mayor, rubber stamping and signing things, meet-and-greets and speeches -"

"Speeches?! What kind of speeches? Speeches to who?!" The only speeches Thaddeus had ever given were to his son as he was growing up about cleaning up and getting up off his lazy ass. None of which had any effect.

"Well Mr. Mayor," She consulted the electronic, hand diary surgically embedded in her palm. "Today at one you have to present a new hall to the O. F. & P. A. of W."

"O. F. & P. A. of W.?"

"Yes sir, the Organization for Financial & Political Advancement of Women. You'll be expected to say a few words there."

"What do I say?"

"Well Mayor Dinkins always started out by reminding them that if men had to have the babies and women ran the government there'd be no more war, no poverty and complete cooperation between all nations on earth. Total harmony."

"Really? And they bought that?"

"They seemed to."

"Okay. Anything else?"

"You'll probably want to say a few words on their current agenda."

"Which is. . . ?"

"Their support and endorsement of the presidential candidate Hillbilly Crayon and her mandatory castration policy for all men who have cheated on their wives."

"Sounds like a pretty even-handed bunch."

"Tomorrow you will spend the morning with the town council working on the budget and the afternoon is scheduled for moderating citizen's complaints to the city. That will be downstairs in the main hall."

"Fantastic."

"It's televised."

"Thrilled." He wasn't.

Ж

"National Convention of Mayors. Kennedy Convention Center, Boston, March 17th to the 19th."

In a cramped, shadowy room in Lower Manhattan's Bowery district, a greasy little man sat and spoke to the small screen of a computerized GPS location unit on his desk, as he read from a magazine article dictating into the computer.

"Upcoming National Convention." He spoke in a neutral, mechanical tone.

The screen sparked to life and displayed a holographic image of the Kennedy convention center. He nodded in approval as the full color, 3D image slowly rotated on its vertical axis and was accompanied by a short blurt of the event.

"Agenda." He dictated and poured himself another coffee cup full of Jack Daniels bourbon and lit a cigarette. The screen displayed the two day list of events to include the grand finale, the awards ceremony for Mayor of the Year.

"List of attendees." The list appeared instantly. Most notably, His Honor Thaddeus Enoch Pervers was absent.

"Display list of nominees for Mayor of the Year Award." He continued and again the liquid vapor circuits complied. To his delight there were only three nominees listed. A mayor from New Jersey, a mayor from Topeka, no doubt a token entry, and one that he immediately zeroed in on.

A Grinch-like smile crept across his semi-toothless face at nominee number three, the only three time recipient of the award. Johnny B. Bentover, a former boy band member was the Mayor of San Francisco. He was a flaming gay who had just been re-elected to his fourth term of office who apparently was the most popular mayor the west coast had ever seen.

The P. I. went to work making notes and outlining his plan.

Less than an hour later he had referenced the home address of Johnny B., contacted a P. I. colleague in Frisco and, along with some instructions, arranged for him to tap into the CCTV feed in Bentover's high class apartment building in the Frisco Heights area of town.

Two days later a package arrived at the New York, Bowery address containing three to four hours of collected digital footage of the mayor going about his daily business entering the apartment building, getting into the elevator and entering his upscale apartment.

The little P. I. immediately went to work perusing the footage and again was more than pleased at the half dozen scenes of Bentover kissing his boyfriend goodbye at the apartment entrance, in the lift as well as down stairs by the revolving door of the front entrance and of the two occasionally strolling the halls hand-in-hand.

47 hours and 37 minutes later, with the aid of a BX-3, Sony video editing suite, a laser disc burner and his massive porn collection, the little P. I. was proud of what he had produced. What he had been hired to produce.

Three days later Snodgrass received what he had been waiting for, a plain brown paper wrapped package with no return address.

Ж

"You don't mind me asking, just what exactly you planning S.O.S.?" Moss probed as Snodgrass opened the Federal Express package in his private office at the inner sanctum of the Northside Gentlemen's Members Only Private Club.

"We are going to persuade this guy Bentover to forgo the award he believes he is surely about to win and in turn nominate our boy."

"How we gonna do that?" Moss asked with the innocence of a not-too-bright child.

"By taking away his strongest advantage, his 'gayability'!"

"But everybody knows he's gay!"

"Everybody **thinks** they know he's gay! Lemme tell you something, there's one thing you can always count on with the American public, especially when sex is involved."

"What's that B.S?"

"Guilty until proven innocent, Mr. Moss! Guilty until proven innocent!" He finished unwrapping the package, removed the mini-disc and slid it out of the sleeve to examine it.

"Huh!" Moss exclaimed as he scratched the flat side of his head, the part on top.

"By presenting scandalous footage backed up by photos . . ." There were also a series of flawlessly doctored 8X10 glossies in the package. "We undermine his entire persona. Take away the one thing he's built his whole platform, livelihood and popularity on through sympathy and guilt!"

"His political prowess?"

"NO YOU MORON! He has no political prowess! He's a puppet with people telling him what to do every step of the way, just like any successful politician! I'm talking about taking away his gayness!"

"Like turning a black politician white so he can't play the race card when he's backed into a corner on a controversial issue!"

"Yes."

"Like turning a female politician into a man to take away her crutch and force her to use reason and responsibility!"

"Exactly!"

"LIKE MAKING A MINORITY CANDIDATE A MAJ-"

"ENOUGH! You get the idea!"

"Sorry." Moss fell back in his seat. "Okay, then what?"

"Then we threaten him with the 'S' word!"

"OH GOD! NOT THE 'S' word!" Moss declared. "What's the 'S' word?!" He challenged.

"STRAIGHT! When homos out there get wind he's straight and not really one of them, they'll tar and feather him quicker than a drag queen gettin' a chubby in a bar room full of sailors!"

"You really think that'll work?"

"Watch and learn Mr. Moss! Watch and learn."

Snodgrass popped the mini-disc into the player and switched it to 'play'.

The screen showed Bentover entering his apartment building and going about his daily routine. But when it came time for him and his boyfriend to kiss goodnight, he was instead, in turn, playing tonsil hockey and strolling through the halls hand-in-hand with a beautiful, voluptuous blond, a green eyed, large breasted brunette or a non-descript but gorgeous, short, exotic Asian.

"You getting the picture now Mr. Moss?"

"I'm watching and I'm learning B.S! I'm watching and I'm learning! No wonder you made it all the way to the senate!"

Ж

The brown Ford Cordova with municipal plates pulled up outside the imitation, lemon yellow clapboard house on the country road. The driver came around and opened the passenger's door.

"I won't be long." Pervers informed the driver as he stepped out and approached the front door of the house.

As he entered, the familiar sights of the velvet Jesus paintings and smells of Clorox bleach called to mind his childhood. His rotund mom sat on the living room couch, eating snack cakes, mesmerized by the T.V.

currently showing *As the World of the Doctors Turns.*

"Where's Pops?" Thaddeus asked as he removed his coat and sat down opposite her and kissed her on the cheek.

"Out back, hanging another flag. Says he wants the rebels to know he's a patriot when the revolution starts." He shook his head and looked down. She muted the sound.

"You sounded troubled on the phone Yankee Doodle. Everything alight with you and the little lady?" His mom asked eyes still glued to the T.V.

"Well, she ain't exactly little no more. Guess that's why I love her." He added as his mom reached for another chocolate cup cake from the large dinner plate on the end table next to the couch. "But no, there ain't no problems in that department."

"What can I do you for Ring Ding? Is it about your dad?"

"No, just . . . what about dad?"

"Well Coffee Cake, I been waiting for the right time to tell you this. When you rang up earlier I thought maybe you found out from somebody else."

"Found out what?!"

"Well, he ain't ya real dad." Thaddeus was genuinely shocked at this familial revelation. "I mean Billy Joe Bob is a nice guy and all, but your biographical father, well let's just say he was only in the picture for a little while."

"How short a while?"

"About one night to be exact."

"But . . ."

"You wann'a Moon Pie?" She held out a sweet cake from the twelve pack she had just torn open. He shook his head no. "I find when I have to deal bad news a Moon Pie is just the thing to make me feel better." She gobbled the five inch, artificial chocolate covered disc in two bites.

"Thanks, no. What about dad?"

"Well Sno Ball, I had to take the best deal in front of me at the time!" She reached into the drawer under the coffee table and produced a small, purple vinyl photo album. She passed it to her son. His eyes nearly fell out of their sockets when he opened it, aghast at the stunning, pin-up of a beauty that stood before him in more than a dozen digital snap shots.

The 30 year old photo of his younger, more vivacious mom rivaled anything he had heard about in *Playmate*, *Maximum* or *Big-Uns* magazines. 'Heard' about but not actually seen since the Catholic Majority made it an offence punishable by ten years in prison to possess any nude photos of women back when George W. Bush III appointed Oral Roberts II Attorney General.

Of course, due to the overwhelming propagation of gays, 57% of the American male population had gone homosexual in frustration at the state of the country, nude pictures of women were still allowed for lesbians and naked pictures of men were okay for those light on their feet, but strictly forbidden for the declining hetero population in fear it might make them deviants.

Thaddeus was surprised, shocked and impressed all at same time. He passed the album back to his mom.

"Now Oreo, how about you tell me what's on your mind? Why you called over?" Thaddeus shifted in his seat and cleared his throat.

"I just don't understand how people can be in public office where they's meant to do good things for society, help people and pass laws that's supposed to protect folks, but wind up putting them in jail and taking their stuff!" He confessed.

"Uh huh." She grunted as she pitied the pathetic naiveté of the man before her.

"I mean, life just ain't the same since I been a politician! We took young Taranjello to the city for the day to see how he'd like it, you know should we ever get ourselves a proper house like, and-"

"How'd he'd take to it?" She asked.

"Hated it! Couldn't wait to get back out to the country! Said he'd never leave the two bedroom apartment we have again!"

"After only one day in the city?!" She grabbed another HO-HO from the plate next to the three remaining Moon Pies. "Well least ways he got an education." She consoled.

"I don't get it mama!"

"Get what Turnover?"

"How did we come to this? Did you know that under Civil Forfeiture laws last year alone, 62,000 seizures with a net worth of $2.5 billion were taken from people who were never charged with a crime?"

"Oh, my little Twinkie cake, them's some big numbers you got rollin' around in your head! But, when it's all said and done, The Lord moves in mysterious ways. I mean they's all kind'a things we don't understand! Where does the daylight go when the sun goes down? How does bread magically turn into toast and how do the Lipton people get tea bags from leafs? I mean, those things don't just grow on trees!"

It was only through their conversation that afternoon that Thaddeus began to realize he had had the good fortune to have been raised in a mixed marriage household. His father was a Blinder and his mother was a Dweeble Head. But they got along fine.

His father firmly believed that one of the things that made America the great country that it was is that it gave his parents the constitutional right to be as stupid as they wanted to be and no amount of educational laws could force them to change that.

Thaddeus was still not placated.

"And that ain't the worst of the laws! Judges now have complete domain over evidence and they passed a law to eliminate juries altogether! I mean, I don't know if

I can be part of that kind of system!"

"Well Ring Ding, best thing I can tell ya is trust your heart, people gonna tell you all kinds'a things but do what you think is right and to heck with everyone else! Forgive my profanity. My daddy used to say opinions are like buttholes! Everybody's got one, some are bigger than others but at the end of the day they all stink! He was a wise man, God love him." Thaddeus smiled and relaxed.

"Okay then. I knew you was the right person to come to!" Thaddeus smiled in relief.

"Now, best you go. Your father's gotta get up early in the morning if we gonna have a proper supper tomorrow night. Them squirrels ain't gonna hunt themselves, know-what-I-mean, son?"

"I know what you mean, mom! Love you! Thanks for the talk."

"Love you too son. And don't you fret none! Jesus is watching which means things gonna work out just fine! You'll see." He bent over and hugged her. "I'm just glad me and your father could see you amount to something before our hereditary dementia set in." He gathered his things. "Course for him I think it's already too late." She nodded to her husband outside in the back yard. Thaddeus peered through the glass of the patio door to spy his father hanging a string of mini American flags in place of the clothes line running between two beech trees.

"I gotta get going mom, somethin' I gotta see some people about." Thaddeus concluded.

A POW WOW WITH FOUO

CHAPTER NINE

🙢

It was the Friday evening before the big client presentation to the FUBAR's by the public relations people and for the first time since the last S&L scandal (the sixth in the last forty-seven years), things were looking pretty grim at the FOUO ad agency.

Snodgrass et al were due in at nine sharp Monday morning and Bloodbank-Leech's people had gotten word that the politicians had such confidence in the Madison Avenue boys that they had already booked time on all the TV, radio, Facebook and other 115 social media outlets for the entire next week. They intended a full media blitz with all the impact of the 9/11 attacks.

The primary sticking point for Bloodbank's brain trust was the exact thing that all commercial ad campaigns hinged on, a slogan. They didn't have one.

'Your vote is not completely useless.'

'Don't vote for the other guy!'

'Preserve with Pervers!'

'Standing behind you no matter how much you bend!'

Flushed with excitement the young aide burst through the front door of the crowded meeting room at ten after ten that night.

"I got it! I got it!" He waved a slip of paper above his head.

"You got what God damn it!" The supervisor yelled.

"Our campaign slogan!! Thaddeus Perver's campaign slogan for a more intelligent, happy and progressive future! Just like you said Bloodbank!"

Bloodbank looked at the words scrawled across the

slip of note paper the aide handed him. He read it aloud.

"You can't help us if you're stupid! What the hell does that mean? That's the best we have?"

Bloodbank looked over at his team supervisor stretched out across three chairs as she begun to snore.

"Change it to; 'You can't help . . . no, fix stupid. Yeah, that's it. 'You can't fix stupid!'" Leech ordered and thrust the paper back at the copy boy.

Ж

That Monday morning a party of three consisting of Senator Snodgrass, Moss and O'Shea were followed by an entourage of 36 as they entered the one hundred seat presentation theater. They were there to review the plan of attack Bloodbank-Leech and his merry band had been commissioned and brain stormed together for regarding how they would shoehorn their man into the Senate while making it look like he was duly elected by the imaginary, prefabricated, yet-to-be-created electorate which he didn't have.

They were efficiently escorted to the first row where small, cafe styled tables in front of each seat were bedecked with Dom Pérignon, crackers and brie cheese. They were shown to their seats by two of FOUO's junior associates where, centered on each seat was a royal purple folder containing a prospectus.

As opposed to some sales meetings where the bullshit gradually seeped into the pitch as it went on, where the truth is not even secondary but tertiary in the push to sell the product, idea or concept, the bullshit here started right away. Everyone realized this because Bloodbank-Leech would throw the pitch himself.

"Gentlemen, good morning and thank you for choosing For Office Use Only as your promotional ad agency!" He triumphantly announced as he took the stage. "I am Bloodbank-Leech, founder and CEO of the most successful company in the industry and would like to start by asking you a simple question." He nodded and the lights slowly dimmed as a film screen gradually lowered from the teaser curtains above the stage.

"My team and I, that is I with a capital 'I' and team with a small 't' of course, have thought of, no built, nay . . . engineered a campaign strategy nothing short of Biblical proportions!" He carefully strode to the other side of the stage.

"So what is it we are talking about? Allow me to tell you Senator Snodgrass! I envision a P. R. campaign of monstrous proportions! A campaign that has never been attempted and launched before!"

O'Shea flipped through his copy of the prospectus and Moss slid slightly forward in his chair. Snodgrass was unimpressed.

"What is it exactly that we are talking about when we talk about the free electoral system in the United States of America?"

Several in Bloodbank-Leech's team raised their hands as if asking to go to the toilet. Moss and O'Shea shrugged while Snodgrass' personal entourage took vigorous notes. Snodgrass set both hands on top of his gold plated cane and leered.

"We are talking about that indomitable quality which allows men to go beyond the beyond. That which motivates people to great heights of achievement!" He produced a laser pointer from his pocket and stepped to the screen. "Allow me to elucidate!"

Moss, a puzzled look on his face, leaned in to O'Shea who reciprocated by meeting him halfway.

"It means 'to explain'." O'Shea quietly elucidated to Moss.

"I wish you would." Snodgrass snipped.

"We are talking about nothing short of a belief system! A system of beliefs creating the ability of people to believe they can choose their leaders."

"Allow **me** to tell **you** what you're talking about!" Snodgrass yelped recognizing the well-worn tactic.

"You're talking about M.O.C.! The manufacturing of consent! We been using that maneuver for years!"

"Exactly!" Leech shot back.

"Now that we've got that straightened out, what exactly is your plan Mr. Bloodbank?" Having never met Snodgrass face-to-face Bloodbank was puzzled by the unexpected hostility but welcomed the challenge.

"Most people call me Leech."

"Okay Leech. Let's hit the beach! What are you looking to sell us with your speech?!" A giggle rippled through the audience.

"Very well Senator." He moved back to center stage. "I see the opening salvo in your war unfolding in three stages!"

"And what would those stages be?" Snodgrass queried."

"Stage one, stage two and stage three!"

"Makes perfect sense!" Moss volunteered.

"Moss! Your mother have any kids that lived?!" Snodgrass grumbled.

"Stage one, faith." Leech pressed on.

A large motif of the antiquated religious symbols, a crescent moon, a cross and the Star of David, appeared on the large screen behind him. "Faith by the people that with an upturn in the economy there will be more money in the future." $100 dollar bills began to slowly seep and ooze from the ancient mythical symbols. He paused to let it sink in.

"Faith in your man by making it not only desirable but 'trendy' to back him by the big wigs and trendy to vote for him by the public. So trendy in fact that it will become untrendy not to vote for him. If you vote for the other guy you will no longer be part of the crowd, the cool crowd. You'll be treated like a conservative in Hollywood, ostracized because you'll be seen as stupid and uninformed. Why, you'll be almost un-American!"

"How exactly?"

"AHHH! How you say?!" The screen quickly faded into an animated circle of people of all colors, shapes and sizes in a large circle all dancing and smiling. "Gentlemen, we intend to not only make it trendy to vote for your man, Tony Anthony Pervert-"

"That don't sound right does it?" O'Shea leaned in and whispered to Snodgrass who held up his hand to stay Rick's question.

"Like the L.A. police forcing an innocent black man to confess, we intend to use peer pressure to vote for your man!"

"Not only trendy but socially unacceptable not to vote for him!" The animated figures, all but one, suddenly turned outward and crossed their arms in anger at the one now isolated in the center to indicate he had been ostracized.

"Next, hope!" The slide faded out and a new one faded in. It was a head and shoulders shot of the old comedian Bob Hope, his giant ski-slope of a nose dominating the screen. "The one thing the human soul can't . . ." Leech broke eye contact with Snodgrass and glanced up at the screen. It was the first he had seen of the image. He angrily stormed over to an assistant off to the side. "What the hell is that?!" He quietly demanded nodding up to the irreverent allegory.

"We Googled 'hope! It's the best we could do on short notice!" The assistant nervously shot back. Leech stormed back over to center stage and continued.

"Hope, the one thing the human soul can't live without! When you lose hope you give up. You give up, you die. Common knowledge."

"How exactly do we go about giving the so called people hope?!" O'Shea queried.

"We pitch hope from the angle that they, the people, will share in that money, the riches, in the future combined with the charity of the government to let the people keep more of their money."

"Comic relief. That's good, I like that." Snodgrass commented.

"This brings us to the last of our tri-pronged strategy." He pressed the remote and a slow rolling slide show of starving African children came up on screen. "The best way to establish a sympathetic following is to attach your campaign to some charitable cause. For who needs the benevolent charity of ourselves more than those who don't have it?!"

"Which charitable cause you had in mind Mr. Leech?" O'Shea called out.

"Doesn't matter! You're not really going to do anything for them anyway and most of the money you collect will be funneled through and siphoned off for your own campaign promotion. The only time you'll really have to give any actual cash to the charity you choose to use as a front is when you do televised promos of actual donations!"

"How exactly does that work?" Sydney inquired.

Bloodbank nodded to one of his people and she quickly scurried over to Snodgrass and passed him a small, hardbound manual.

"Everything you need to know about the manipulation of charities is in this instruction book."

Sydney glanced down at the publication given him and read the title.

The Handbook of Operations for the Clinton Foundation.

"And here's the best part . . . it's all tax deductible!"

"I like this guy!" O'Shea leaned into Moss and commented. Snodgrass smiled and nodded.

"Charity. All of the great campaigns of the past have attached themselves to and allegedly worked towards a cure, a treatment, the elimination of some devastating something-or-other."

"What if it's something can't be cured like cancer or something?"

"All the better! You get that much more mileage out of it." Bloodbank bragged. "Also, if we are wise and use the charity of a really hopeless cause, and I strongly suggest we do that, then we establish an information dissemination program! You know, the fight to spread 'awareness' angle." Leech threw in air quotes for emphasis. "We fight to help the cause of blah. Our goal is to raise awareness of blah, blah. People have to know about the tragic cost of terrible, TERRIBLE blah, blah, blah. And how better to do this then through the Pervert foundation?! Attaching the word 'foundation' makes it sound legitimate."

Leech was confident he was winning them over.

"It's Pervers! Not Pervert damn it!" The senator snapped.

"But, here's the important bit, whatever said charity is, it must appeal to all genders. Male, female, gay, lesbian, cross-gender, trans-gender, bi-sexual, bi-curious, surgically enhanced transsexual, beastial, and trans-miscellaneous!" Leech added.

"That it?" Moss asked.

"Not quite. Another, just as important feature of your campaign is that it must be short, frequent and episodic. We can't stress people's attention span for more than one or two seconds at a time!"

"Sounds logical." O'Shea agreed.

"We gotta get the people pissed off about something. Something not really that important and not so built up that it becomes dangerous. That's also important! Something that can be built up to seem really important."

"Such as?"

"Such as a war, revolution or insurrection somewhere in a far off Third World country preferably someplace nobody's ever heard of."

"Revolution's always good. We can tie in with the American revolution back in 1873!" Moss added.

"1876 you idiot!" O'Shea corrected. "Don't you even know your own history?!"

"And finally, but most importantly, the make believe enemy!" Bloodbank announced. Snodgrass sat up straight. "An enemy which must be insurmountable, never before heard of, built up to be very real, immediate and potentially devastating and must be presented as being only able to be subdued by your man, Anthony Preview Thaddeus!"

O'Shea again open his mouth to speak but was stayed by the hand of Snodgrass.

"What's the tent pole of the whole campaign?" Queried Snodgrass.

"It doesn't matter, nothing really matters once we get in the swing! Except for my fee of course. That will have to be paid up front."

"What the hell you talking about, 'doesn't matter?'"

"I'm talking about N times B to the fifth!"

"Speak English man!"

"NBBBBB! No bullshit backing by big business! We'll run the entire campaign on donations from the public to show how much they really want 'him', their own man, and how little influence the fat cats, the big business interests, the lobbyists really have on him."

"We buy the right people, he builds a sufficient public profile as the only man who can do the job and the ignorant masses of sheeple will do the rest!"

"What about the press and all their bullshit hard-hitting questions?" O'Shea challenged.

"Bullshit is small potatoes, we just have to make sure they do their job!"

"And what's that Leech?"

"We make sure they focus on sniping the candidates, scandals, blowing the little stuff all out of proportion exactly as John Q. Public has come to expect!"

"What about the issues?"

"That's the beauty of it! By controlling the issues selected, picking your own ground to fight on, he can't look too stupid."

"Remember, if Senator Ted Kennedy had been driving a Volkswagen he would have been president."

"What the hell is that supposed to mean?"

"It means sir that because VW's are watertight they float so when he went off that bridge-"

I KNOW VW'S FLOAT GOD DAMN IT! I mean where's the god damned correlation?"

"Truth doesn't matter! What people **believe** to be the truth is all that matters. A great man once said: 'Perception is 99% of the truth'."

"That's clever! Who said that?" Snodgrass queried.

"You did senator!" O'Shea said.

"I did ? You sure?"

"YES SIR, when you were called up in front of the Senate House sub-committee investigating the illegal mayonnaise lobby."

"Oh, yeah."

"Also we win by employing the perfect campaign slogan." Bloodbank added.

"And what would that be?"

"You can't fix stupid!'"

The room fell silent for what seemed an eternity. None of Sydney's entourage spoke. None of Bloodbank's people uttered a sound until finally Sydney spoke.

"I like it!" Snodgrass finally declared and a collective sigh of relief filled the small auditorium.

Ж

Thaddeus' mind remained at a loss as to why or how, being mayor only a few months, the National Association of Mayors was able to locate, contact and reserve a place for him on such short notice at the convention. Before receiving the invite he didn't even know there was such a convention much less an association of national mayors.

It was less than a week ago that he received the invitation package and he never dreamt that United States mayors were treated as such a privileged class but when he read the first class flight agenda, saw that the Presidential suite at the Boston Hilton had been reserved for him, and read the scented, flower-festooned note briefly explaining that all expenses had been paid compliments of his constituency, he thought he had seen it all.

Of course he had to put his bewilderment on hold while he looked up the word constituency

The driver of the stretch limo flagged him down at the airport and drove him to the hotel. He played with the magician's window most of the journey into the city and when he got bored with that he played airplane pilot with the radio dials in the back until the chauffeur disabled the radio from the front and told him it was bad reception due to the increased hover traffic as they approached the city.

Not sure what else to do with himself on his three day visit he spent the first day perusing the city sites, taking photos with his Eye Phone-12 and enjoying the Guinness beer, Guinness pie and the Guinness stew which was the pride of the traditional, bland Irish food featured in the restaurants and pubs of the greater downtown Boston area.

He visited Faneuil Hall, Fenway Park and the Freedom Trail. At the remarkably low price of $27.50 he drank a glass of whiskey at the Bunker Hill Bar, a second at the U.S.S. Constitution Museum and another at the Old State House.

He slept well that night.

Bright and early the next morning, after a sumptuous breakfast buffett, he found himself taking in the convention.

Pervers pondered the latest conundrum to invade his formally simple life as he showered and dressed in the Presidential suite of the Hilton however, the festive, circus-like atmosphere which greeted him as he passed through the expansive lobby of the Kennedy Convention Center wiped his concerns away while lifting his spirits.

At the convention center he was overwhelmed by the various displays of the three storey structure which presented an array of confusing terminology and lexicon to be dealt with. He passed by booths for *Internal Affairs*, strolled by tables advertising *Municipal Accounting Services* and stands offering help with *Fiscal Budget Management*. Additionally there were places where one could learn how to invest in external and internal relations.

There were kiosks boasting the latest developments in departmental oversight and smaller stands squeezed in here and there manned by volunteers and advocates of all the usual causes such as feeding world hunger, fighting war in Africa and various agencies metastasising money for cancer research.

In the adjoining hallway there was a booth petitioning for lobster's rights, another advocating a bill of rights for plants sponsored by the special interest group petitioning the Federal Ethics Committee on Non-Human Biochemistry for the ethical treatment of flowers. He passed another protesting the negative portrayal of snakes in film and television and the Asperger's Pride Movement.

Once in the hanger-sized main hall he was accosted by the exhibitions of the primary sponsor of that year's National Mayor's Convention, The Law Enforcement Association of America.

Predominated by police devices advertised to 'help control your population', the theme of the three day exhibition was proclaimed by the giant sign which hung overhead above the main wing of the hall;

Making the Streets of Your City Safe for Your Citizens!

"The L.E.A.A. - violating criminal's rights so they don't violate yours!"

Plotting a course through the labyrinth of stalls Thaddeus approached the information desk with a query.

"How do the L.E.A.A. intend to do that?" He asked pointing up to the banner.

His question had not risen out of cynicism of any strand but mindful of the latest infotainment broadcasts boasting the 27% increase in police violence across the country.

"Do what sir?"

"Make the streets of my city safer for the people? I mean how exactly to make them safer from heavily armed criminals?"

"Well, by replacing the street's with more heavily armed police, how else?!"

"And who will be watching the heavily armed police?"

"Watching the police? Why would anybody want the watch the police?" Thaddeus stared at the association rep before responding.

"Because it's a fact that police have a tendency to get heavy handed when they know they can get away with it, especially if nobody's looking over their shoulder."

"There' no proof of that, besides, police can't do their job right if somebody's watching them all the time!"

"How many unarmed men and women are killed by police each year in this country?"

"This year only 2,068! Down from 2076 last year. Which proves the system works! And the best system is to replace the criminals with more heavily armed police! It's just common sense."

"Of course." He wandered away digesting the conversation.

"You have a good visit sir!"

"Thank you."

He wandered over to the first booth where there was an array of strange looking devices on display. He and the vendor greeted one another and he pointed to an item on the display counter between them.

"What exactly is this thing?"

"That there's a taser shotgun! Fires up to 100 taser rounds at once up to 100 meters away! These here cartridges allow up to 50 quick reloads thus minimizing the alleged threat to the peace officers by suppressing the law breakers and allowing rapid fire capacity. Good for college demonstrations, protests, church socials which might get out of hand. That sort of thing."

Carefully watched by the hillbilly cop behind the display table he next ran his hand over something labeled the Blinding Laser Dazzler. Because Thaddeus sported a suit and tie the weapons dealer smelled a juicy deal in the works he shifted to sales mode. The cop/weapons dealer carpied the diem by volunteering a short lecture on the 'fatal but non-lethal' offensive defensive weapon.

"It'll dazzle you into disorientation by zapping your ass with two low powered diode laser beams! Causes prolonged, intense headaches, ear splitting ringing in the ears and projectile vomiting! Comes with a 24 hour battery, just in case!"

"An Invisible pain ray?"

"Kind'a cool, ain't it?!"

"Interesting. What's this one?"

"Well sir, that's the new anti-personnel microwave transmitter. Technically called the Active Denial System, or AiDS for short."

"Sounds like something out of *Star Wars 27; Rise of the Boil*."

"It works like an open-air microwave oven!" He enthusiastically relayed. "Imagine you had a giant microwave oven mounted on the back of a truck, or better yet on the back of a an M1-27 Abrams tank! Safer that way." He added. "You just pull her around to where the trouble is and slap them homos with a dose of AiDS!"

Thaddeus lifted something from the table that looked like a kid's 1950's plastic water gun.

"Now that one's a real doozie! It a projecting, focused beam of electromagnetic radiation to heat the skin of its targets up to 130 degrees!"

"That's pretty hot! Sounds like it could be fatal."

"It is! But that's okay."

"How so?"

"It's been approved for use."

"By whom?"

"By the manufacturer of course! Up to a 130 degrees, Pretty cool huh?!" He chuckled. "Or not so cool!" He elbowed Thaddeus.

"Can it be used to cook burgers too?" Pervers wryly commented.

"The NYPD call it the bye-bye effect!"

"Clever."

"Oh not as clever as what the LAPD used to call it. The FTSE! The Fry The Scumbags Effect!"

"Oh, that's much better." Thaddeus commented while gazing at another of the futuristic toys.

"Screaming microwave that pierces the scull and renders the perpetrators unconscious by causing mini shock waves in the brain casing." The enthusiastic little salesman offered. "Good for busting up unwanted protests."

"Side effects?"

"Not many. It may cause a little brain damage from the high-intensity shockwave created by the microwave pulse, but what the hell, they should'a thunk about that before breaking the law, right pardnor?!"

"What about peaceful protesters?"

"Ain't no such thing! All protesting disrupts the natural order of things." The salesman, now in high gear, instinctually moved to ye another gadget "You've no doubt heard about white noise, pink noise and purple noise, but what about brown noise?!"

"Never heard of brown noise." Mayor Pervers replied.

"This baby will give you an education!" He said as he held up the pride and joy of all his toys, a shoulder mounted gadget that resembled a WWII bazooka. "It emits sonic rays at just the right frequency."

"Just the right frequency to do what?"

"To make the protesters shit they pants!" He charged the weapon and pointed it at a group of nearby school kids on a field trip.

"NO! That's alright." Thaddeus yelled as he slapped the muzzle down and away. "No need, I believe you."

By now it had become clear the Thaddeus that the L.E.A.A. et al had adopted the attitude that they were engaged in an arms race. An arms race in which the opponent was the general public.

"It's effective up to a good 200 yards."

"And if you're closer?"

"Well, any closer than 50 yards and there's probably gonna be some permanent damage."

"And ten yards?"

"That's not good."

"What does that mean?"

"Probably bad."

"How bad?"

"Death. Maybe. Probably."

"I thought this convention was for mayors to help improve their ability to manage their cities?"

Will Mayor Thaddeus Enoch Pervers please come to the information desk. That is, Mayor Thaddeus Enoch Pervers to the information desk please.

The announcement over the house P.A. came as a surprise but also as a welcome relief which allowed Thaddeus to escape the hall of horrors he had inadvertently wandered into.

Upon arriving at the information desk the information he received informed him of the answer to the question he had been pondering since leaving Brubaker, Ohio less than 49 hours, thirty-seven minutes and twelve seconds earlier. To wit: who was responsible for his being in Bean Town? Home of Cambridge, MIT and the place where everybody parked their caa in Havaad yaadd.

A message was handed him which requested his presence in the Crystal Ballroom bar of the Hilton Hotel at half past seven that evening. Semi-formal dress optional.

The message was unsigned.

Ж

Later that evening, as he sat at a two top table in the center of the Stars and Stripes lounge of the hotel and the waitress brought him his second Thomas Jefferson whiskey sour, he prepared to watch the floor show, due to start in a few minutes. Again the waitress who was draped in a stared and striped mini dress sporting red, white and blue wig and red sparkly shoes made her way over to Thaddeus' table.

"Sir, there's a group of gentlemen at that corner table who would like you to join them." Thaddeus looked around as he handed his money to the patriotically festooned waitress who refused it. "It's paid for sir. On the gentlemen who wish you to join them sir."

"Well, that's mighty kind young lady but tell them I'm waiting on someone."

"Yes sir." She scurried away to relay his message only to scurry back seconds later.

"Sir they asked me to tell you that they are the people you're waiting for."

"Oh! Okay, tell them I'll be right over."

"Yes sir." The walking flag responded then fluttered away.

A minute later Thaddeus was on his way over to the corner table where the scheming triumvirate patiently sat.

"Remember, no commitment, we just feel him out." Snodgrass quietly reminded the others as Thaddeus approached the table.

"Mr. Pervers, very happy to make your acquaintance." They shook hands. "I'm Senator Snodgrass and may I introduce my associates Mr. Rick O'Shea and Mr. Peter Moss."

"Gentlemen." Thaddeus was immediately uncomfortable as he took the fourth chair which faced Moss leaving Snodgrass to his right. O'Shea flagged the waitress and indicated for another round.

"We understand you're doing a bang up job out there in . . . in -" The senator stumbled.

"Ohio" Rick prompted.

"Ohio." Snodgrass added his compliment which dripped with condescension.

"You've heard of me?"

"Oh heck yes! We read all about you!" Rick re-enforced.

"All about you! I always say you can tell a lot about a man by his biography!" Moss added.

"Well, thank you sir. That means a lot coming from a genuine senator. But the truth is I'm only at it few months —"

"Now let's don't berate ourselves! The fact is you jumped in, took the reins by the hand when needed and saved a town from the certain doom of a rudderless ship and took them back onto a course of peace and prosperity is all that matters!"

"Well . . . I don't know about all that—"

"Of course you do!" Moss moved behind him and took his jacket and hung it on a nearby coat rack.

"Thaddeus, you don't mind if I call you Thaddeus do you?"

"No, not at all Senator."

"Call me Sydney! Please!"

"Okay, Sydney."

"After all Thaddeus, I feel like I already know you!" Pervers began to relax. "May I tell you a story?" Thad nodded as the floating flag in the fancy footwear brought more drinks.

"Once there was a man, a poor man, and every day, without fail, he played the lottery. Day after day without fail, he bought the same ticket number. Into the same grocery store and laid his money down as he went. Finally he won!" Moss smiled and nodded at the happy event in the story. "So he packed up his wife and kids, moved out of their one room apartment and bought a mansion. But not an ordinary mansion, no, no. He was part of the new rich elite now, so he could have whatever he wanted. It so happens he wanted a crystal palace like the ones his mom read to him about in storybooks when he as a kid." Pervers, identifying with the protag's sudden change of fortune paid attention. "After a while the man got bored, because he didn't have to work, and his wife suggested a hobby. So he took up collecting."

"What'd he collect, what'd he collect?!" Moss excitedly asked.

"Chairs!" Sydney snapped. "After a while this man's collection grew. Bent back chairs, arm chairs, Queen Anne chairs, all sorts of chairs. But there was a problem."

"What was the problem Sydney?" Moss again piped in.

"I'm about to tell ya, now shud-up will ya?!"

"Sorry Sydney!"

Meanwhile the waitress who had delivered the drinks and overheard the story, drifted away from the table but hovered within earshot arranging some silverware pretending to set a neighboring table.

"The problem was the house got real crowded. Soon there was no room for the family. They couldn't eat dinner, they couldn't watch their favorite game shows and so the wife finally gave him an ultimatum. Either the chairs go or I go!"

"She must have been pretty-" Moss was cut off by a scowl from Snodgrass.

"Turns out he wouldn't get rid of the chairs, so she took the kids and left him. Finally the inevitable happened. Having spent the last of his fortune, he brought home one too many chairs and as he stuffed it into the house one of the crystal walls cracked and shattered. This started a chain reaction and the whole palace collapsed to the ground!"

"Whew!" Moss mumbled.

"Because the damage was self-inflicted the insurance company wouldn't pay him. Now the man was homeless, penniless and alone. Back worse than when he first started out." Sydney sat back, sipped his drink and made eye contact with Thaddeus who failed to pose the obvious question forcing Sydney to press his point. "Do you know what the moral of the story is?"

"No Sydney, what is it?" Pervers pushed.

"People who live in glass houses shouldn't stow thrones!"

Moss laughed in an overtly exaggerated manner. Sydney considered giving his colleagues a nasty look but glancing over he observed that Rick already had one. Moss quickly clammed up. Thaddeus stared like a dog looking in a mirror for the first time.

Observing that Pervers remained unimpressed Snodgrass nodded and smiled at the others, a nod and smile which were in reality a clear signal to back the truck up with a fresh load of bullshit to pile on.

"Look, I know that on the outside I must seem like a pretty honest guy-" Snodgrass pleaded.

"No, not really." Sydney was taken aback by Pervers frankness. O'Shea snickered. Moss stared blankly. "I mean, you are a senator which means you're either a business executive or a lawyer. Or both."

"Okay, I get it."

"My secretary in Brubaker tells me about 70% of you guys are lawyers so realistically if there was a scale of dishonesty-"

"I get it!" Snodgrass took a moment to collect himself from the unexpectedly turbulence. "Lemme ask you something Pervers. Do you believe in America?!"

"Well, it's the only country I live in, so I suppose I like it good enough, yeah." He absently answered. "Except sometimes back in the factory when we had to wait around all day because of -"

"I'll take that as a yes. Since you do believe in America then we want you to join us! America, Americans and everything American needs you! Join Team America Thaddeus!"

The request both puzzled and took Thaddeus off guard.

"What exactly does America need me for Senator?"

"To help us, help our team." Rick jumped in. "We want to get away from the dirty politics of the past. The name bashing and mudslinging." Rick O'Shea commented.

"The name calling, negative innuendo and derogatory remarks!" Sydney added.

"And the saying bad things about each other too!" Moss proudly contributed.

"We want to make you-" Rick began.

"RUN FOR, we want you to run for!" Sydney quickly corrected.

"Oh sorry, **run for** the Senate."

"As our candidate!" Moss chimed in.

"Senate!? THE UNITED STATES SENATE?!" Thaddeus fell back in his chair. "You got your wires crossed fellas!"

"As **the people's** candidate!" Snodgrass added.

"ME, A SENATOR?!" "I don't know, that's . . . that's a . . . a-!"

"Think of it! No more financial problems, ever!"

"Prestige, respect!" Rick O'Shea added.

"And money!" Moss triumphantly added.

"Your own office in the nation's capital, Washedupton P.C.!"

"And money!" Moss parroted.

"I mean, we're just getting settled in over at the court house in Brubaker." Pervers protested.

"You could buy anything you want!"

"Only don't buy no glass houses!" Moss quipped with a giggle a second before O'Shea smacked hum in the back of the head.

"This country's in trouble Thaddeus. You know it, I know it. The whole world knows it! This two party system is a joke!"

"Especially when the party platforms are creeping closer and closer to each other every day!"

"Bipartisanism is killing us! Except for war, higher taxes and no real progress the Congress hasn't given us a thing in last twenty years!"

"THIRTY YAERS!" O'Shea argued.

"Problem is, only we have the power to do something about it! The Congress refuses to do it. The people can't do it!" Snodgrass pleaded.

"They could if they had the balls!" O'Shea sniped.

"That's an argument for another day Rick!" Snodgrass fought to suppress his frustration at maintaining control of the sales pitch. "The bottom line is the system isn't working like it's supposed to!"

One by one they leaned into the table and spoke with more intensity. Sydney put an arm around Thaddeus.

"It hasn't for years!"

"The system isn't evolving." O'Shea added.

"There's no progress!"

"It's completely stagnating."

"Yeah, and it's staying the same too!" Moss babbled.

"We think it's time for some new blood." O'Shea demanded.

"A fresh approach."

"Something new!"

"The old system has failed. Time to call it a day."

"The Great Experiment is over! We need to rethink things."

"Let's don't forget Einstein's definition of stupidity!" Moss appeared to be on the verge of saying something profound. "He said, 'Expecting different results when doing something different all the time doesn't work!'" Rick hung his head.

"Well senator Snodgrass, you've kind'a caught me off guard." Thaddeus finally confessed.

"Uh huh." Snodgrass sat back and decided he, they, had done all they could and the ball was now in Pervers' court. O'Shea and Moss sat back too.

"But I promise I will think about it."

"Well Thaddeus, we hope that you will." Snodgrass offered his hand and they shook.

"Here's my card. We'll wait for your call." O'Shea stood and shook Thaddeus' hand.

"Call us!" Moss added. The triumvirate sat silently until Pervers took his leave and was out of sight. Rick turned to Snodgrass.

"I'm not sure he's the right guy for the job." O'Shea shared his reluctance. Moss just shrugged. Snodgrass gave his opinion.

"To tell you the truth, I'm encouraged by this lack of sophistication. You know, like women with small breasts."

"What the hell's that supposed to mean?" Rick challenged.

"Most men like them big, not me I like them small." Sydney defended.

"Why for crying out loud?"

"Small breasts are a sign of intelligence."

In the next room the curtains parted and the floor show began.

THE DREAM

CHAPTER TEN

Ж

Thaddeus found himself frantically running down a cracked and decaying urban sidewalk moving swiftly under his feet. The steel and glass edifices of the buildings around him were gradually melting and slowly evaporated into a scene of wide open, empty space. He stopped running and looked around as he fought to catch his breath.

The earth began to crack open and trees slowly forced their way up through the ground and a bright, blazing sun shone down on the rolling hills which appeared first in the distance then began to slowly, but steadily creep closer and closer. A minute later the hills stopped advancing. To his left he noticed there was scattered shrubbery but mostly wide open field. Now he was standing in a rolling, plush green country field sprinkled with daisies and butterflies flittered around. To his right he saw a dirt road lined with more shrubbery trailing off into the distance.

A minute later he heard the whinny of a horse off to the side, behind the heavy brush on the left. He moved closer to inspect.

A tallish man, maybe in his sixties, sat legs open, next to a white horse which appeared a bit fidgety. The man, reins in hand, had obviously fallen from the animal.

"You okay?" Pervers ventured.

The man, dressed in a white, hemp blouse, 18th Century breeches and brown riding boots got to his feet, brushed off his clothes and righted his white powdered wig.

"Yes. Damn horse!" Pervers was shocked at recognizing the man.

"General Washington?!"

"Morning Thaddeus! Apologies for the awkward entrance. How are ya son?"

"Sir, how do you know . . . where'd you come from?!"

"Virginia, why do you ask?" The man steadied the horse.

"I mean, why are you here, why am I talking to you?"

"Consarn it, I thought the electorate would get smarter with time! It's a dream you moron! Where do you think all these clouds and hills suddenly came from?!" Following Washington's gesture Thaddeus looked down to see a thick blanket of fluffy white clouds covering their feet and the ground. "Did you think you were suddenly in London?"

"I just . . . it's just that . . ."

As opposed to the wise, benevolent father of the country he had heard about in history class it was a surprisingly cynical General Washington who confronted the confused Mayor Pervers.

"It's just that you are the greatest American ever to live! I'm a little-"

"I'm BRITISH DAMN YOUR EYES! Just because Cornwallis and those other snobby bastards wouldn't give me the King's commission!" He suddenly broke into a sarcastically exaggerated English accent. "'Sorry old boy, too bad you were born in The Colonies!' I had no choice! I had to join with the rebels. And we kicked their asses, didn't we boy?!" He patted his horse's neck and smirked. "I didn't care about The Americas being independent nations! I thought it was a ludicrous idea! We're British! Besides, you know what a pain in the hind quarters it is to start a country? I just wanted the Redcoats out so we could have free trade. Bloody taxes were killing us farmers! Tobacco prices were set to triple in one year! Man can't survive in conditions like that! I'd, we'd of all preferred to continue negotiations."

"That didn't exactly work, did it? Because of King George I mean." Thaddeus pointed out.

"TO HELL WITH KING GEORGE! It was those idiot farmers at Concord! I distinctly gave the order, 'Shoot over their heads. Over their heads! Just scare them a little!' But noooo! Do they follow orders?! Those yahoo farmers had to go and kill the Brits which pissed them off and then . . . well you know the rest. Regrettable incident. The whole thing."

"Regrettable?! Look what you did! You created the United States of America which inspired the French Revolution, the Irish Uprising and a whole lot of other revolutions against colonial tyranny!" Thaddeus blurted out, shocked at his sudden recollection of his school lessons. "We're a world power now. Well, we're number four at the moment but-"

"I'm still not so sure it was the right thing to do." Washington shook his head until Thad's words sunk in. "What do you mean, 'number four'?! Please don't tell me the Brits are ahead of us again?"

"Oh hell no! They're like sixteenth or twentieth or something."

"Well, at least that's something."

"But you're the father of our country!"

"Father smather! I only wound up the general of the army because nobody else wanted the job! And believe me it wasn't from lack of trying! Those idiots in the Congress approached everyone else first! Jefferson, Adams even Franklin!"

"Thomas Jefferson turned them down?"

"Yeah, that's how desperate they were! 'What are you crazy?!' He told them. 'The British? They got thousands of guys from all over the world, they're filthy rich and the guns! You ever seen the size of their guns?!

Makes a man embarrassed to remove his breeches at night.'"

Washington took up the reins of his horse and guided Thaddeus and himself out around the bushes and on to the road where they began to meander out towards the hills.

"So you became our country's greatest icon by default, by . . . by accident?! How come we never learned that in history?"

"You'd be surprised what you don't learn in history my son!" They walked for a bit as Thaddeus digested what he had heard.

"Did you really end up leading the country by accident?"

"No, no of course not. There's no such thing as accidents. Einstein taught me that."

"Einstein? But he . . ."

"Yes, Albert Einstein, you head of him? I became the leader because I lost a bet. A bet of sorts, it was at the gaming table at any point. It was At Put we were playing."

"At Put?"

"A card game. You probably know it as poker."

"Poker?!"

"Was your mother a parrot?! Yes, poker! I'm terrible at the game! Seven Card Stud anyway. Five Card Stud I'm an animal, won a set of sterling silver teeth off Paul Revere one time! But Seven Card, forget it! I might as well be tits on a nun. Balls on a priest. A Republican in Congress!"

"Interesting."

"Anyway, we were all hitting the grog pretty heavy that night and Franklin folded early, Adams had a Full House and God be he damned, didn't Jefferson come into the last hand with a Royal Flush! A **Royal** Flush! How ironic is that when we're sitting there trying to determine who is going to lead the fight against the King of England!"

"You seem to use a lot of profanity when you talk!" Pervers observed.

"It disturbs you?"

"No, it's just that I thought all you guys, the founding fathers, were hard core Christians! Heaven, Hell, eternal damnation, all that?"

Washington stopped dead in his tracks and stared at Thaddeus.

"So we were wrong, there is no god, paradise or angels. So sue me! It's all the political agenda of the churches. Only way they could get into politics."

"Oh."

"You people haven't gone back into all that superstitious rot have you?" Washington asked with genuine surprise.

"No, not really. There's still some die-hards, but they're dying out, replacing truth in favor of reality." They paused by a side road. "So what can you tell me? I mean about what's ahead?" Thaddeus ventured.

"Well, eternity as it turns out, is fairly boring. There's the occasional visitor, like yourself, but with no need to sleep eat or fulfil any other biological functions . . ."

"Not even sex?"

"Nope, no sex."

"WOW! That has got to suck!"

"It's not that hard. No pun intended."

"Thanks for being so honest!"

"Don't get too attached to honesty either."

"How do you mean?"

"I'm not too certain about that 'honesty is the best policy' shit either! There'll always be folks like Jefferson waiting to cut you off at the pass, one step ahead and swoop in to take your winnings."

"Like with the cherry tree thing!" Thaddeus proudly displayed what little American folklore he knew.

"What cherry tree thing?"

"The tree you chopped down then when your father asked you didn't lie about chopping it down?"

"Gosh-all-Potomac! Why would I cut down a cheery tree? I love cherries. I invented cherries jubilee for crying out loud!"

"I did not know that."

"That damn Frenchman gets all the credit but I used to make it for Martha."

"Oh, how thoughtful."

"Especially when my mother came to visit. They didn't get on very well." George became thoughtful. "This tree, was it cursed with the black rot, the blight or something?"

"What's black rot?"

"It's a fungal disease common amongst fruit trees."

"Never mind. Why are you here? I mean why appear to me? Even in a dream?"

"Not the slightest idea Mr. Mayor. Central booking scheduled this meeting and we're seldom told the why's or wherefores, those people at Central Booking move in mysterious ways. I'm just grateful to break the monotony of hanging around for eternity. Last visit I had was ages ago. Some fellow named Bush. Claimed he was talking to God about starting some holy war or something."

"THAT'S IT!" Thaddeus suddenly yelled. Washington and his horse jumped. "Sorry! That must be it! I'm faced with an important decision. You must be here to give me advice! Like how to deal with the Electoral College."

"College? What have the colleges to do with government?"

"You know, the Electoral College! You guys set it up!"

"Oh, you mean the College of Electors!"

"Yes! Because of that and because there's only the Democrats and Republicans, things are pretty screwed up down there." He looked to the ground. "It is down there, isn't it?"

"No, it's more a quantum mechanical thing, at least that's how Tesla explained it to me, but let's not get into a turgid, metaphysical, categorical, ethereal argument about it. It's not that important. I know what you mean. The great Adams-Jefferson-Burr row! I told them that Electoral system was a bad idea but I was out voted. Damn that Jefferson! Anyway, I died before it was tested."

"Okay, back to my problem. What do I do if I wind up in Congress? I mean, how do I deal with the economy, race relations and all this 'equality' bullshit?! Women to be equal to men, all men wanting to be equal to each other! Especially this two party thing? Nothing gets done! They just hamstring each other at every turn!"

"Firstly, don't be fooled. Americans have fallen into that bottomless pit where-by they advocate that greatest of all falsehoods, 'equality' means the 'same'. It does not. Just as no two words in the English language mean exactly the same thing, neither too can any two men be the same. Believe me young man, all men are not created equal! I've seen some of Jefferson's slaves at Saturday bath time!"

"Huh!" Thaddeus declared. Washington put an arm around Pervers and adopted a more fatherly tone.

"You're struggling with the knock-on effects of political correctness and the false belief that we should all be nice to all people all the time, even to the morons, idiots and imbeciles!"

"Well, shouldn't we be?"

"HELL NO! They're idiots, morons and imbeciles! You know stupid! And you can't fix stupid! America is dangerously ensnared in the propaganda of 'false equivalency' coupled with the political correctness of 'being nice' to people which in reality just means lying about how stupid, obstinate or uneducated they are.

You've got to learn to call a spade a spade and not beat around the fucking bush!" Thaddeus feigned deep understanding by looking down and nodding. Washington continued. "And never lose sight of the fact that all this is agitated by the popular press in order to build and maintain their audience. Money is the new mantra, isn't it? I mean we started this whole thing to establish an independent economy now it's gotten out of hand. It's become a matter of money's not everything, it's the only thing!"

"I think I see what you're saying. But who decides who's stupid and who's smart?"

"Look, this two party thing, we had a few parties back then and they were always at each other's throats. But never forget, political parties may now and then answer popular ends but they will always likely become potent engines by which cunning, ambitious and unprincipled men will be able to subvert the power of the people to secure for themselves the reins of power of the government and destroying afterwards the very engines which have lifted them to unjust power."

"That's pretty intense!"

"Well if that means good, thank you. That was part of my farewell speech back in . . .back in, ah. . . .'78 I think."

"Thank you for sharing it. That explains a lot."

"Bottom line Thaddeus ` is, at some point you have to clean out the shallow end of the gene pool son! It's as simple as that."

"So what you're telling me is -"

"You can't fix stupid!" Washington turned to leave. "I really appreciate the visit and I wish you the best of good fortune with your important decision whatever it is, but they're calling me back now."

Without warning General George Washington and his white horse turned and wandered up the side road. Thaddeus watched as they slowly became transparent and disappeared altogether until they were nothing more than a memory.

Thaddeus turned and stared off into the distance as the hills slowly receded back out to the horizon. He suddenly felt tired and lay down under a nearby tree where he promptly fell asleep.

When he awoke, in his own bed, he found his wife soundly snoring next to him and saw it was light outside. Thaddeus sat up in bed and contemplated the night's experience. He decided that his dream meant something, that it wasn't just a dream but a vision. A visitation with a message.

The message was that although Americans had voted through several female, Jewish, black, mulatto, Hispanic, gay, bi-transvestite presidents nothing had really changed. Nothing, it seemed, could free them of the slavery of the two party system.

He was convinced that the United States of America was ready to take the giant leap which would set it on a new course to freedom and prosperity. The path to truth, justice and the Am . . . another way. He was firmly convinced that the 600 million oppressed people of America were ready for multi-partyhood.

As he fixed breakfast that morning his musings grew bigger and more grandiose.

Happy but no longer satisfied in his two room apartment, the fantasy of his own home, something he never dreamt of much less seriously considered, seemed even more possible as he began to consider in earnest the FUBAR's offer of entering into the life-long contract and allowing them to buy him a seat in the senate.

By the last sip of his morning coffee Thaddeus Enoch Pervers had made the decision he would sign on the dotted line with the Snodgrass Triumvirate and enter into the United States Congress under the banner of the newly created FUBAR Party.

AMERICAN FREE ENTERPRISE

CHAPTER ELEVEN

Ж

It is written that in the beginning the theory of American free enterprise was that everyone had the opportunity to improve his financial status in life through hard work, diligence and ingenuity.

Unfortunately the reality of life is that, except under the law, all men are not created equal. Especially in terms of industriousness, ingenuity or honesty.

It is taught that the original framers believed they were establishing a system where-by anyone would have the opportunity to build a life, raise a family and pursue happiness. However, somewhere along the way, years later, a new breed of man evolved which strayed from the original concepts and changed the interpretation of 'free enterprise'.

These new men interpreted American free enterprise to mean that to be American you were supposed to grab for everything you could and hold onto it until somebody smarter came along and was able to take it away from you.

Eventually laws were made to prevent others from taking your things away, unfortunately access to these laws was determined by how many things you had that is, how rich you were. The more things you owned the easier and more access to these laws you had.

Soon the laws, which were 'passed' without consent of the people, became so convoluted that no one could understand them.

A culture developed and a cult was born from this bastardization of the free enterprise system whereby a handful of men evolved dedicated to depriving a man from what was rightfully his.

These men were called 'politicians'.

Curiously there were no scientists, physicians, artists or mathematicians among these men, only lawyers. Lawyers who gradually promoted themselves to something they called 'judges'. This seemed a strange title because, the word 'judgement' had been generally taken to mean a balanced determination of all the facts. Curiously it seemed that their judgement was always somewhat skewed to favor the other lawyers. These judges soon became the ultimate deciders in who could take what away from whom.

To the astonishment of the formerly naive population, these lawyers and politicians became very rich and were relabeled, 'the elite'. They were the elite by virtue of the fact they were rich.

Gradually the population lost their naiveté and became aware of the fact that these men were professional liars with no rules, no morals and no limits on what they would do to get what they wanted. They lived and worked, for all practical purposes, in the vacuous, chaotic world they ostensibly evolved to prevent and they stole everything from the people.

When they were caught red-handed stealing, cheating and lying, they simply hired a lawyer to go before a judge and were either found innocent or let off with a light sentence. On more than one occasion they simply changed the law so that it no longer applied to their particular situation. After all, they were lawyers, they could do this. After a while the population had become completely devoid of all their naiveté.

By then it was too late.

Thaddeus, who had been boning up on his U.S. History, closed the big book over and went to sleep.

Ж

With the combined influence of his parent's failures in life, the essentially pointless job of mayor of a small town and the ghost of George Washington ringing in his ears, Thaddeus Enoch Pervers had decided to accept the offer of the FUBAR party of buying him a seat in the U.S. Congress.

Purchasing a seat in the congress had become much easier than it had been in previous years. Earlier there were efforts by citizens' interest groups to establish and enforce laws regarding how and when and from whom an American politician-wanna-be could get his funding. These were called 'conflict of interest laws'. But much as other lawyers had established loop holes to 'get around' the established rules of the courtroom, politicians had chipped then hammered away at these rules by first manipulating the law to make it more difficult for them to have an effect and then ultimately by creating laws restricting their effectiveness altogether.

Total victory was finally achieved back at the turn of the last century when the Supreme Court was cajoled and bribed into ruling against any restrictions by anyone about giving money to the candidate of their choice.

It was then only a matter of one electoral cycle that the rich jumped from controlling 97% of the nation's wealth to the present day 99%.

Of course Thaddeus, like the majority of American citizens had no real knowledge of this dynamic, which is precisely how the bad guys got the upper hand in what was formerly considered the greatest nation on earth.

Of course all that's ancient history and, as everyone knows, you can't change history.

Ж

It was in the very back of the back room of the Northside Gentlemen's Members Only Private Club, or the NGMOPC, where Thaddeus headed to finally meet up with the founding members of the FUBAR Party, Sydney, Rick and Pete.

It was up on the fourth floor of the club he found the attendant that the desk clerk at reception had informed him would be waiting.

"I'm here to meet Senator Snodgrass." Thad announced.

"You must be Mayor Pervers."

"Yes, yes I am."

"The Senator has instructed me to escort you to him as soon as you've arrived. Please follow me." Without waiting for a response the tuxedoed club attendant turned and walked away.

With Thaddeus in tow he led Pervers out of the main room, turned left into the main corridor and continued to the T intersection twelve doors down. Here they took a right, ascended a short flight of ornate stairs turned left and stopped in front of a well-oiled mahogany door with an engraved brass plaque which read:

Executive Washroom
Level 12 Members Only!

"This way Mayor Pervers." With a gold plated skeleton key selected from a small ring the attendant unlocked and held open the door then followed Thaddeus into what was an ornate toilet.

"Here you are, Your Honor." While pleasantly thrilled at the attendant's use of formal address, Pervers was puzzled at what was expected of him next. He stood still as he perused the detailed tessellation of tinted, tiled art work on the walls and floor. The row of sinks with, their glimmering brass fixtures, lined the wall behind him and was smartly aligned below a row of bevelled glass and framed mirrors.

Standing in front of the first toilet stall he looked down and saw the seals which adorned the floor in front of each of the four stalls, each closed off by a polished, mahogany door. They displayed in turn the great seal of The Freemasons, The Knights Templar, The Skull and Bones and The Illuminati.

The attendant, now standing off to the side, loudly but not too loudly, cleared his throat.

"Pervers, you there?" Came a voice from behind door number one.

"Yes sir." He didn't know why he answered in the submissive but it seemed he should.

"Good, good! Glad to see you came to your senses!" It was Senator Snodgrass. "I assume you're here to accept our offer?"

"Well, you see sir, I've given it plenty of thought and -"

"Good, good! I have a good feeling about you son. Knew it the first time I saw you. Now, here's how we have to approach this thing." The senator's comments were punctuated with the unpleasant sounds of his bowels being emptied and it became objectionably obvious that Snodgrass hadn't had a solid meal in some time. Either that or he had been eating Mexican for the last three days. "First we get a sit down with O'Shea and Moss. Greenspan?!"

"Here senator!" The attendant barked back.

"Them other two show up yet?"

"Yes senator. Both are in the Blue Room awaiting your arrival." The attendant remained at his proper place in the corner by the sinks.

"Let us just take care of the paper work and then we can get busy." Snodgrass added.

Remembering how decrepit the old man was Thaddeus leaned over and whispered to his escort as he gestured with one hand as if he were wiping himself.

"How does he, you know . . ." Just as he did the stall door opened and Snodgrass accompanied by a second attendant stepped out from inside the cubicle. The number two man held his rubber gloved hands out in front of him as he walked behind the shuffling Snodgrass.

"Let's us get over to the Blue Room so we can get started on this operation!" The senator instructed as the first attendant stepped forward and washed Snodgrass' hands then carefully dried them.

Attendant number two meanwhile disposed of the gloves, donned a new pair from a sink side wall dispenser and took up his station back inside stall number one next to the toilet bowl.

As the three exited Thaddeus quickly peeked down and spotted a pair of legs in each of the other stalls standing ready next to the toilets for the next executive club member to arrive and take care of business.

"You know the old saying; 'Money talks, nobody wipes!'" The first attendant whispered to Thad.

Ж

The Triumverate's plan to establish a new political party when so many others over the decades had failed seemed to be coming along swimmingly and now that they had found the right FNG, it seemed doomed to succeed. They had the money, they had the connections, they had the money and they had the knowhow. But most importantly, they had the money.

They met once again in the private conference room of the NGMOPC. With Thaddeus now firmly on board and sitting in on the meeting they got down to business.

"We need a platform." O'Shea started. "You know to base things on."

"What for?" Moss the lawyer challenged.

"So the people know where we stand!"

"They don't need to know where we stand!" Moss argued.

"Why not?" Thaddeus asked.

"Because, it doesn't matter. We can tell 'em whatever we want and once we're in, the game is ours. I mean, we can't get fired!" Moss countered.

"But we gotta get **in** first!"

"So why would you want to tell people where you stand? Giving them details only backs us into a corner and invites criticism! That's why we have to be as general, non-committal and as vague as possible! Besides, that's what the people expect!" He pleaded. "You start getting too specific about what you're going to do about the thousands of problems we get now in this country and folks are gonna get suspicious. They ain't prepared to have somebody in office who knows what the hell he's doing! Or worst yet who that really gives a shit about changing anything!"

"Alright, I'll tell ya exactly what we're going to do." Snodgrass loudly interrupted. "We approach Hatfield of the RNC and tell him we want our boy to run on the red ticket and we're willing to sink a load of cash into him. Do whatever it takes." O'Shea sat forward with interest. Moss was puzzled. "Then we quietly approach McCoy, the new chairman of the DNC, and say we wouldn't dream of having candidate Pervers run on anything but the blue ticket." Thaddeus had gotten used to the idea of the title 'Mayor Pervers', but the sound of 'Candidate Pervers' was beginning to sound even better.

"That's a dumb idea!" O'Shea declared.

"Your daddy not wearin' a condom was a dumb idea! Now shuddup and listen will ya?!" Snodgrass attacked. "We make it clear to both of them that this is strictly hush-hush. Keepin' it out of the press is critical, any hint of a leak and we're out. No candidate."

"No candidate and no support!" Thaddeus voiced his understanding.

"And we all know what that means! No support and no money!" Moss blurted out.

"See Moss?! You ain't as dumb as you look." Sydney quipped.

"I got a lunch with some guys from the P.C. Rotary Club on Friday. They're all dyed-in-the-wool blue staters." O'Shea volunteered.

"Perfect, you can drop a hint there, quietly of course, no mention of Thaddeus, that way word'll leak out back to McCoy."

"Consider it done." O'Shea confirmed.

"I'll set something up with the RNC for next week." Moss nodded. Snodgrass turned to Pervers.

"Thaddeus, absolutely crucial you keep this quiet, got it?" Sydney reiterated. Thad nodded. "Once we get close enough to election time, say ninety days out, we can assess the polls and make a decision."

"What if they're tied?" Pervers asked.

"Don't worry about that. I'll deal with that."

"What do I do in the meantime?"

"Get back to your office, pretend to be mayor for the next six weeks or so and when everything is set, we'll get in touch."

"What'll happen with the mayor's office?"

"Who gives a sh-" Rick O'Shea started but Snodgrass held up a hand to cut him off.

"Pick yourself a successor, somebody you trust can do the job, we don't want nothing coming back on us later. But make no announcement. By the time we're ready to make our move we'll have a good excuse all drawn up for you as to why you're leaving. We want you, The National Mayor of the Year, clean as a whistle when we launch."

"Sounds like you fellas really have a handle on what you're doing!" The former production line worker spoke with absolute confidence.

"Hey Sydney, why not use that? From Town Council to Mayor in less than a year. Winner of The National Mayor of the Year award!" O'Shea suggested.

"Maybe drum up some phoney stats about how he revamped the budget, saved the town money etc . . .?" Moss jumped on the suggestion band wagon.

Unnoticed by the others Thaddeus winced at the mention of 'phoney' stats.

"We'll certainly bring that up but we'll leave the PR to the PR boys." Like a group of Drinking Bird toys perched in front of tall glasses of water they all nodded rhythmically.

"That's right! They can do everything with one big computer stimulation." Moss added.

"I didn't know any better I'd swear you lost a few heat tiles on re-entry boy!" Sydney mumbled under his breath. He wobbled to his feet to indicate the meet was over but, unused to such extreme physical stress, almost immediately fell back in his Queen Anne chair and composed himself.

"Now I suggest we have a drink, order dinner and get a good night's sleep. We got a big day ahead of us tomorrow!" They again all nodded in agreement.

An attendant with a hover chair was summoned, Sydney was loaded up into the hover device and they all moved the party to the private dining room to seal the deal with a meal.

THE CAMPAIGN LAUNCH

CHAPTER TWELVE

Ж

Being a bit steeper of an uphill climb than expected things hadn't been going well for the senate campaign over the last six weeks. Although Snodgrass still had tremendous influence on The Hill and throughout the P.C. area, several factors conspired to throw up barriers to his goals.

Inter-party rivalry, a constant stream of terrorist attacks across the world and the steady attention paid by the media to the current crop of female politicians in both parties and their finally catching up to the men in positions of power provided a steady diet of headlines for the profit oriented networks.

Very few, even the bravest of networks, had the integrity to report that the female politicians were just as stupid, narrow minded, short-sighted and dishonest as any of the men politicians in their respective parties, but stories with other angles flourished.

These were just a few of the factors Sydney had to overcome in attempting to make potential allies who were gun shy about throwing their lot in with an unknown.

It was then that the concept of reorganization and a new angle of attack came up in conversation.

It suddenly dawned on them that what the FUBAR's needed was something they had never before thought of. Something which required forethought and planning taking into consideration all the different ways things could turnout.

"What about a misinformation campaign?" Snodgrass suggested to the group now gathered in the club.

"Why not? It worked for Teddy Roosevelt!" Rick lent his support.

"Almost worked for Senator Joe McCarthy!" Thaddeus who, unbeknownst to the others, had been reading up on American political history as of late added.

"Didn't work too well for Chuck Duff!" Rick countered

"Duff was an idiot! He couldn't organise a pissin' contest in a brewery!" Snodgrass countered.

"Did you know him?" Asked Pervers.

"Knew his wife."

"We could get Thaddeus to be vice president, kill the current president, then they'd have to make him President." Moss finally piped in.

"You need a lobotomy!" Sydney offered.

"Besides, it's been tried once or twice before!" O'Shea said.

"According to the history books it's been tried 17 times before!" Thaddeus informed.

Impressed, all eyes turned to Pervers who carried on with his train of thought.

"It seems to me, what we gotta do is, what politicians have always done in the past, come up with an enemy. Somebody the people can get together against, learn to hate." Thaddeus proposed.

"You mean like the teachers?!" Moss queried.

"No! People don't hate teachers! After the lawyers, cops, judges and politicians all got themselves vilified the teachers are the only ones the people agree on that are doing some good for society, even if they do get paid the equivalent of a paperboy and got their work year slashed in half! Besides, manipulation of the education unions through bribes, graph and illegal threats took care of that. I'm talkin' about somethin' really, really bad! Something so evil, so heinous that even former President George Bush -"

"Which one?"

"What!?"

"Which George Bush?! The first one, the second one or the Grandson? There was three of them, Americans aren't exactly fast learners."

"Don't matter!"

"Oh, okay. But I get what you mean. Find an enemy then convince the people that we're . . . ahh, Pervers is the only one who can save them!" O'Shea conceded when Sydney suddenly hit on an idea.

"Rick get your people to see if they can't find some Third World country we can invade, or maybe one that's recently been invaded or maybe one thinking about invading somewhere. Don't really matter, as long as invasion is somehow involved."

"What good'll that do Sydney?" O'Shea challenged.

"Better yet, find one **about to be** invaded! Try the Middle East or maybe Africa. Those people invade each other like a station wagon load of relatives showing up in your driveway at Thanksgiving!"

"But what if there just ain't nobody just now?!" Moss asked.

"Have you learned nothing in all your time in American politics?!" Rick admonished. "There's always somebody peeking over the backyard fence looking to take something's not theirs! Besides, if we can get someone else to do the invading, we save time, money, planning and after a month or two we can swoop on in and rescue the country while using up all that war surplus we got stored up and all at a minimal loss of our own idiots, I mean soldiers!"

"What war surplus?" Moss asked.

"The war surplus from the last war! What surplus you think?!"

"But we ain't had no war recently, at least not any real war."

"It don't matter bonehead! We always got a mess load of war surplus stored up some place because they always overproduce from the last war to maintain the profit margin! DAMN it man, ain't you never shopped at Costco?!"

"What about a different kind of enemy? Like some kind of evil bird flu?" Moss threw out.

"Be real will ya?!"O'Shea objected.

"Monkey flu?" Moss countered.

"No flu! No cold, virus bacterium or infections of any kind! Infections require bodies and plenty of 'em. If we want bodies all we gotta do is pick a fight with somebody, make it look like they started it and have a war! Then we'll have all the bodies we need, damn it! If people are gonna pay attention we need a disease free, bird free, monkey free enemy! As long as it's lethal."

"How do you feel about kidnapping, psycho killers, fake Third World terrorists or otherwise radical/politically motivated leftist groups threatening to attack America?" Thaddeus proposed.

"That's always been a pretty good way to ignite political backing for an unknown!" Rick O'Shea conceded.

Snodgrass perused the group.

"Yeah, yeah that's not bad. See what you can come up with and get back to me."

Ж

It had now been eight weeks, three days and four hours since the leaders of the FUBAR party had gone to work calling in favors, making deals and buying whoever was necessary to get Thaddeus a senatorial seat.

A campaign headquarters was set up in downtown Washedupton, D.C. as a front, a slogan had been drawn up, posters, flyers, buttons and hand-outs had all been produced and commercial air time featuring professional actors, technicians and cameramen had been invested in. The slogan, "You Can't Fix Stupid!" was now front and center in the public eye.

In short everything required had been done to make it look exactly like all the other well financed political campaigns in an effort to avoid anyone asking awkward questions when Pervers was ready to finally be installed in office.

Problem was the August deadline to register for the elections was less than forty-eight hours away and they still had a long ways to go. Even Snodgrass himself was sleeping less soundly.

Then one night the phone rang.

On the other end of the line, in Houston, Texas a man in green scrubs lifted a white sheet from a naked, pale white, cold and dead 99 year old who, despite being no longer of this world sported a broad smile. The Coroner stared down at the limp lump of formerly functioning protoplasm on the chrome gurney, and immediately realized this was information he should share with his good friend Sydney Snodgrass way out in Washedupton P.C.

After he hung up, based on the information he had just received from said coroner, Snodgrass decided to call in one last favor. He rang down to the all night attendant in the club's reception and asked him to put another call through. He would wait by the phone for the call back.

Governor Otis The Duke' Oakham of Houston Texas, a Republican, was elected on a platform of promising a 100% conviction rate in Texas courts and was also a lifelong buddy of Sydney Snodgrass.

It turns out that Oakham had been caught cheating on his wife of 37 years with a Dallas Cowboys cheerleader. It wasn't so much Oakum cheating with a cheerleader that ticked her off but that it was a Dallas Cheerleader that really tipped the cart.

His wife, reluctant to accept the news in the benevolent spirit in which he had hoped, informed him through her platoon of lawyers that he was facing a very ugly, no-holds barred, I'm-gonna-reduce-you-to-dust divorce.

Based on their iron-clad pre-nup which would give the ex-wife-to-be a hefty chunk of everything including fifty per cent of the hunting lodge in San Jacinto, 28 1/2 feet of the 57 foot, custom made Chris Craft Commander down in the Gulf and all of the 1967 Spice Red and polished chrome Chevy Corvette.

From Otis' viewpoint this was an unacceptable scenario. So he turned to get help from Sydney Snodgrass, known in earlier days as 'The Fixer'.

A week later Oakum's wife suddenly agreed not to file for divorce, (ever), go back to work and look the other way when ever Otis decided to engage in an extra marital dalliance.

Backed by photographic evidence, Sydney had arranged for her to be caught red-handed, having it off in a Houston motel room with three members of the Texas Rangers baseball team, only one of which spoke English. The live goat in the room was an unexpected bonus.

Copies of the photos were sent to her at the monthly Daughters of the Alamo breakfast in San Antonio along with a neatly hand written note.

When you swim with sharks my dear . . .

Ten minutes later, back in Sydney's room, the phone rang again, it was the call back. Sydney answered.

"Okay, get me Governor Oakham as soon as he comes in. Tell him someone'll be down in the morning with the cash." Following a short discussion the matter had been settled.

What the coroner had passed onto Sydney and had already been reported to the governor is that a one Jubile P. Gadfly, a Republican senator from the panhandle district and who was a shoe-in for re-election, had just bought the farm.

"What the hell are you doing?!" Thaddeus challenged when Pete Moss later informed him of Sydney's new tactic. "Governors can't interfere with senatorial elections!" Thaddeus had played along willingly stretching the limits of his integrity as far as he could. But now he began to have serious reservations regarding the FUBAR's efforts if not their motives.

"He's not interfering he's 'appointing' in time of unforeseen crisis!" Sydney explained to Pervers.

"Well what the hell is a 'forseen' crisis?! A disaster you see coming at the last minute?!"

"EXACTLY! Kind'a like when your mother-in-law-pulls into your driveway unannounced you know, because she just felt like 'dropping by'."

"That still doesn't give a governor the right to appoint a non-elected candidate to the Senate! Senators have to be elected! Besides, state and federal governments are supposed to be separate, joined as one under the constitution but separate!"

"And they are Thaddeus, they are!" Sydney tapped Pervers on the knee to reassure him. "Exactly in the same way a street walker and her pimp are two separate individuals!"

He all but ignored Perver's argument as his mind raced ahead to the phone calls he had to make while he tired of the basic lesson in modern civics he was being compelled to give. "Moss, talk to this guy will ya?" Snodgrass instructed. Pete the councillor took over the lesson.

"Thaddeus. . ." Moss assumed the air of a trusted guardian, even though he was a lawyer. ". . . back in the early part of this century there was a case which resulted in what we call The Palm Sunday Agreement! It came out of the what's her name . . . the Schiavo case I think it was. A case in Florida where a woman was veged out and was kept alive on tubes and machines. You gotta remember, this is before we had suicide parlors where you can just go in pay your 1200 bucks, watch a movie or two and drink your Kavorkian Cocktail and it's *Good Night Irene*! Hell back then those idiots all thought life was 'sacred', holy or had some intrinsic meaning somethin' nutty like that." Thaddeus stared as Moss spoke. "Well anyways, the docs wanted to yank the tubes outt'a this girl, you know, shut her off from the gas pumps till she ran out gas, shut her down until she gently coasted to the side of the road."

In the background Sydney continued on with his phone conversations.

"Well why didn't they just-" Thaddeus interrupted.

"I'm getting to that, I'm getting to that! The family said no but couldn't pay the up keep on her. First it went to the local courts, then to the Federal courts before it came back down and went back up again." Moss sipped his double martini with three olives. Sensing they were in danger of losing their new meat puppet Rick jumped in.

"There were so many goddamned courts, lawyers and judges involved in that case that to this day nobody knows where the hell the line is between the Federal government and the states! That fuckin' little ruckus we had back in the 1860's didn't settle shit about a state's power except to decide that might does make right! And Lincoln's boys had the factories and raw materials so they could make more guns and so they won that little pissin' contest. And that's the name of that tune Gladys!"

"Besides," Moss remained in lawyer mode. "There's a provision in the Fifteenth . . . or is it the Sixteenth Amendment, one of those amendments in the teens that allows a governor to appoint a senator if one dies. Or is it if he quits? I don't exactly remember but I'm pretty sure it's legal."

"What about the state residency requirement? I'm from Ohio!"

"Look, Mayor Pervers -" Sydney sought to reassure him.

"I'm not a mayor anymore, remember?" He despondently responded.

"Okay, okay." Sydney slowed the pace. "Thaddeus, do you know what the most beautiful thing about the American legal is?" Pervers shook his head in curiosity but mostly in dismay. "It's endless legal system! For every law ever passed in this country, there's a counter law! I mean a law you can use to take that law into the courts and possibly have it reversed or struck down! Even a Supreme Court decision can be changed and they're supposed to be immune from the Congress and the President!" Thaddeus stared at him. "Hell, let's don't even get started on the drinking age, abortion or what kind'a fight went on about the voting age way back when before it was finally settled by the Feds a few years back."

"I'm still not sure I agree with Congress on that one! Fifteen seems a bit young to be able to vote!" Thaddeus responded as he again began to focus on what was being said.

"I see yer point but fair's fair! If they can be drafted at fifteen they should be allowed to think they're making a difference by voting." Moss countered.

"Exactly! Besides, kids are stupider! You can sell them more bullshit!" Rick threw in to the discussion.

"Chisholm v. Georgia, Pace v. Alabama, the Dred Scot case!" Moss again picked up the baton. "And where'd we be without the overturning of Bowers v. Hardwick, a law against blow jobs for fuck's sake! No pun intended. What the hell kind'a law is that?! Of course that opened the way for the homos to go crazy, but they learned the hard way marriage ain't all it's cracked up to be! Be careful what you wish for, hey boys?!"

"Point is Thaddeus," Sydney resumed. "There's so many god damned laws in this country there's no accurate record of all of them anywhere and no fucking lawyer, no matter how crack he is, knows them or can access them all, and even if he did there's probably a law contradicting that law and both can be argued against in court!"

Not completely convinced but not prepared to fight anymore Thaddeus, resigned to the situation, sat back in his seat and nodded.

"What I'm saying son is, our backs are against the wall right now and, after all we've put into this, I have no desire to throw in the towel. What's more, if anybody wants to challenge what my good 'ol boy buddy down in the great state of Mexas is doing by appointing you as substitute candidate for the recently deceased, see ya in court!"

"It's our God given right to use the courts to get what we want!" Pete Moss added.

"And it don't matter who wants to fight us or who it belongs to!" Rick O'Shea threw in.

Thaddeus Enoch Pervers, former ball bearing factory worker, former town councilman and former mayor sighed deeply, sat back and nodded. Sydney fought not to fall over as he slapped, rather tapped, a dismayed Thaddeus on the back.

"Is this a great country or what?!" Rick slapped Thad on the shoulder.

Ж

41/2 HOURS EARLIER . . .

Representative Jubile P. Gadfly, the Republican from the former state of Texas, now known as Mexas, had served his constituency well for over 57 years.

He had done this primarily through the tactic of avoidance. Whenever an important bill arose on the Senate floor he would work overtime surveying the prevailing political winds and if it appeared his vote would matter, he would simply not show up to vote. He was never in any danger from ever being ejected from the party because his constituency was the largest in the party, and because he had been re-elected 28 times. The fact that the held controlling interest in American Oil, inc. didn't hurt either.

Gadfly was less than one year away from his tenth decade of life with a record five thousand Simple, Joint and Concurrent Resolutions, bills, measures and motions having been avoided to date. Despite these accolades and all he had done for the good 'ol folks of The Great State of Mexas, all was not well.

The facts were these:

It was at 14:10 that Friday afternoon in the capitol city of Washedupton, P.C. that Senator Gadfly, with the mind he believed the all-knowing, all-seeing God that controlled everything gave people to control all things in their lives, that he made the decision to take off from his office over on Independence Avenue and make it his business to cease official business for the week and take care of some business by getting down to business with a one Miss Dandelion LeFleur a 24 year old former Washedupton N.A.I., now Dallas Cowboy, cheerleader wanna-be.

Formally the Washedupton Redskins football team, now the Washedupton Native American Indians, was affected one month after the establishment of the Office of Political Correctness, OOPS for short, a cabinet level office established by the passage of the *Politically Correctness Bill* H1099-P a few years earlier.

Just as hypnotists, politicians and by default lawyers, hate people who open their eyes during a session, eyes were opened and a slew of secondary laws was passed. The PC Police, commonly referred to behind closed doors as the 'Thought Police', were established a year later as part of the republican platform and now numbered in the tens of thousands.

Stricken from the lexicon were words such as 'janitor', 'waitress' and 'dinosaur'. The official PC verbiage, (a 427 page manual was available on line), had deteriorated into Sanitary Engineer, Sustenance Transport Technician and Pre-petroleum Being.

As words increasingly became used to disguise as opposed to illuminate, 'racist', 'sexist', 'homophobe' or 'bigot' became weapons. Weapons used to derail careers, imprison opponents and lie about the actual motives of the politically motivated. Starting at the top it was only a short time before these practices filtered down through society and these destructive legal actions became the norm until it was commonly held that truth had become an insult.

In yet another example of the lawyers overstepping their bounds, laws were passed without these terms being clear cut or well defined thus leaving them open to interpretation, the single biggest danger of American law.

Even when uttered during a clumsy attempt at humor or construed in the artistic expression of a photo or painting, a crime could be charged.

Self-censoring became so dominant in most Washedupton workplaces that co-workers were compelled to communicate only by electronic means and most face-to-face encounters were discouraged, unless it was to report a politically incorrect colleague.

The few who bravely bothered to address the fact that it had become uncomfortable to even discuss anything which could remotely be considered controversial, were dismissed and blacklisted by the infomedia, and ergo society.

Ironic that in a democracy, an ideology founded on competitive ideas and freedom of speech, such a disease should evolve.

And so it was the professional football franchises who were some of the first casualties of the *Politically Correctness Bill*. The Bill had been guaranteed to pass with unanimous approval as soon as it was introduced on the floor of Congress. It would have been considered politically incorrect of anyone who didn't vote for it.

That afternoon the ninety-nine and a half year old senator Gadfly made his way via taxi to the outskirts of the city north of the Beltway to the Beltsville district and to a brown stone walk-up on Belt Street in the Beltsville North Park Estates.

It was herein that there was a two bedroom apartment which he maintained for the one Miss LeFleur, at tax payer expense of course, under 'miscellaneous expenditures'. Along with the $40,000 furniture allowance he was allotted by the GAO he was also allotted 8,200 square feet of living space. With this level of prosperity their relationship remained on firm footing and was now more than seven years old.

So as he entered the apartment no formalities were called for and they got right down to business.

As soon as he came into the bedroom she temptingly shed her shear, black negligee, seductively removed her garter belt and sexily rolled down her black, seamed stockings then patiently waited the usual ten to fifteen minutes while he struggled out of his trousers.

Following a passionate three and a half minutes in the sack they laid side-by-side.

He lit up a Gurkha Black Dragon cigar while she fired up a pre-rolled spliff of Panama Red laced with Thai stick and they reignited the conversation they had left dangling after last week's visit.

"But don't the people have to vote on something like that?" LeFleur innocently inquired.

"Nope! Don't matter we vote for them." He confidently shot back.

"I did not know ya'll could do that." She idly mused. Amongst the smoke scented room he continued the lesson in American jurisprudence.

"We can do anything dahling! We's The Senate." He got up and poured a whiskey. "The only time American votes actually matter is when they get to vote at a Hollywood preview on how a movie ends, phone into a reality TV show or when they's in a group discussing whether to eat at Burger King or McDonald's."

"Huh!" She declared. When they had extinguished their smoking materials and returned to bed with their seats in the upright position, they decided to go again.

Less than two minutes into their renewed activities, the senator mumbled something into LeFleur's ear. Her fake panting obscured what he said and so she asked him to repeat it. He didn't answer. She asked again. This time he responded with a deep sigh and went limp. Both kinds of limp.

Like the victim of a recent earthquake, it was the better part of twenty minutes before Dandelion LeFleur was able to shove the dead load of a Senator off her, extricate herself and fall over onto the floor.

Suffering the normal side effects of a weed-induced paranoia, it was a full hour before she could pull herself together, call the police and deal with the fact she had just fucked a man to death.

The assigned detective patiently took notes as she spoke and it was with poised pen he ventured further.

"Where there any last requests of the deceased ma'am, any last words?" He discreetly inquired as the gurney mounted and white, linen mummified body of the senator rolled past in the background.

"Oh my yes! Jubile was a great oralist in the U.S. Congress! Did you know somebody once told me, after hearing him speak at a fundraiser, he had a mouth could talk the chrome off a bumper hitch!"

"I think the word is 'suck', Ma'am.

"Huh?"

"It's suck not talk the chrome off a bumper hitch." She stared wide–eyed at the cop.

"Well I still don't get it, but I'm pretty sure it was a compliment."

"Yes Miss LeFleur." The only past events the jaded lieutenant was interested in were those of the last hour. He pushed on. "So, back to the facts ma'am. What would those last words have been, ma'am?"

"He pulled me close and said; 'I'M CUMIN'! I'M CUMMIN'!' And then he went."

"Can I quote you on that Miss LeFleur?"

Ж

Almost as suddenly as it started, the campaign to buy Thaddeus Pervers a seat in the U.S. Congress was over. How it ended was no less a fluke then how it started, with a kidnapper being shot to death by the police. How it ended was with a phone call about a man who had been fucked to death.

Not believing in karma, fate or coincidence, (unless it had to do with car accidents), Thaddeus Enoch Pervers would never have guessed or accepted the ironic coincidence of Jubile's untimely albeit unique demise.

It seemed a butterfly had flapped its wings in Thailand however the consequences were in America. The butterfly had been a prostitute in Washedupton P.C. and the consequence was, in spite of Snodgrass' frustrated efforts, the intended outcome.

Thaddeus Enoch Pervers and company owed a debt to Miss Dandelion LeFleur of which they were both unaware and could never repay.

SNODGRASS BACK IN BUSINESS

CHAPTER THIRTEEN

☆

Few men get a second chance at life, much less a third or fourth. As different people deal with the impending inevitability of their own deaths in different ways, Sydney Snodgrass dealt with his through the most common technique known to man - denial.

Shortly after his forced retirement at age ninety he manifested this most common human emotional reaction to bad news in the form of continually finding, grooming and propping up young men in the world of politics to do his bidding for him.

If Sydney had a son, that is if he married and if he was ever compatible with any female he didn't resent or who wasn't revolted by his very nature and if they had bumped nasties long enough to procreate, the son would have had no choice as to his future life and endeavors. He would have been his father's successor in all things political and judicial. If this theoretical child had been a girl Sydney most likely would have, much like the ancient Spartans, left her at the foot of the mountain to wither and die. Such was the track of his personal belief system.

Now, with Thaddeus Enoch Pervers firmly seated in the puppet structure of the U.S. Senate, and following a ten year absence, Sydney felt himself back in the game.

However, like all high ranking, career politicians whatever or however much they have, it is never enough. Unbeknownst to Pete, Rick or Thaddeus, there dwelled deep in Sydney's heart, something greater, something insatiable. Something described, in the words of that great trial lawyer J. Pete Moss, Esq., "an anterior motive".

As with most people of his philosophical bent Senator Sydney Snodgrass, Ret. had secrets.

Even with all the modern medical technology money could buy, and he did buy some over the years, such as the entire geriatrics wing at Justin Bieber General Hospital, a private oncology clinic in central Baltimore and several dialysis stations strategically placed around the Belt Parkway, Sydney was only months away from buying something else - The Farm.

Whatever his level of denial he was a practical man and to that end Snodgrass kept a rotating file of six wills, three written and three living wills, that were recorded. The recorded wills were kept as back-ups for the three written wills and all were certified and notarized.

With a total net worth of $125.2 billion Snodgrass was decidedly in the upper 1% of the U.S. population that controlled the nation's economy.

The first pair of wills divided his estate equally between his surviving heirs, all cousins.

The second pair were in the event he decided his heirs didn't deserve anything and were to be instituted if he, near the end, decided he was pissed off at everybody in which case his entire estate was to be donated to the Arlington County Puppy and Kitten Hospital.

Ж

The old two bedroom house, which the Pervers had occupied for the last year and a half, faded in the rear view mirror of the brown Ford Cordova carrying the Pervers family. It left the cul-d-sac and headed for Interstate 70 to drive east. As Brubaker was west of Columbus they settled in for the nearly 500 mile trip with Thaddeus driving while Taranjello was riding shotgun and acting as navigator. Prudence, now approaching twice her previous weight, was stretched out in the back with the rest of the luggage. The moving van would follow a few hours later.

With the first one hundred miles behind them Thaddeus pulled over and, Taranjello having finally passed his driver's test the fourth time around, took the wheel.

Taranjello was a happy little camper after they had switched off driving and they did so as to allow Thaddeus to be able to review the list of rules and responsibilities he would encounter next week when he began work as a U.S. senator. Thaddeus became absorbed in his booklet and Prudence continued to snore away soundly in the back. A round the third hour into the journey they hit their first snag.

"Dad which way?" He asked as a barrage of overhead signage bore down on the boy and they approached a five way intersection with on ramps, detours and off ramps. Thaddeus glanced up from his reading. They were just outside Cambridge Township, Ohio. Thaddeus returned to his reading as he issued commands.

"Left onto the service road. We can use it as a bypass the clover leaf then cut South on 77."

"Left it is!" Taranjello responded as he promptly turned right at the 70-77 intersect and headed deep into West Virginia. Oblivious to the navigational error Taranjello drove, Thaddeus read, Prudence slept and pines trees zipped past.

An hour later, after they had passed the sixth or seventh, four-way intersection each featuring a McDonald's, a Burger King, a KFC, and a Dunkin' Donuts they decided to stop for gas.

"Dad, there's a sign coming up on your side can you read it?"

"Ahh yeah . . . Brobdingnag County Line, Township of Lilliput." Thaddeus glanced up and read the sign then took the road atlas from the glove box.

"I don't see it on the map!" He related to his son.

They took the next off ramp, pulled off the highway onto a four lane black top which, fifteen minutes later, narrowed into a two lane blacktop which five minutes later turned into a two lane dirt road which gave way to the first man made structure they came upon, a rundown Exx-O-Co gas station. Three of the four pumps wee adorned with, 'Out Of Order' signs.

Beneath a faded tiger attempting to pounce from a punctured and dilapidated billboard sat an old man in a chair leaning back against the one story wooden building.

His grey hair, wrinkled face and faded bib overalls tagged him as the attendant, although he was also the owner. He adjusted his battered Atlanta Native American Baseball cap as Taranjello pulled the car up between him and the row of mostly dysfunctional pumps and got out to stretch his legs.

"Howdy." The man greeted.

"How are you? We need some gas." Taranjello informed.

"Well this here's a gas station." The man reassured.

They exchanged several nods. "I'll just go round back and start the pump." The attendant was back a minute later.

"How far till we get to the state line?" Thaddeus asked.

"Oh, you got a ways yet. Just keep on til ya'll reach Morgantown then south on Route 79." As he pumped the gas the meagrely-toothed individual eyed Pervers up and down. "Hey, you talk funny! Where you from boy?"

"We're from the other side of Ohio."

"Just passin' through are ya?"

"Yes. On our way down to P.C. I've just been elected state senator. I start on Monday."

"WHHHOOOOEEE! I do declare, a real life senator! Wait'll I tell Darlene!" Attracted by the war hoop Taranjello wandered back over towards the two. Thaddeus was pleased at the notoriety however passing, but was anxious to get back on the road.

"Thank you, thank you very much, ah . . ." He started to climb back into the car and like a puppy the man trailed behind him.

"Eugene, Eugene Amos Corn!" They shook hands. "Say! I got's an idear! How's about you come over to the hall with me and have a quick jawin' with Jim-Bob?!"

"Who's Jim-Bob?" Thaddeus asked.

"Why he's the Mayor!" The shocked attendant replied.

"Mayor?!" Perusing the surrounding area he saw a few houses in far the distance and a converted barn acting as a hardware store across the road from the gas station but not much more. "Where exactly are we?"

"This here's North Vrindaban! Famous county wide for the *Can't Beat My Meat* chain of butchers & grocery stores! Now they's mostly closed down, all except the one in town. They turned that one onto a fishing store."

With Prudence asleep in the car and not due for another feeding for an hour or so, Thaddeus decided to accept the invitation and climbed into the rickety Ford pick-up truck the man indicated. Taranjello followed suit.

Enroute to the town hall Eugene filled Thaddeus in.

"Ever since the two parties, The Jackasses and the Fat Asses-"

"You mean the Democrats and Republicans?"

"We quit calling them that a long time ago! No disrespect if you're one of them Mr. Senator."

"As a matter of fact I'm not. I'm sort of an independent." Suddenly Pervers felt a small swell of pride.

"You mean there's another party?" He asked. Taranjello leaned forward from the back seat and poked his head between them.

"Daddy here's the first member of the FUBAR party!" The teen bragged.

"Huh! A third party!" Eugene mused and shook his head. "That just don't seem very American." He mumbled. "But, don't nothin' surprise me no more about politics in this country! As I was sayin', ever since they came together as one and agreed not to agree on anything and the trouble started at the factory after the government sold off them states to China and Canada, this place turned into one big slum."

"How are the people getting along?" Thaddeus inquired.

"I ain't gonna lie to ya Senator! Things ain't doing so good."

"Call me Thaddeus."

Thaddeus saw what the gas station owner meant as they pulled onto Main Street of the small town.

The two dozen shops were mostly abandoned store fronts. There were less than half a dozen people on the street, counting the two old men sitting in front of the barber shop one of them being the barber, and the road hadn't seen maintenance in a number of years. But something else caught his attention, the children.

Back at the gas station there were three young kids, grade school aged, playing around the place. They all appeared inordinately small and when Eugene revealed their actual ages as they spoke in the truck, Thaddeus was surprised. He put it down to the financial dilapidation of the area and the fact that they were only fed one full meal a day, but sometimes two on Sunday which accounted for their stunted growth.

Now seeing the kids walking with their mothers about the town, he realized the children's stunted growth was not only due to malnutrition but more wide spread then he at first realized

"You's a senator, let me ask you something. Is it true we's in debt for $444 trillion dollars?"

"I'm not sure of the exact figure but, it is up there."

"We used to consider ourselves middle class, the wife and I, actually most of the people around here, but once we lose the house -"

"You may not lose it."

"We have until the fifteenth to pay the three months in arrears plus the interest. The last factory in these parts got sold to the Koreans and they're closing it down next week, moving all the machinery out to the west coast. Guess there's more Koreans out there or something. That's another 500 people out of work. That makes over two thousand this year so far."

"How many in the town all together?"

They pulled up in front of the *Master Bait & Tackle* fishing shop.

Used to be upwards of 35,000 a few years back, but ever since the closures there's less than 5,000 now. Mostly people with land and them who's trying to hold on to their homes and shops, people like Jim-Bob here who's still got all these closed up shops. There's plenty of property, just ain't no work."

They entered the spacious tackle shop and even Taranjello was quick to see the space had formerly served as a small supermarket. Behind the single display case sat an early, middle aged man with dark hair reading a fishing magazine. The place was festooned with fishing paraphernalia of all shapes and sizes which hung from all four walls and the ceiling. Most of it dusty. An array of posters cluttered the two front windows.

"Jim-Bob! Get off your fat ass boy and meet a real life Senator all the way from Washedupton P.C.!" Jim-Bob quickly sprang to his feet, made a cursory attempt at brushing back his hair and extended his hand.

"I'm actually from Ohio, not Washed-"

"Senator Pervers, this here's Jim-Bob Stone, Mayor of North Vrindaban!" Eugene performed as if introducing a relative to the king. The two shook hands as Taranjello wandered over to the wall to inspect the fishing rod display.

"Eugene was filling me in on the financial situation of your town Mr. Mayor."

"Ohh, call me Jim-Bob. Everybody else does."

"Okay." The three took seats around the display case and Jim-Bob produced three long necks of Budweiser from a large Styrofoam cooler.

Perhaps as a knock-on effect of having been a mayor, but for unexplained reasons, Thaddeus' mind shifted into a sort of command mode and he began asking relevant questions.

"How many markets did you have Jim-Bob?"

"Oh, in my heyday I had upwards of a dozen markets spread out over the whole county." Jim-Bob answered, his braggadocio tempered with shame and embarrassment at being less of a man due to his financial failures.

Thaddeus sat back and thought for a moment. He considered how Brubaker, the factory owner, used to combine his factory's efforts with those of other industrial institutions to bolster production and keep people working when times were lean.

"Mr. Mayor," Thaddeus started, "did you know that the farmers of this country, in spite of only comprising less than 2% of the population, are producing 100% of all the food for the country with an annual surplus of nearly 40%? And even though the scientific advancements that have allowed this had been mishandled by the Paris Hilton Administration, as well as successive administrations, most of the surpluses still exists."

"I don't follow."

"Well as you probably read in the papers, the nation's farmers, thanks to the Republican controlled union People Who Plant Things in the Ground For a Living, are paid to destroy all their excess crops. Donating the millions of tons of excess crops to the starving of the third world nations was consistently voted down in Congress because it was 'communistic' in nature. Even as a potential way to help offset our debt."

"Well, it's common knowledge that that sort'a thing is a step on the way to socialism which is the first step on the road to comm'anism!" Jim-Bob commented.

"My point is, there are no laws against domestic, charitable distribution. As a matter of fact, I know some farmers over in Ohio who'd be glad to donate excess crop yields to you folks! All you'd have to do is go up there and get them!"

"Damn Mr. Senator, that'd be mighty white of them Ohio folks!" Jim-Bob declared as Eugene was suddenly struck with a another idea. His second that month.

"Hell, Virgil's got all them trucks left over from when his delivery business folded after the factory closed!"

"Who's Virgil?" Thaddeus asked. Jim-Bob took up the question.

"Virgil Minors, he's the mayor of South Vrindaban. But I don't know how keen he'd be on helpin' folks from North Vrindaban!" Taranjello had wondered back over to the pow wow area and had been listening.

"Why not?" The teen asked. Eugene and the mayor exchange glances but it was Eugene who responded.

"Way back when, even before the latest housing bubble burst, North Vrindaban and South Vrindaban were just plain old Vrindaban. Then as things was getting good, financially speaking, some folks started getting greedy and raising prices more and more so's they'd take in more money. Wasn't no time till the folks over on the south side of the county started having two different prices for everything. One price tag for tourists and out-of-towners and a second, higher price if they knew you was from the north side."

Jim-Bob took up the narrative.

"Folks over here on the north side had no choice but to re-irate, and do the same thing!" Thaddeus ignored the abused vocabulary.

"Was only a matter of time before both sides drew up charters to split the town in half." Eugene concluded.

"You think this Virgil will see reason if I speak to him?" The two locals again shared a glance but this time with broad smiles.

"You'd do that for us?"

"Government is supposed to be there to help the people! And I'm supposed to be a representative of the people."

"That's fantastic!"

"I'll speak with Mayor Minors and follow through and arrange something as soon as I'm in P.C. In the meantime I'll contact the farmers over in Ohio and have them start puttin' their excess aside."

"But Dad, what about processing and packaging all that grain and raw food material?" Taranjello again made a surprise contribution to the effort. "It would take less than an hour a day to process the amount of stuff these people need and with the factories only working a few hours a day I'm sure you can convince them to squeeze it through the line."

Thaddeus was pleased at his kid's efforts.

"Guys, while we get this underway you might want to clean up a couple of your closed up grocery stores and talk to a couple of people about coming back to work!"

"You got it Senator!"

Back at the gas station Eugene dropped them off and the Pervers made ready to make the short trip over the abandoned railroad tracks to the south side of town. Eugene approached the vehicle as Thaddeus prepared to pull away.

"I don't know how we could ever repay you Thaddeus!" Pervers put a hand on the gas station owner's shoulder.

"You pay your taxes Eugene?"

"Absolutely Mr. Senator!"

"Then you're already paying me! Let's get me over there!" The vehicle pulled out.

"Dad how you gonna convince the people in the south to work with the people in the north?"

"It's been done before! Leave it to me."

Ж

About two miles down the black top which was state Route 17, they passed a sign.

Welcome to
South Vrindaban, Brobdingnag County

Under the salutation were the words, "Home of the - ", with the adjoining noun painted over in black paint. A minute later they were parked down the street from the town center.

Thaddeus thought it better if he approached the hostiles alone but upon Taranjello's insistence he let his son tag along.

The two walked up the block of what appeared to be the reverse reflection of North Vrindaban with the exception there was a red brick, two story, Antebellum styled building in the town square.

They spotted a parked cop car with an elbow hanging out of the driver's side window. Smoke drifted up into the still air above the cruiser.

"What's that?" A curious Taranjello whispered into his father's ear.

"Cigarette smoke. This state is one of the places they used to grow tobacco before the ban."

"If it's illegal then how come he's smoking?"

"He's a cop." Thaddeus signalled for his son to hang back as he approached alone.

"Excuse me officer. I'm looking to find Mayor Minor?" The overweight cop perused Thaddeus up and down.

"Why, what's he done?"

"Nothing, that I know of. I'm Senator Thaddeus Pervers and this is my assistant." Taranjello was shocked as Thaddeus gestured over to him. "We're here from the nation's capital on a fact finding mission."

"Yeah? What facts you tryin' to find?"

"The fact of where I can find your mayor. That is if he's in town." The cop directed them to the Tick Toc Coffee Shop a few doors down.

In a battered red vinyl booth along the wall of the obsolete eatery Thaddeus and his son sat across from an extra out of *Deliverance*, aka Virgil Minors, Mayor of South Vrindaban.

Like the policeman on the street and every other town resident they had seen since stepping out of Eugene's pick-up, Virgil Minor, though noticeably emaciated stood well over six foot six tall.

The population's borderline gigantism was due to the unusually large radioactive and chemical contamination of the existing food supplies caused by the Cleveland area industrial waste run-off far to the north on Lake Erie. Since no one could fight the big corporations the intermittent successes at cleaning up the major rivers and tributaries of the Midwest around the

Great Lakes were constantly countered by Big Business' continued success in the courts.

Because of their financially backed political influence, the petrol chemical companies could afford to buy land then manipulate regulations to suit themselves. Even the low 'acceptable' levels of industrial contamination took a significant toll over time. The result was constant contamination of one level or another.

Even as they sat Thaddeus had to look up to make eye contact with Minor.

"Virgil, I'm a member of the senate sub-committee on Small Town Support investigating problems in America." Taranjello looked puzzled.

"What that got to do wit me?"

"Well it has to do more with your people Mr. Mayor."

"You ain't one'a them com'nists are ya boy?"

"No sir, I'm from another party, but that's not why I'm here. I want to talk to you about a plan."

"What kind'a plan?"

"Me and my aide here came to investigate general house hold eating practices, school lunches and fast food eating habits of various rural areas." Taranjello was impressed with his father's ability to bullshit so early on in his political career.

"Uh huh."

"That and the unemployment situation in the area." That seemed to garner Virgil's attention and his eyes became just a little less dull. Thaddeus quickly realized that as slow as the mayor of North Vrindaban was this guy clearly had him beat and it wasn't long before he came to the realization that the mayor of South Vrindaban was just as stupid and small minded as the mayor of North Vrindaban.

"Look, Virgil, this area has been devastated by the closings and the people aren't doing so good." Slowly, one by one the dozen or so diners perked up and tuned their ears into the two man conversation. "Now, you do want to help your people, don't you?"

"Course I do! What'a you intimidating?"

Must be something in the water! Thaddeus mused to himself but pushed on.

"I have connections up in Ohio which I think can help."

"What kind'a connections?"

"In the agricultural industries."

"Uh huh."

"If you can find it in yourself to work together with the folks of North Vrin-"

"I KNOWED IT, I KNOWED IT!" He slammed the table with his hand and jumped up. "As soon as you started using them fancy words like 'general house hold eating practices' and 'school lunches' I knowed you was up to something!"

"All I'm asking you to do is listen to the plan."

Virgil looked around and suddenly realized that the entire diner of giants were staring at him. He sat back down and became quite.

At this response Thaddeus quickly hatched his plan.

"They got retail outlets, storage and advertising facilities already in place. You've got transport and distribution capabilities. I can supply your people with the commodities. Together all this will create jobs! Think, Virgil, how nice it would be to see people going back to work again! The markets full of food, the shops bustling and the streets filled with traffic again!" Virgil was visibly deep in thought. Not too deep, probably less than six inches deep, but it was a start. "And all due to you Virgil Minor, Mayor of South Vrindaban!"

Virgil again perused the now silent, motionless dining room, all eyes glued on the battered red vinyl booth as the waitress at station six kept pouring coffee until the customer's cup overflowed onto the table.

"In addition to that Mr. Mayor, money. The cash flow would set in almost immediately. Of course the grocery stores, as would the other shops, offer significant discounts at first to get the ball rolling, but once it started the whole place'd be back on its feet in a matter of a couple of months!" Pressure in the room mounted.

"What I gotta do?" Virgil asked.

The place instantly broke into cheers and applause followed by a standing ovation. Negotiations resumed as the small crowd settled.

"I'm going to setup a meeting with Jim-Bob and yourself and you two can work out the details! I'll be at my desk in P.C. first thing Monday morning and I'll get my secretary to contact you with the details. Meanwhile I'll work things out with my friends up at the farms in Ohio so you can start receiving goods. Deal?"

He extended his hand. They shook and the people cheered again.

"Meanwhile, I want you and your wife to have dinner on me!" In unison the diners all said 'EEEEWWWW!" and clapped again.

"Where's the nearest fine dining restaurant in these parts?" Pervers innocuously asked.

"The Don Knotts exit! Best KFC in the state!" The waitress at station six called over.

"No it taint neither!" The grill cook yelled through the service window behind the counter. "The McDonalds over to the Joyce DeWitt Rest Stop. They has a booth now!"

"The Stonewall Jackson Intersection! There's a Whopper Meal Deal on all this week!" Someone else called out.

Little realizing he would nearly start a riot with such a simple question, Thaddeus examined the map he had with him. He had to find a way back to the highway via a different intersection than they had come off anyway.

He advised of the nearest one by the Mayor. Everyone knew this intersection because it was different from the all the others with a McDonalds, a Burger King, a KFC and Dunkin' Donuts. Instead there was a McDonalds, a Burger King, a KFC and a Denny's.

It was late that evening that Thaddeus and family got back on the road with a stop off at the Conchata Ferrell Denny's where he gave the head waitress $100 and informed her the two mayors would be by with their wives and that the money was to pay for their meals.

It was once they were back on the highway that Taranjello suggested that when they reach Washedupton Thaddeus look into the goal of regulating industrial waste disposal in the Cleveland-Lake Erie area to clean up the Chippewa Valley.

"Eugene told me it's been contaminated from the turn of the 20th Century!" Taranjello informed his father. "That's got'a be like a thousand years ago!"

"Not quite, but I understand what you mean." Thaddeus answered.

It would be a week later that word would reach Senator Pervers that the dinner he had arranged between the two minor dignitaries deteriorated into a name calling session followed by a short bout of fisticuffs. The dinner ended when the sheriff of North Vrindaban showed up and arrested the mayor of South Vrindaban, the sheriff of South Vrindaban ordered the arrest of the mayor of North Vrindaban. Following a twelve hour negotiation a prisoner exchange was finally arranged.

The failure of the détente diner was over before it began leaving the situation between North Vrindaban and South Vrindaban essentially unchanged.

Ж

They drove for some time that evening unaware that due to road works on the highway they had been detoured due east. Due to the detour and some bad directions at a truck stop given by a Pakistani with little or no English, they found themselves along a large river in an upscale neighborhood with a long line of big schools.

Thaddeus deduced these were universities and so the neigborhood was that of Laputa in Cambridge Massachusetts, a suburb of Boston. The river was The Charles and they were now just outside the Massachusetts Institute of Technology alias MIT and, as it was getting dark, that's where they pulled over.

With the national atlas opened across the steering wheel and Taranjello manning the flashlight they heard a tap at the side window. Thaddeus set the two inch manual aside and lowered the window. Outside stood a studious looking young man about forty-ish, clutching a small stack of text books.

"You folks okay? Get turned around back on tha motorway did ya? Sum'a them turn offs can be wicked bad!" He showered them with Bostonian.

"Motorway?" Forgetting he was in a faraway territory Pervers was temporarily thrown by the lexicon of the foreign language as it lingered in his cranial lobes. He laughed. "Yes! Is there an on ramp close by, to get back on the highway I mean? We're trying to make it down to P.C."

"Tryin' fa P.C. tanite?! Not gonna make it! Tell ya what, pahk ya cah round back in the yahd, and I'll help ya find a room."

"Thank you, that's very kind."

"When ya get round back make sur-ah ya lock ya doo-wahs! Afta dahk this area can be wicked bad!"

He gave some quick directions to a motel, Thaddeus thanked him, rolled up the window and they drove away.

"Dad! What'd he say?" Taranjello leaned in close and asked.

"These people originally came from Britain son, so they suffer from a genetic speech deficiency."

"What's that dad?"

"They can't speak English."

"Ahh! That's too bad. They seem real nice."

Ж

They found the motel, checked in and later that night Taranjello sat alone in his motel room reading about the Cambridge area in the tourist's guide. It gave a brief description of the background of the Laputa area in Cambridge and featured the main characteristics and sights.

He read how, being a scientific community where all its residents were scientifically literate, they were completely rational and the only region in the country to become unencumbered by holy books or other superstitions. It is they who were responsible for all the major discoveries which have improved life and dragged nearly all of mankind out of the Stone Age.

All except for the Middle Eastern countries which still wallowed in the Sixth Century desperately clinging to their Iron Age war god and on whom the rest of the civilized world had given up in favor of civilization and humanity. Taranjello also read how it was most likely out of frustration that the average Middle Easterner had half the luxury, half the convenience and therefore half the opportunity to advance their lives as the average Westerner and that was probably why they kept giving rise to the evil cults who subsisted on butchering, bombing and killing each other along with any Westerners who tried to help.

Ж

Early the next morning the desk clerk/owner, hoping to boost business in the midst of the current twelve year recession, and who had last night gotten wind there was a genuine senator in his place of business, notified the local paper which sent a reporter to run a story in the early morning edition announcing that Washedupton higher ups stayed at this humble little motel.

The real interest in the story however was because senators and representatives no longer visited their districts, not since the first rapper was elected and drive-bys became a constant danger.

That morning when the Pervers crossed the motel parking lot and entered the crowded lobby to check out, dozens of people were milling around in the small area. The people took pictures and uttered 'Wow' and 'Oh-my-gosh!' as expressions of their wonderment.

The city's mayor, having seen the story in the morning paper as he had his breakfast of rehydrated chowder, artificial baked beans and soy raisin toast, decided to seize the opportunity to connect with a Washedupton big wig in person, an honor he had never been afforded.

As the Pervers were leaving a black, stretch limo pulled into the narrow car port in front of the drive-up office and a well groomed, uniformed chauffeur hopped out, opened the rear passenger door and called over to the senator. Thad told Taranjello to take the bags to their car while he investigated.

Upon poking his head into the rear window of the vehicle Thaddeus was introduced to mayor Sean O'Dwyer Fitzgerald-Kennedy.

"Senator Pervers, great to finally make your acquaintance!" He thrust out his hand. "I was just on my morning drive and since I was in the neighbourhood . . ."

"Pleasure to meet you your honor." Thad reciprocated.

"Senator, I wonder if I might impose upon you for a brief period and show you around our lovely city?"

"Well, Your Honor, the truth is we've already lost-"

"THAT'S FANTASTIC Senator! It's a nice Saturday for a drive, isn' it? James!" He yelled out to the chauffeur. "Help Mrs. Pervers and the boy into the car."

"But Mayor Fitzgerald-Kennedy-" Thad began to object.

"Oh! Don't be so formal! You can sit up here in the V.I.P. seat!"

Minutes later the Pervers found themselves on a tour of 'Beantown' accompanied by a detailed lecture given by the Lord Mayor himself.

A quick trip along the Charles River led out to the downtown area and around the Boston Common then it was out past Fenway Park as the mayor talked constantly.

However, the tour was not without information which Thaddeus found himself increasingly engrossed in.

He discovered for example that due to a spate of the Commonwealth's laws back in the 2020's forbidding all references to race, culture or ethnic origin, almost all vestiges of the people's cultures had vanished. Culture was no longer allowed to be taught in schools, speaking foreign languages was ruled 'racially prejudice' and 'safe spaces had to be provided for none English speakers before Spanglish was ruled the official national language.

Protests began.

Protests over Columbus Day, St. Patrick's Day, Martin Luther King Day, Susan B. Anthony Day, Menachem Begin Day, even Liberace Day were, one by one, added to the holiday list in response to protests by an increasingly ill informed electorate.

As a knock-on effect of these state laws, which surreptitiously crept into the legislature one by one every time a politician needed a boost in the polls, the number of holidays celebrating each American ethnicity reached 366. There were simply too many official holidays for the standard calendar to accommodate.

A solution had to found. So all ethnically related holidays, even religious holidays because they were ethnically motivated, were deemed 'racist' by the Department of Ethnic Neutrality and so were made illegal.

Even Labor Day was struck from the calendar when the managers went out on strike in protest.

They wanted Bosses' Day.

Pervers began to realize that it appeared where everyone is occupied with the sciences, or only their own discipline, they were unable to see or relate to the city crumbling around them. The population not only became culturally ignorant, but completely ignorant to all spheres and areas outside their own areas of expertise.

As an unintentional learning outcome Thaddeus also realized that the people the mayor referred to had apparently been isolated for so long, trapped in their circle of undergraduate school, graduate school and post graduate school after which most of them stayed in the safe confines of the university teaching and engaged in research, that they had become essentially blind to the situation throughout the rest of the United States.

Outlying schools suffered and combined with a plethora of pointless, government subsidized courses such as *How to Watch T.V., Elvis as Anthology, How to Get Dressed, Lesbian Dance* and *Gender Studies*, courses people had lost the ability to hold intelligible, informed conversations regarding their own history, art or philosophy.

Here too he was made aware of the need to re-invigorate investment in advanced education in general when he was told about the great-great-great grandson of N.D.T. the great Astrophysicist who singlehandedly forced the government to reinstate science teachers as legitimate teachers after being banned from schools by the religious right under the fourth Bush administration.

"James, pull over here." The Mayor directed. It was an abandoned factory parking lot facing the wharf and the bay beyond.

"Look outside senator. Tell me what you see." Thaddeus was greeted by the cool sea air as he stepped out of the limo.

The first thing which caught his eye as he slowly perused the expansive, empty parking lot was an abandoned shopping cart a few broken up wooden pallets scattered amongst faded parking lines. Highlighted by broken glass sparkling in the morning sun he watched discarded newspapers and McDonald's wrappers drift across the macadam.

But a few dozen yards further out he spied strings of abandoned and dilapidated fishing boats slowly bobbing in their slips all along the harbor. Over three dozen of them.

"This processing and cannery factory used to employ about two thousand people and their family members." The water quietly lapped up against the boats. "The boats supported another six dozen families in the Boston area alone."

"Over fishing?" Thad speculated.

"No, companies moving to foreign markets to escape unregulated foreign competition, higher Federal, state and government taxes, unrealistic minimum wage laws all combined with skyrocketing housing prices." Thaddeus digested the information. "The last of the sea side industrialization shut down when the companies shifted operations to Guatemala and El Salvador where the legal working age is 10 and there are no minimum wage laws, so the fifty cents an hour the American companies pay them allows them to hire five or six thousand new kids a year."

"That's alot'a kids!"

"Yes, but this is offset by the average number which die each year from industrial accidents, malnutrition, and starvation or the ones who are kidnapped and pressed into service in one of the three dozen revolutionary guerrilla armies infecting those areas."

"That many?"

"Forbes, Putnam, Pearson Productions and Pfizer Pharmaceuticals, along with Dow plastics all gone. I mean, it's bad enough when this dynamic struck the small towns in the Bible Belt or former western states, but the third largest urban settlement on the Eastern Seaboard?!"

Later, over some Irish coffees, where Prudence passed out after the first one, the mayor pleaded with the senator to do something to financially revitalize the Boston area.

Thaddeus bid the mayor farewell and even though it wasn't his district, promised to do what he could once he took up his duties down in P.C.

Forty-five minutes later, once back out on the road, Thaddeus spoke to Prudence and Taranjello as he drove.

"America is turning out to be a far different country then I thought it was." Thad quietly confided as they drove away and headed back towards the interstate.

SENATOR PERVERS

CHAPTER FOURTEEN

Ж

With the unexpected delays finally behind them, now heading south, the Pervers passed under the large green road sign announcing their exit from Massachusetts and less than two and a half hours later they were entering the outskirts of the megalopolis of what was formally New York City, Philadelphia and now known as the Greater P.C. District.

It was two days after setting out that the Pervers had finally come to the end of their journey.

Thaddeus pulled off Route 270 and onto the eight lane access road into the city.

With renewed vigor he made a self-commitment, as a newly appointed senator of the United States Congress, to attack his new job and was determined to use all the influence he didn't have to rectify any problems which came across his desk.

Twenty minutes later the Pervers were checked into the Hotel Houyhnhnms on the outskirts of the capitol. It was there in the hotel lobby that Thaddeus met with a Mr. Jon Johnson, personal aide to Senator Redressal, Secretary of Private Affairs. Jon Johnson had been sent to receive the Pervers and help them get settled in. Just as back during the first Lump administration, a smooth transition of government was paramount.

Redressal always made it his business to take personal charge of new personnel and get them 'settled in' so to speak. He liked to keep an eye on things, as he saw his job. It was the thing which kept his rice bowl full.

As Secretary of the Office of Private Affairs of Others it was Redressal's job to determine whether or not a given citizen might pose a potential problem to the country's security. If said citizen or citizens were determined by his office to be potentially detrimental to The State, the S. of P. A. of O. was authorized to take unilateral action to redress the issue. Of course said action could only occur after the mandatory two or three hour investigation of the individual or individuals concerned. After all, there had to be controls, this wasn't a police state. Redressal sensed the Pervers posed no immediate threat. For now.

After being shown to their hotel rooms, where they would spend the remainder of the weekend while their new house was in final prep, they quickly unpacked, showered and were then taken out to the suburbs to view their new abode. It was everything Thaddeus had promised Prudence all those long years ago when they first married.

The two story, split level ranch, although more than ten years old was in good condition. Prudence made a mental note to replace the ugly polished Canadian cedar siding with a beautiful lime green plastic siding as soon as they were settled in.

Johnson led the way up the path as he moved to open several latches on the specially installed front door leaf which allowed the opening to widen an extra 12 inches. This to accommodate Prudence's increased girth which, although not yet having reached Jaba the Hut proportions, remained unrestrained in her efforts to gain such globular girths.

Mrs. Pervers was then pushed through the door in her new hover wheel chair which had been gently floating outside the front door on the porch.

"Lights please." Johnson quietly ordered as they passed through the vestibule into the main room.

Lights activated. A smooth female voice responded

as soft illumination slowly rose to fill the room. A large staircase sat off to the left with the other ground floor rooms ahead and to the right.

"The entire structure is voice activated. There are remotes for all the TV's-" Johnson informed.

"ALL the TV's?!" Taranjello gleefully questioned.

"Yes, counting the kitchen there are four. Also for the surround-sound stereo featuring the latest Bose Advanced Lifestyle, Series VI system as well as the conveyor to the upstairs toilet which features an extra-large tub with an optional shower feature and an array of digital temperature settings. Also voice activated of course."

"Of course." Taranjello echoed.

They made their way through to the chrome festooned kitchen off to the left. It was complete with appliances, wall and floor cabinets and a large center island.

Still getting the hang of her new contraption Prudence's floating chair bumped the kitchen door frame as they entered.

"Hey! There's no doors on this fridge!" Taranjello declared as he stood in front of what looked like a standard, two door, upright fridge sans doors. From the front the complete interior was visible with glass shelves and bottom drawers albeit all encased in a translucent, greenish mist. Although it had not yet been stocked it did contain a handful of items. A carton of orange juice, a wrapped sandwich and a butter dish with half a stick of butter sat on one of the shelves.

"The food's left over from the workers, cleaners and such. Taranjello, hand me the orange juice please." Johnson directed. Taranjello stared through the mist at the carton.

"How do I get it?"

"Same as you do from your old fridge. Reach in and take it."

The boy hesitated but reached in through the gel-like gas, grabbed the juice and pulled it out. A sound like that of squashing tomatoes or a grotesquely fat man sitting down at the dinner table emanated through the room. Once out he held it up.

"There's no gel on my hand! And . . ." He held the carton to his cheek. "It's ice cold!"

"It's an advanced form of a Freon based refrigerant." Johnson smirked. "Stable at room temperature, once activated lasts up to a year and can be recharged. No more opening and closing the door to get your food plus, you can make out your grocery list from across the room!" He reached over and pressed a button on the side of the large island in the middle of the room and all the fronts of all the cabinets slowly turned clear. "Same with your food storage." He pressed it a second time and the shiny chrome fronts returned to normal. "If you grow tired of the chrome a simple reset will afford you the option of Canadian maple, pine or oak fronts for all the cabinets. No need to redecorate. Shall we continue the tour?" He led them out to the dining room.

"Everything in the house is compliments of the various manufacturers. All the senators have them."

"So, we're being bribed by big industry?" Thaddeus half challenged.

"Oh hardly **big** industry senator. None of these companies employ over 5,000 people!"

"UUGGGHHH!!" Suddenly they heard a ruckus back out in the kitchen.

Something had possessed Taranjello, still fascinated by the modern fridge, to experiment by seeing if he could cram his entire head into the space between the orange juice and the sandwich. He succeeded where upon he immediately found out he couldn't breath. The boy managed to push himself free and fell to the floor.

"Not exactly the sharpest knife in the drawer." Thaddeus quipped to their guide. They returned to the tour.

Prudence meanwhile had steered her hover chair over to the staircase and was experimenting with the wall mounted lift which towed her and her large form in the chair up the staircase to the top landing. She enjoyed it so much she made several round trips.

"The main and guest bedrooms are upstairs, all equipped with temperature controlled beds and remote controlled, tinted windows with built in night shades in the windows."

"Nice." Pervers answered.

"We'll be ready to move you in as soon as the moving craft shows up later this evening. It shouldn't take long, meanwhile we've booked you in the Huey Long Senatorial Suite on the 49th floor back at the hotel for the night."

As they made their way back out to the front door Johnson handed a small gift wrapped box to Pervers.

"What is it?" He opened it to find a square slightly larger than normal cell phone.

"It's a Kaspersky 3000 photo/document printer. It allows you to print standard sized documents directly from your cell phone.

"Thank you Mr. Johnson, that's very kind of you. Must have cost a fortune!"

"Not at all! $5,000 retail but, Kaspersky ships them to us by the dozen."

"I see." He commented examining the device.

"Senator, you are requested to report to the Senate Monday morning for the ten o'clock session which will start promptly at about eleven, eleven thirty."

"Okay."

"You are scheduled to have lunch with a senator Hurley at twelve and your office will be ready by half past one. Senator Snodgrass set it up for you."

"Senator Snodgrass? Very good."

"Will there be anything else sir?"

"No thank you. You've been most helpful."

"Well, here are the house keys and if you're ready I'll drop you and your family back at the hotel."

Johnson turned to go.

"There is one more thing."

"Yes senator?"

"Didn't the Democrats pass a communications bill last year?"

"Oh, that! That was something different. No relationship to Kaspersky Electronics."

Ж

"Senator Pervers, Senator Pervers sir!" A bell hop scurried along behind him as he headed for the hotel exit that afternoon. He stopped to allow the bell hop to catch up. "Senator Pervers sir, you have a phone call." Thaddeus glanced over at the busy front desk. "Ah, you can take it in the green room." He pointed over to a door to the right of reception. "It's sound proofed."

"Thank you."

Pervers made his way over to the four by five room, closed the door over and picked up the wall phone.

"Thaddeus! How ya getting' on son? Got everything ya need?" It was a familiar voice.

Thaddeus had temporarily forgotten about his mentor/godfather Sidney Snodgrass. In all that time it really hadn't occurred to Thaddeus what had become of the old goat.

"Senator Snodgrass, nice of you to call! This place is fantastic! I've never seen any place like it!"

"Well, we here in the government strive to keep things as far removed from the difficulties of everyday life as possible." He assured. "Besides, I can't just forget my favourite protégé, now can I? Getting settled in alright? Ready for the first big day at the office on Monday?"

"Just trying to understand the whole system. You know, how everything works out here. It's a bit different."

"You're not in Kansas anymore, Dorothy! But things are not really all that complicated." Snodgrass sought to explain 'the system'.

"We can't control the ballot boxes, too many people watching. We can only partially control those with enough money to launch a campaign on their own."

"Can't they be denied party backing if they go too far off the rails?" Thaddeus challenged.

"Theoretically, that is we used to could, but once folks like Lump came along with his billions and being part of the Upper 1% and wielding all them rich connections, the party leaders on both sides decided it made more sense to compete for their candidacy and get them into the party rather than keep them out. Hell, they gonna run anyways, might as well get them and their money on your side, know what I mean?" Sydney explained the prevailing logic.

"Uh huh." Thad mumbled.

"On the other hand we certainly can't control the electorate, at least not outright."

"If you can't control the electorate outright then how do you control the election?" Pervers' questions had ceased to be didactic in nature and the answers he was receiving began to water the seeds of discontent.

"Blindingly simple son. Don't have to. Just control the nominations. Tell them who they can vote for. Once the 'candidates' are made public, all we have to do then is control the news and hell, since they're corporate sponsored, that's easy!"

Having been born, schooled and gone to work and married in the same small town for his entire life, Thaddeus never really had any exposure to the alternative life styles of other Americans. To that end he had learned a lot on his detoured journey from the little town he left behind in Ohio.

Since leaving the confines of the ball bearing factory in Brubaker and being exposed to more of the nation he had been inadvertently 'sent back to school' as it were.

He learned about the loss of the middle class and the devastation of their children's future. He was made aware of the unbelievable, unexplained and incomprehensibly large national debt. Sydney further informed Thaddeus how in his nearly 100 years of political service the dangerous loss of national identity evolved with everyone more concerned about their own little slice of the pie, victimhood and complaining rather than uniting as a country under one goal caused the national motto *E pluribus Unum* to metamorphose into something more akin to *E pluribus discordia*.

But most importantly he was made aware of the destructive cultural fractionalization America had deteriorated into and which gave way to the country's current tribalism and identity politics, and how that virtually paralyzed political advancement.

It was at this point Thaddeus realized that, intentionally or not, he had been being re-educated by Snodgrass.

Now, sitting there in the booth, talking with the old senator, his education began to crystalize.

Ж

With the missus commanding the movers out at the house, Taranjello off somewhere and Thaddeus not due at the office until Monday morning Pervers had some time to kill that Saturday.

He considered going over to the office to have a peek at his new place of work but instead drifted into a swank restaurant with the intention of getting some lunch however, he spotted the back room where there was a bar.

He went in, pulled up a stool and ordered a Bud Extra Lite. He paid the twenty dollars and sat forward on his stool, leaned on the bar and became consumed in thought.

Things seemed to be moving fast and he began wrestling with his new life choices. Was all this wealth and privilege 'supposed' to happen? Or was he violating some preordained cosmic order in violation of the rules? He ruminated over all the stories of those who rose too quickly to the ranks of the rich and famous only to suffer the inability to adjust and go down in flames only to crash and burn.

Feeling a bit despondent Thaddeus decided to call his old BB Stacker buddy Joe. Not wanting to use his government cell he flagged down the 105 year old bar tender.

"Excuse me, is there another phone nearby?"

"Why yes sir. In back, next to the toilets."

A minute later he was entering his universal PIN and the phone was ringing.

"Joe! It's Thaddeus!"

You old bastard! How ya doing? Everybody's been reading about you in the papers! Looks like you're doing pretty well for yourself!

"It's going okay. Certainly getting a view from the top. The bigger picture if you will!"

Speaking of big, how's Prudence?

"Bigger."

Taranjello?

"Not bad, considering. What do you say to a get together some time? Hash out old times, maybe share a beer? They got some great bowling alleys out here. And you know the best part?"

Tell me.

"I hear nobody in these parts can throw a ball worth a shit! We'd clean up!" Thad spoke with child-like enthusiasm.

I'd clean up, there's no points for gutter balls! They both laughed. *Let me call you in a week or so and we'll talk about it.*

"Okay, sounds like a plan. If ya miss me leave a message with my secretary. I think they already have me listed."

A secretary?! Wel! ecxcusssee meee! Mr. Big Shot! You take her easy!

"Tone down the brouhaha about me back there, will ya! Not like I'm gonna make much of a dent out here."

Well just make sure you get your share of the pie before it's all over!

"Thanks! Talk soon Joe."

THE O'NARABLE GENTLEMEN O' THE UNITED STATES CONGRESS

CHAPTER FIFTEEN

⚜

Snodgrass had more sense than to just throw his personal investment, the brand new senator Pervers, to the wolves and so had arranged for a senior senator friend, Senator Hurley from New York to take Thaddeus under his wing.

James Jacob Hurley, J.J. to his multitude of friends and those who wanted to be his friend, was old school with emphasis on the word 'old'. His 1940's style, Irish gentlemen's fashion sense, complete with walking stick, had come in and gone out of fashion several times in the past century but remained a trait all who knew the man identified him with.

Tall and slender he carried himself well and the collagen injections combined with his annual plastic surgery allowed his face to belay his one hundred and nine years.

Snodgrass had arranged for Thaddeus to meet Hurley for lunch in a restaurant just off Connecticut Avenue a week before the new Congressional session was to convene.

The manager escorted Thaddeus to a table in the back, next to a well-lit picture window with a view of the Capitol building where Hurley waited and the two politicians ordered drinks and food. After the meal, which was lightly sprinkled with small talk, the conversation solidified and became more serious.

"Senator Hurley, do you recall a time when corporate influence in the Congress was somewhat limited?"

"Yes, yes I do." Hurley responded with an ignition of faded recollections. "From the very beginning corporate influence, to a limited extent, was considered normal. But I have long ago given up any hope that this or any future government will ever return to any semblance of normalcy."

Thaddeus was drawn to the fact that Hurley distinctly paced his words which were enunciated with surgical precision yet flowed like silk.

"Normalcy' meaning the Congress functioning on a productive level to help bolster the country which now sags so low that nothing short of a direct invasion is going to pull these people together again!" Thaddeus was surprised by Hurley's candidness as the veteran Senator's third Manhattan began to release any inhibitions he might have had. "Quite simply the government has given up on the people and the people have, as we are well aware, have given up on the government."

"I know that part but, what I wanna know Senator is, how did it get like this?" To his own surprise Thaddeus found himself unexpectedly but sincerely invested.

"With each new election cycle the word 'hope' is bandied about. Hope in the future. Hope that they'll be changes in the way things are done. Hope in the new president elect." Hurley sipped again. "Things change alright, but like all evolutionary processes changes aren't always for the better. Science tells us there were dozens, maybe hundreds of offshoots of hominids before nature settled on Homo sapiens, the now dominant species, or so it's rumored. I've seen some pretty crafty chimps at the zoo." He paused to choose his words. "It's pretty much the same in political systems."

"I see." Thaddeus digested Hurley's thoughts processing them as suggestions for his own future.

"The first Continental Congress wanted George Washington to be king. He declined."

"Yeah, so he told me."

"What?!"

"I mean . . . that story's old, to me. I heard it before . . . from teachers. Read it also. In history books."

"Uh huh." Hurley sipped his drink and continued. "Washington argued against being a king because they had just broken with a monarchy and so they put their heads together and came up with a modern democracy. Or what used to be democracy. Slavery was abolished and eventually blacks got the vote, as did women but nothing much changed politically speaking. Gays got to marry and have kids, good or bad as that was, but again nothing really changed as far as the political system was concerned." Hurley flagged for another drink. "Unfortunately there gradually came a point, sometime around the first two decades of this century, the people of America no longer saw themselves as a cohesive population with a national identity but rather an autonomous, unconnected collection of residents who happened to reside in the same country."

"I've read that before. But how could it get to that point when just two generations before that patriotism was still the norm?" Pervers queried.

"So shocked by their first real lost at war, against the communists in what used to be Viet Nam, now Hunamviet province in China, they turned inward and put their own personal interests ahead of the country's. The people forgot John Kennedy's words completely. 'Ask not what your country can do for you ...'"

"Ask only what you can do or yourself!" Thad added.

"Exactly. They gradually saw themselves as whites, blacks and Hispanics first. Gays, lesbians and straights above all else. Farmers, industrial workers and businessmen before they were Americans." Hurley turned and stared out the window as he spoke. "We used to call that tribalism."

"I've heard of that. It's one of the first signs a society is-" Hurley held up a hand and cut him off.

"A few wily politicians saw this and decided to exploit the situation. They observed that the people had ceased to be a people who controlled their government and lost the ability to tell the politicians what they wanted from that government in such a way as to make the leaders listen. When things started getting too violent in the streets, as tribalism will to do, the politicians were able to step in and say the government needs to sort this out."

"Well they should if it got too violent." Thad concurred.

"Well they did and that's when the people abdicated control to the politicians. Politics affects people, gets their dander up. Even when they don't realize it. Taps into their base morality, you know? What everybody thinks is right or wrong." Hurley shrugged. "Right around the time we lost that war the people in this country started to lose faith in what the country stood for, to vote more and more along the fracture lines established during that time and to follow the example of their leaders by adopting the 'me first' attitude."

"But we all pulled together before, when there was a crisis! In the past!"

"In the distant past! Only way back, during the first two World Wars, and that was largely because people realized that America could actually be beaten again by another country. But memories fade fast in this land my boy." Hurley sat back and sighed. "A country's government should be controlled by its people, not the other way around. Ever heard of the Celts?"

"You mean like on what used to be St. Patrick's Day?"

"Yes, before it was outlawed as being racist."

"Uh huh." Too captivated by the senior senator's observations 'uh huh' was the best Thaddeus could do.

"The ancient Celts had a helluv'a cultural tradition. Whenever they were beset by devastating wars, plague or crop failures, they would ceremonially have an all-night celebration-"

"Like drinking and feasting kind of celebration? That's a bit weird! Celebrate disaster!"

"An all-night celebration following which they would, with his full cooperation mind you, march the king out to the swamps and kill him."

"Fuck! That's intense!" The waitress shot a disproving glance at the table as Thaddeus fell back in his chair.

"Sorry!" He mouthed over to her. She flipped him off.

"Point is up into the 21st Century monarchs claimed they got their powers of rule from the gods. The ancient Celts, like all others, accepted this, so when things weren't going so good for the Celts as a people, they would send the king back to the gods."

"That's too bad."

"How so?"

"I mean that's too bad in we can't do that today." Thad pointed out.

"You're not the first to make that observation Senator! My point is, we were the first to establish a country supposed to be controlled by its people, not the people controlled by the leaders. Leaders are for leading but have evolved into rulers who want to control and when they sense they are losing control they turn to lies through misinformation. But they are not the sole perpetrators!"

"Are you suggesting the fractionalization . . . the deterioration of American society is the people's doing?"

"Well, look who showed up for school!" By his fourth drink Hurley's inhibitions had fully evaporated.

"Are you suggesting the failure of the present government is the people's doing?"

"Hell Yes!"

"But . . . how are the people letting the - ?"

"By bitching and moaning like a bunch of school kids who were told playtime's over!" Hurley paused to corral his anger. "I was speaking at a university last month and some bonehead professor pipes up with, 'Wars have become political tools!' I immediately cut him off with 'Wars have always been political tools!' I said. 'Tools where you bet the number of lives lost against the potential damage to your poll numbers and whether or not you can flaunt it as some kind of a victory when it's all over! No shit war is a political tool! War has always been a political tool, you tool! How the hell do you think we became the most advanced vestige of modern civilization?! Peace treaties?' Fuck that Ivy League theoretical bullshit! This is the real world. Deal with it. Millions of men and women before us have now, like it or not, it's our turn!"

"How'd he take it?"

"Not so good. No sense of humor." Hurley grunted. "They terminated the lecture, I was escorted out. And they refused to pay me."

"Well that's pretty small of them."

"It's okay, I'm Irish. My Jewish lawyers threatened to sue them on racial discrimination grounds, I got paid."

"Okay, so how do you really feel senator?" Thaddeus asked oblivious to his own sarcasm. Hurley pushed on.

"Some have proposed the argument that with all but the total collapse of the government under the two party system, the 'Great Experiment' has failed."

"Is that what **you** think?"

"Son, at the risk of sounding too much like an evasive politician, I'll be dead in a handful of years and so it don't really matter all that much to me."

"That is pretty evasive." Thaddeus agreed. "But I don't expect to be dead in a few years."

Hurley was taken aback by this comment.

"You tryin' to tell me you're goin' in there, into the senate, with the intent of making a difference?" Hurley challenged as he nodded out the window towards the Capitol rotunda peeking above the tress.

Thaddeus shrugged and punctuated his suddenly blatant naivety by looking down at the table and twirling his half full drink glass.

"I'm not sure what difference I can make, whether or not I'll score any points but I'd sure like to have a clear picture of the playing field before I suit up. You know what I mean?"

Hurley fell back in his seat and smirked before responding.

"Well, if you're sniffing around asking me what I'd do if I had my youth back, knew what I know now and had the opportunity to go back in there," He again nodded out towards the Congress. "I'd lock all the bastards up! Every last one of them!" He snarled. Thaddeus smiled.

"You mean like a military coup de grâs?"

"It's called a coup d'état. And no that's not possible. You'd have to control the military for that. I just mean something to put the fear of God into them. Hell, can't even do that anymore! Most of the churches are closed." Thaddeus looked at him in puzzlement. "We ain't got a god anymore!" Hurley clarified.

"Sure we do!" Thaddeus insisted. Now Hurley looked puzzled. "Money!" Blurted Thaddeus. Hurley laughed.

"You'd probably have all the backing you'd need in that department but, then what would we do for a government?"

"Good question."

"Aww, I'm just babbling. Tee many martoonies!"

Hurley joked and held up his empty glass. "I got to run." He stood and gathered his coat and briefcase. "Good luck at the session next week." J.J. said. Thaddeus stood as well.

"Thank you senator. Your advice means a lot."

"Just keep your head down, pay attention and get familiar with the procedures. Best way to get on top of your opponent is to use procedure. Nobody can get around that. And never let emotion get the best of you. Stick to the facts. Hard to argue against the facts."

"Procedure. Facts. Yes sir. I see why Sydney picked you to be my mentor! I researched your record you've served on more committees than any other congressman!"

"A mobile segment of petrified matter agglomerates no bryophytes, m'boy! Never forget that!"

"I . . . I won't sir. I think."

"And never forget; people are capable of committing shocking atrocities, we all know that. But they are also capable of achieving miraculous heights! That is the nature of this animal we call society." He donned his jacket. "We must all decide, each for himself, whether in our time here we will commit or achieve."

As Hurley left Thaddeus retook his seat and stared out at the rotunda of the Capitol.

Unsure if it was nerves, fear or excitement his body tingled and, unlike back at the ball bearing factory or any time since, his thoughts began to clear as never before and he felt an unfamiliar sense of purpose seep into his mind.

Ж

The House of Representatives and the Senate, the two chambers of the U.S. Congress that make up the legislative branch of government, have a difference in function.

The U.S. Senate proposes and considers new laws, approves or rejects presidential nominations, provides advice and consent on international treaties, and serves as the high court for impeachment trials. Although the U.S. House of Representatives also works on new legislation, only the Senate performs the other three duties.

Additionally The Congress, as a whole, has the power to override a presidential veto. However, a two-thirds majority vote in both the House of Representatives and in the Senate is required to do this. The exact number depends on how many representatives vote; therefore, the actual number is subject to change.

Thaddeus' first Congressional session was Friday morning at ten.

It was a clear, cool day outside, the halls hummed with activity and he felt a strange type of energy. As he entered the chamber at half past nine his scalp tingled from the buzz and excitement of a place he had only seen in movies.

"I wonder if this is how Jimmy Stewart felt way back when?" He whispered to himself while he stood in the back lobby peering down the main aisle to the floor at the Speaker's prominent desk centered on the back wall of the expansive chambers.

J.J., his new mentor had already arrived and sat in the row directly in front of Thaddeus and as Pervers sat J.J. turned to speak to him.

"Morning senator."

"Morning senator." Thad smiled like a school boy.

"They set you up with your senatorial orientation yet?" Hurley asked.

"My secretary told me to report to the orientation center right after the session ends."

"Good."

"Who's that fat fella sitting over there?" Thad queried.

"That's the Republican Whip, Robert R. Ropey. Steal the I-teeth right out'a your head!"

"He's dishonest?"

"More crooked than five miles of country road. After you shake hands with him count your fingers, make sure you've still got five."

"What about that little skinny, grey haired fella on the other side?"

"Democratic Whip, Senator Emmet Brown. Total nut job! Continually mumbles out loud. Talks to himself out loud when he's really serious."

Tipsy O'Brien, The Speaker of the House had opened the proceedings by calling the session to order and was reviewing the agenda.

Knowing he, along with two other newbies, was to be sworn in that morning, Thaddeus was stressed about how to conduct himself.

Thaddeus launched into eliciting more advise from his surrogate mentor who was now otherwise absorbed in the current argument being presented to the floor by the senator from Kansas.

The rep, who had a string of two dozen, high interest loan companies throughout the mid-west was fervently arguing in favor of the massive, private predatory lending industry prevalent throughout the more impoverished states. As the current presenter addressed the floor Hurley made a short phone call.

"I got'a run Pervers. Get over to your office and check in as soon as they take the vote, you're sworn in so you can get to your orientation."

"Vote? What vote?"

"The vote on precatory lending!"

"How should I vote?"

"The Democrats are gonna vote to enforce the law against, but it don't really matter how you vote. The House is gonna vote against so nothing's gonna change. See ya at the commissary for lunch!"

"What about a debate, what about the overall outcome?"

"Never let the facts get in the way, son." Hurley tapped him on the shoulder as he breezed past. "Only muddles up the conversation." Hurley's use of sophistry as a technique to deflect the truth clearly signalled to Thaddeus that the truth was seen as something to be avoided not sought out.

Later after the session outside the building as Pervers started down the steps of the Capital Building a female reporter with a cameraman dutifully schlepping behind her slid up to Thaddeus.

"You're the new freshman senator from Ohio aren't you?"

"Yes ma'am, yes I am."

"I'm LaKesha Filet Minyon, do you mine if I axe you a few questions?"

"No, not at all." He brushed back his hair and smiled at his impending first press interview. She signalled to the cameraman to roll.

"In light o' the fac' that recent surveys indicate that most, if not the majority of the Senate is horribly out of touch wit reality, 'on the ground' as it were Senator, can you tells us how much would a typical lunch, or say a simple loaf o' bread would cost in Eugenia, Ohio, your own, home state?"

"I guess . . . I guess that would depend."

Having used this question more than once in the past to show how out of touch most upper echelon politicians are, the reporter smiled at the fact that she had cornered the freshman senator to the point where he was forced to evade the question. She smiled over at the cameraman who pulled a close-up on Pervers as he scratched his chin. Expecting a question about the sinking economy, unemployment or military spending, Thaddeus was shocked at the bread question.

"Well, I've never been to Eugenia, but I imagine not

much more than any other small town, say Lima, also in my home state of Ohio. Are we talking about white bread, rye bread or whole wheat?"

"You pick."

Senators Out Of Touch With the People. Yet Another Detached Senate Convenes! She fantasized the full blown, front page feature stories based on her tactic, and again smirked. Thaddeus cleared his throat.

"Well, Wonder Bread, the brand we use in my house, is typically around $3.59. Tastyee Bread is the brand I imagine most lower income folks would buy, it goes for around a dollar less. Sunbeam's breads go for a little more in most supermarkets. Now if we're talking about rye, my favorite, Pepperidge Farm rules, I love that stuff! I pay 5.89, a little high I'll admit but it's worth it."

Her mouth fell open. The cameraman smirked.

"What's **your** favorite bread Miss . . . I'm sorry, your name again?"

"Ah . . . Sunbean. I mean Sunbeam."

"Well Miss Sunbeam, what's your favorite bread?"

"Not my name . . . that's not my name. Sunbeam. Sunbeam is the bread. The bread I eat."

"I know the bread, I was just curious as to what your name was again?"

"I'm . . . my name is LaKesha . . . Filet Minyon."

"Oh! Nice to meet you LaKesha. I've seen your broadcasts!" He smiled. "You have any other questions you would like to field?"

"No, no thank you. Thank you for your time senator."

"Call me Thaddeus." He offered. "Feel free to phone my office if I can be of any further assistance." He added as he turned and left.

"Ah . . . thank you." She stared as he walked away. "We'll tape a sign off later." She said to the cameraman as she gave the cut signal and handed him the small radio mic before walking away.

"At least he sounds like he's in touch with the real world." The cameraman commented as they took the steps back down two at a time.

"Shuddup Marv!" She quipped.

On his way across town to his office Thaddeus was struck with a thought. Had his newly found colleagues, the people who he now surrounded himself with, become infected with what the Germans call 'Realitätsfern'; total disconnection from reality, in this case Realitätsfern visa vie the electorate? Over relying on polls, nearly 100% of which came from the Press? If so, it would explain a plethora of social problems.

His mind wandered to a more personal situation. If he were to become serious about making his mark on this town, at least one person he trusted would be of great help.

Was there possibly a place for his fellow BB Stacker Joe in this big circus they called Washedupton P.C.?

Ж

That afternoon, after checking in at the office, Thaddeus headed back to the Capitol building to meet with Hurley at the west entrance for lunch.

"Why didn't we meet at the main entrance? I saw a sign, the commissary is just on the other side of The Crypt."

"Well, we're senators, we always take the long way around the barn. Besides, this'll give me a chance to give you the grand tour."

"Oh, guess that's why I'm the freshman senator."

Hurley led him down the marble laden corridor and assumed his tour guide status.

"The U.S. Capitol, is the 'People's Building', 30,000 square feet in the footprint alone. Just over 500 of it public." Thaddeus chuckled at the irony.

"Up here there's the office of a rep from Georgia, Paul Bunyon, old 'Mr. Science is the Devil's playground!' kind'a guy." Hurley lectured as he pointed towards one of the many dark oak doors along the wide and endless hallway. "Last time he ran, a professor of literature at Athens University started a campaign against him, but the Professor didn't run himself. Instead he proposed to the County Board of Registration a candidate by the name of Charles Darwin."

"Okay."

"The board approved the submission and Charles Darwin made the ballot."

"What happened?"

"In a town of 10,000 Darwin got 5,000 votes."

"True story?"

"Look it up. It's in the record."

"Remarkable!"

"Gets better. In the same speech about environmentalism Bunyon explained how although Jesus our lord and savoir hates science, he never the less helped the good senator singlehandedly kill a Kodiak bear in Alaska and later a 1,000 pound male lion in Central Africa just last year. Despite the fact that there's no sign of the bear and lions of that size are extinct."

"You ever actually talk to him?"

"Yeah, once." Hurley affected a mock southern accent. "'All that stuff I was taught 'bout evolution, embr'ology and the Big Bang is all lies, lies straight from the pits of Hell!'"

"Sounds a little loopy to me!"

"It gets even better! He's recently been appointed as co-Chair of the House Committee on Science, Space & Technology."

"Kind of like Apple appointing Lady GooGoo head of their research division isn't it?" Pervers admitted.

"Then there's Frank Trents." He indicated the office two doors up to their right. "Republican from Arizona, officially the least effectual Congressman in P.C. Of the some 45 bills he's sponsored to date, none has been passed. None has even been considered serious enough to take a vote on."

"That's pretty ineffectual!"

"Senator Jackson of Illinois asked someone on the floor to explain a balanced budget amendment. Trents volunteered, took the floor then waffled on about creationism for twenty minutes."

"We can do that? Bullshit about anything?"

"When Senator Trents was challenged by the Speaker about wasting time, he concluded by saying that abortion was more devastating to blacks then slavery."

"Jesse Jackson the Fourth? Wasn't he indicted on blowing nearly $100,000 of his campaign contributions on a vacation for himself and his wife?"

"Caught red-handed yes, indicted no."

"Who's that, heading towards the exit?" He nodded to a short, hefty late-middle aged woman click clacking across the highly polished floor.

"Best stay away from that one. Shirley Jason-Lee, also known as 'The Queen of Mean' Arrived on the hill about twenty years ago and it only took about a week before the first of her staff members quit. Each year *Washedupton Magazine* runs an article, 'The Meanest Bosses in the District'. Lee has never finished outside the top three. Multiple sources have quoted her as referring to her employees as 'morons, idiots and stupid motherfuckers'. Even gives them numbers because she's apparently too stupid to remember their names. Sad part is no member of Congress has sponsored more failed amendments."

They turned and passed a frazzled gentleman as they turned and headed down another hallway.

"But for wasting the people's time she pales in comparison to Congresswoman Mary Bochminster. Bochminster's pushing a bill based on the notion that the

HPV vaccine causes mental retardation and that there is a direct relationship between the Swine Flu outbreaks we've been having over the last century and Democratic presidencies."

Thaddeus felt himself sinking deeper into bewilderment with a detour into despair

"The fella we passed back there was Representative the Right Reverend, George Kleinhammer, one of the ones that didn't adjust too well when the states backed away from financial support of the churches and rescinded the millions in tax breaks they were giving 'the chosen ones', what we used to call 'holy rollers'."

"I understand it had to be done! Those tax dollars went to medical research, doing all kinds of good. Besides, who follows these whack jobs?" Thaddeus questioned.

"Well in George's case he built his reputation on how he can perform gay exorcism and 'out the evil spirits who inhabit the soul of the damned'."

"Isn't there something can be done about these nutters in the government?! Check that, I mean running the government?"

"Good question but don't forget son, to give an indication of how things operate here, the Supreme Court itself has yet to give a ruling on the most important case we've all been looking for. A ruling we been waiting on since way back in the late 1990's."

"Which ruling is that?"

"A ruling on the constitutionality of the Constitution." Hurley tapped Thad on the arm. "Have a quick glance to your left." Thad complied. "That's Sam DeLaurentis, Republican out of Tennessee."

"I read about that guy! How the hell can he have a running tab at the local abortion clinic?"

"That was just a bit of journalistic sarcasm, but it might as well be the case. He's knocked up four women in the last six years, two of them his own patients, none of whom are the woman he's married to. Having a baby by another woman could get a little sticky. Especially being a three time House Representative who's political platform is founded on being an anti-abortion zealot!"

"What an asshole!"

"He's got more frequent flyer miles racked up at his local abortion clinic then a pilot has flying transcontinental on a weekly route. As a family doctor he's regularly asked to speak at his parish church, on family values. On the floor he's known as the Tennessee Tomcat."

"Other senators know about this?"

"Practically all of them."

"And nobody does anything about it?"

"You know how cops protect each other no matter what?"

"It's legendary!"

"Times that by ten and that's the situation in the House and Senate. Rat somebody out and you're history."

"Why does his head look like a giant lemon?"

"Bee pollen. He takes sixty pills a day for his allergies."

"Allergies to what? Common sense?"

"The agency DeLaurentis founded with taxpayer's money started with a budget of $2 million, it's since ballooned to $130 million annually."

"They find anything?"

"Oh yeah! So far they've burned through nearly two billion investigating the effects of prayer on AIDS, UFO's and The Real Bermuda Triangle."

"This place is a fucking madhouse! How do they get away with it?!"

"Easy! The people have come to accept all their shenanigans as part of the price of doing business. That plus no one believes most of what they read in the press, at least those of us who still read the press. So exposing them is near impossible. Factor in the public's apathy coupled with the belief that this is the 'greatest country on earth' and the bitter pill of truth is a lot easier to swallow."

J.J. finished his comments just as they came to the main entrance to the floor where the main chamber door was propped open and the senator from Texas was concluding his remarks to mostly empty seats. His voluminous voice reverberated through the chamber.

"I just want to make it perfectly clear that if anything I said on the floor this morning has been misconstrued to the opposite effect I want to apologize for that misconstrued misconstruction. Thank you for your understanding. And thank you Mister Speaker, the gentleman yields."

Hurley turned to Pervers and smiled.

"Questions, comments, snide remarks senator?" Hurley asked.

"I need a drink!"

"Well then shall we head down to the commissary? I'm told they have a lovely mint julep recipe!"

Immediately following the tour and a short lunch Thaddeus took his leave of J.J. and made his way back to his office over on Independence Avenue near 11th Street across from the famed Martha Stewart memorial statue complete with drug induced smile and Supercuts discount haircut.

He entered, went around behind his desk and flopped into his high backed, leather padded swivel chair. But before he could get settled in, his secretary Barbara, reminded him of his senatorial orientation back in the Capitol.

"I've just finished my orientation."
"How was it?"
"I'm completely disoriented."

THE GOLDEN RING

CHAPTER SIXTEEN

Ж

Time passed and Senator Thaddeus Pervers learned the essential elements of a bill and how to cobble one together. He was rarely allowed to speak on the floor but was unexpectedly sucked into the debating process several times and by all accounts acquitted himself well. Progressively building confidence, he diligently attended and voted in every round of sessions where a vote was called for.

Which, for the most part, proved pointless.

He quickly picked up on the accepted technique of not wasting his time reading bills or motions proposed by the other side. As they would be voted against by his side, they were never going to achieve the required majority to pass anyway. When he questioned why automatically voting against the other side was accepted as standard procedure, he was told because said content of the proposals was not the primary consideration. All that mattered was which side got the most bills passed through Congress by the end of the each fiscal year ergo, voting against opposition bills ensured the other side accomplished as little as possible.

Bipartisanism agreement was considered synonymous with blasphemy.

The second most important thing was to do whatever was required to make the other party look bad and being able to claim the other side never passed any bills was one powerful argument against them come election time.

This, reinforced by always being able to trace and blame any scandals which arose back to the other side, ensured the opposition party year-long bad press and forced them to focus undoing the cluster fuck they were portrayed to be in what till passed for the press. This of course essentially stalemated congress, but that didn't seem to bother anyone.

In any other career filed if you didn't produce whatever it was you were supposed to be producing, you would be shown the door. This however, wasn't just any career field! This was The United States Congress.

Before he knew it Thaddeus was well into his second year and he discovered that he was no longer considered a freshman senator. He would now be allowed to present bills that would be voted down, propose proposals that would fail and suggest suggestions that no one would listen to.

He felt he was making progress.

He learned to deal with the wild animals that stalked the halls of the Congress and in particular that most uncivilized species known as Lobbyus domesticus. A parasitic creature which could usually be found stalking along the walls and halls of the Capitol building just prior to a congressional session, especially one where a vote was going to be taken.

He learned how to intimate a promise without really promising to promise on something he knew he couldn't deliver. So adept at the convoluted language of The Hill had he become that few challenged him on his abbreviated verbiage. They automatically interpreted, 'I'll see what can be done' and 'I'll put feelers out' to mean he would do it. He found this most useful.

The daily ten to three, (sometimes two), work routine went on until . . .

Late one afternoon things changed.

Thaddeus received a sealed message from a page as he was leaving a session to return to his office. With his mind cluttered by things to be done he pocketed the envelope until he got back to his desk on Independence

Avenue.

Once back at his desk he opened it and read the short note contained therein.

Meet me at the club tonight. 18:30. Urgent.
SS

Sydney Snodgrass had called a meeting with Thaddeus.

Snodgrass, relying on reports from Hurley's people for updates on Thad's progress, had not been in regular contact with his protégé since he entered the senate, so Pervers was both surprised and relieved to finally hear from his surrogate father.

He arrived on time and was greeted by name at the Northside Gentlemen's Members Only Private Club, Washedupton branch, by the doorman who informed Pervers Senator Snodgrass was waiting for him upstairs.

On entering the private room he was surprised to find they were alone.

"Shouldn't we wait for the others to arrive?"

"Tonight will be just us." Sydney informed. "What I want to talk about is just for you and I. For now anyway."

"Oh, okay." Thaddeus made himself comfortable. Sydney fixed him a white wine spritzer.

"How's it going, over all I mean? You feel like you're getting in the flow of things? Fitting in?"

"I guess so." Another useful lesson Thad had learned when not sure why he was being approached or questioned about something, was to respond with non-committal answers.

"J.J. tells me you've got some pretty strong feelings regarding the state of the Senate. More than a little upset about the way things are done." Sydney showed his hand and the intended reaction was elicited.

"**Not done** more like!" Thad clarified.

"How so?" Sydney prompted, suppressing a smirk.

"Gun control, drugs, police brutality, military spending the crumbling domestic infrastructure! In the nearly two years I've been on The Hill, save for the re-election of congressmen, virtually nothing has gotten done! Some of the so called laws have even gone backwards!"

This was exactly the reaction Snodgrass was hoping for. He sat back and smiled.

"Sixteen cities have declared bankruptcy since the last election! How can we reduce the national debt when we can't increase the tax base? How the hell can we increase the tax base if unemployment keeps rising and they won't pass a comprehensive minimum wage law? What are people supposed to pay taxes with?! Pigs and goats?" Pervers attituce was gradually approaching the exact temperature Sydney Snodgrass secretly sought.

"Well than, let me ask you this; How would you feel about taking things to the next step?"

"What next step?" Thaddeus questioned as he polished off his wine and signalled for another.

"You know, taking it to the next level."

"I don't follow." Thad replied. Sydney hung his head.

"Declaring your candidacy!"

"You mean for re-election? But the Senate race isn't until-"

"The Presidency Bonehead!" He slammed the table as hard as he could which, in his dilapidated physical condition came across as a child's frustrated tap. When he finished chocking Thaddeus sat speechless.

"Look, it's just under sixteen months until the November election, enough time to organize ourselves, get the needed backing and declare you as a candidate."

"But . . ."

"There are only sixty-two, sixty-three candidates so far declared and registered themselves for the next election. Probably won't be more than seventy or eighty by the deadline. Ronald Lump's already served his legally allotted four terms -"

"Still can't believe he got that law through the Congress!"

"Money talks nobody walks, son! That's the law of this land as well you know it. At any rate he's not eligible to run again. The GOP's only have about twenty-four possibles, the Independents have nineteen, the Greens only about a dozen and the rest are from the parties nobody ever votes for because we restrict their promotional abilities and never let them join in any public debates!"

"What about the Socialists?"

"THE SOCIALISTS?! Are you kidding? I don't know why the hell they keep trying, complete waste of time and money. Who the hell is ever gonna vote for a bunch of rabble who preach that the government should take care of the sick and elderly just because they worked their whole lives and can't work no more? Get real! We all get old and die at some point! Tough shit, deal with it! And free education?! Stupidist idea I ever heard of! Somebody ain't smart enough to figure out how to get an education he's probably too stupid to have one! That's the name of that tune, Boy-o!"

"I forgot, there are no poor people in America." In disagreement Thaddeus quipped, unable to curb his sarcasm as he sipped his drink.

"There are no poor in the United States of America! Only those who haven't made their fortunes yet! The very thing that's made this country great, entrepreneurial ability! And don't you ever forget it!"

"How many candidates do the Socialists have?"

"Don't matter! Point is none of them parties have a chance! Which just leaves us against the only two real possibilities. One egocentric old guy and an old woman with enough dirt on her to fertilize half of Africa!"

Thaddeus was nowhere near being convinced.

"I'm just reluctant to take a pot full of money from a bunch of people I don't really know and who are going to invest their hopes, dreams and hard earned cash in me and then watch me lose. Or worst yet, wind up me not being able to deliver what they want. That's all."

"Oh, I see." Sydney sat back in his chair and shifted to a more conciliatory tone. "I understand you're reluctance. That is if you think the time required for the work involved is . . . is more than you can handle -"

"The work involved? If it's anything like being in the Senate . . . I mean the work involved in the Senate is minimal. The actual time on the job is only about 30% of my time. The other 70-80% is trying to raise funds at meet-and-greets and doing favors for people. There's no real 'work' per se. A vote now and then on a bill that's not gonna pass anyway."

"Well, if you're satisfied making the minimal impact you're making now, that is not really interested in leaving a real legacy for yourself. Something for your children. Ah, child and grandchildren. Possible grandchildren . . ."

"Sydney, let me think about it, talk it over with Prudence and all."

"Yes, yes! By all means, talk it over with your wife, better safe than sorry. Besides, you never know, she might not like being called, 'The First Lady', having people wait on her hand and foot and having her own expense account."

"I promise I'll sleep on it." Sydney fully realized that Thaddeus, still under the misunderstanding that the word 'promise' meant that you were obligated to do something, would in fact talk it over with Prudence and sleep on it. He also, in the last few years, had come to know the temperature of Thaddeus Enoch Pervers better than most and so knew, with a 96.8% probability that if he, Sydney, could deliver the means, T.P. would climb aboard the ultimate gravy train.

"Okay. You sleep on it and get back to me. Meanwhile I'll put the wheels in motion and start drumming up support."

"Sydney, don't jump the gun! Let me mull it over!"

"Of course, yes. I meant to say I'll be putting out feelers."

They bade each other good night and parted company.

The scraggly but sparsely sprinkled hairs tenuously clinging to the convoluted rugae of Sydney Snodgrass' snow-capped dome hit the pillow that night secure in the knowledge that his carefully cultivated meat puppet, the man he had invested the better part of three years in, would be his ultimate ticket to the ultimate man on-the-inside as head of what was left of the Free World, President of the United States of America.

All sixty states.

ALL THINGS BEING EQUAL

CHAPTER SEVENTEEN

ℋ

Issues. There were the ones which would never be resolved like gun control, drug abuse penalties and police brutality. But there were others to which most of the senate believed a solution to be within realistic if not desirable, reach.

Problems like government overspending, the immeasurable military expenditure and the out of control social welfare budget which had become the primary contributor of the crumbling domestic infrastructure and of course American education, now rated at 47th out of the top 50 civilized nations.

The twelve year stalemate in Congress had several aspects, but the primary hot button topic was how to balance the budget. It was generally accepted by politicians and public alike that this was an unsolvable issue and so was continually pushed to the background. After all the country hadn't had a balanced budget since the last century and seemed to be doing fine. Fine if you ignored the runaway inflation, the unemployment stats or the giant slump in the economy coupled with the one or two per cent of the population controlling over 85% of the economy.

So that left the most controversial of all the controversial topics; the in-fighting over the topic of people's 'rights' represented by the thousands of citizens' rights groups which had sprung up across the country as calculated by the Victomology Studies Institute, a billion dollar a year branch of the government's brain trust.

The whole mess began when whites, who in reality comprised only 15% of the world's population, the least amount on the planet, began to push back as everyone who wasn't white was considered, by the U.S. government, a minority.

Once the whites had been officially recognized for their diverse cultural differences, much like the two or three hundred recognised Eurasian cultures, under law they officially qualified for minority status, a status they in reality always were but had never been 'officially' recognized as by government polls, registrations or censuses, and so had long remained a status they didn't qualify for.

All the other ethnic groups protested at the whites' reclassification, and in the resulting backlash it was decided, following years of public debate, riots and general unrest, that the only way for everyone to be 'truly equal' under the law was by eliminating the majority all together. And so everyone was reclassified under the law as a minority. The only question that remained was which minority did you belong to?

New 'rights' were defined by the recently passed House bill HR1776 alternatively called the EWD law or the *Everybody Who's Different Bill*. Because virtually everyone now considered themselves some kind of minority, that is different, the Bill could be construed to include virtually all the people of the United States.

It covered Blacks, Whites, Asians and Mexicans. It also purported to protect half Mexicans, mixed race Caucasians and partial half Asians. Under its benevolent umbrella it took in mullottos, Brulés and Bois-Brulés regardless of whether they were considered bi-racial, mixed cultural or half breeds.

It even covered Canadians.

Religiously speaking Jews, Christians and Muslims were covered. It also covered all of the mixed religions such as the Cews, Mistians and Juslims.

Straights, gays, bisexuals, cross-dressers, transgenders, agenders, bigenders, cisgenders and big spenders were all promised protection. Included in paragraph six, clause seven recognition of BDSM, LGBT, S&M's, ATM's and M&M's was afforded.

However, lawmakers were careful to ensure that there was nothing in the bill that could be considered androgynous.

As a matter of fact, it covered men and women so equally that separate Men's rooms and Lady's rooms in restaurants, movie theaters and public buildings were outlawed. This of course caused massive confusion to the people of the civilized world when they visited the U.S. for business or on holiday.

A group of English rugby players, during an extended drink-up at a New Jersey sports tavern in Trenton, became confused at the lack of urinals, now outlawed as per the EWD Bill, and so choose to relieve themselves in the sinks.

A group of professional women tennis players from Parsippany, also in town for a tournament, walked in on the boys and the resulting 27 sexual assault lawsuits caused the tavern to shut down and tied up the state courts for months.

As a result of the sensational headlines, protests by SJW's and multiple arrests due to rioting, the British embassy put out a travel warning to British citizens to avoid travel to New Jersey. The U.S Ambassador in London retaliated in kind by issuing a warning to Americans about visiting the Jersey Islands. However, no harm was done, as few Americans knew there were such things as the Jersey Islands and mistook the warning as referring to some place near Hoboken.

There was however an upside to the financial and political chaos caused by HR1776. The captain of the rugby team proposed to the coach of the tennis team in court during one of the law suits and they were married a week later.

Oprah, Ellen and the *Rachel Maddow Shows*, all

now entering their ninth decade of syndication, covered the event. The tennis captain accepted the proposal on the proviso they have two separate sinks in their bathroom.

The terms 'man' and 'woman' had, in the intervening years somehow metastasized into an all-consuming politically correct cancer, fractionalized into sixty different gender options infected by the warped concept of 'all-inclusive'.

This greatly distorted concept of 'equality' reached such a low point that most work places passed mandatory work place rules requiring all employees to dress in completely androgynous attire so no one could determine what sex they were, spawning a whole new fashion industry termed 'Andro-dress'.

Laws and edicts were passed so that even inquiring about the sex of an individual became a misdemeanour in some places like Oregon, Washington and California, even if you were on a date.

It was only at the moment of truth when entering the bedroom, (providing the standard three page consent form S069 had been mutually endorsed beforehand by both parties), that the participants were legally permitted to know the sex of the person with which they were about to copulate.

Additionally, by edict, the EWD bill decreed that all citizens of the United States must, by the end of the fiscal year, declare themselves a member of the minority of their choice, register with the Bureau of Minorities in Washedupton, P.C. and forever thereafter use the proper, approved government abbreviation following their sixteen digit social security number and assigned minority code when conducting all business with the federal government.

While the concept of 'unity' was sacrificed at that ceremonial P.C. alter known as the U.S. courts, the one disparagement untouched by Bill HR1776, was that the richer remained more equal than the poor.

Ж

Following an abbreviated pow wow with Prudence, who was very supportive of Thaddeus' proposed stab at the next echelon, given it would not only stabilize their current financial situation but possibly increase it, Pervers gave Sydney the go ahead to push the candidacy button.

One of the first steps to insure his possible candidacy was to garner as much initial press as possible. However, rather than hold a press conference first, the skids would need a little greasing. So the big news that the humble Senator Thaddeus Pervers from the Great State of Ohio was throwing his hat into the ring was without brouhaha, leaked to the press. As was the custom this was not called 'leaking', it was called testing the waters and would be monitored for reaction in several of the key demographic areas across the country, particularly in The Polls.

After contacting his sixteen clandestine contacts and his thirteen secret sources Snodgrass then texted Thaddeus that the leak had been sprung. Also Sydney advised he be on the lookout for signs that the news had permeated the agencies.

It was as Thad was leaving his office one sunny afternoon a few days later, that the first unexpected, planned ambush took place.

Like a rat darting out from behind a kitchen cabinet, a reporter, flanked by a cameraman scurried out of nowhere and pounced blocking his path and assaulting his lower face with a microphone.

"Senator Pervers, Diane Wong, Assimilated Press. Can you confirm that you are planning to run for office and if so what in your opinion is the biggest problem in America today?"

Thaddeus had been advised to assume an air of knowing but avoid answering any question directly whenever possible. Also similes and metaphors were handy tools a well.

"Well Miss Wong, stupidity is, as far as I'm concerned, this country's biggest challenge! Apparently common sense has assumed the status of underarm deodorant and those who need it most, don't use it."

"But are you planning a run at the White House, senator?"

"One has to be careful these days who one challenges. For example I learned at an early age not to drink and drive because trees defend themselves very well."

"Senator, you've been in Congress less than three years. Do you really think you're ready, I mean do you think you've learned enough about politics to be president?" The aspiring BaBa WaWa pushed, probed and prodded.

"Miss Wong, I learned enough about working in Washedupton to stop using the phrase; 'How stupid can you be?' Apparently some folks here on The Hill take it as a challenge." He answered before he walked away.

"Asshole thinks he's Mark Twain!" Wong quipped under her breath.

And so it was that Thaddeus had made his first friend in the press.

ЖС

One of the first orders of business for Snodgrass' new FUBAR party was to establish locations for headquarters across the country. It was decided that, as in years past, one main HQ on each coast would be required supported by one branch office in each state, preferably in the state capitols. Preferably close to the capitol building, ideally **in** the capitol buildings as close to the Governors' offices as possible to facilitate all the things necessary to run a modern government. Things like general communication, meetings, the passage of information, pay-offs.

To kill two lobbyists with one stone, it was decided to establish the two coastal HQ's in a couple of the holiest and most sacred places in the country. Other than Wall Street and Hollywood. So some research was required.

Sydney's research team found that despite the fact that 72% of the American public now disavowed any firm belief in a god, as opposed to the Europeans who stood at 97% or the Middle Easterners who stood at a firm 0.1% to avoid getting their heads chopped off, however, copies of the so called traditional holy books could still be found here and there.

Advances in science had gradually nudged the Christian Bible, the Torah and the Qu'ran down the virtual book shelves from the Religion section to Philosophy to Fiction and finally to the same section as the Book of Mormon and the complete works of L. Ron Hubbard, both the red and the green volumes.

These were all now located in the Fantasy section.

With 89% of the world's clergy on welfare fewer and fewer of this genre of book was being produced. But the books still contained all the relevant teachings of the respective religious beliefs as passed down by word of mouth from the respective prophets and on to their faithful followers of the respective clergy as spoken from the mouth of their respective gods all those millennia ago.

They for instance, more or less, all still preached that Abraham begot Yahweh who came in the name of the one true god, the god the Jews borrowed from the Babylonians way back in the Bronze Age. The one the Christians borrowed from the Jews, and rechristened Jesus because Yahweh was too hard to pronounce.

Besides the early Christians didn't have a 'W' in their alphabet so God was easier on the tongue.

Also these books taught that Jesus begot Mohammad who gave them the word of god spelled A-l-l-a-h because the Arabs didn't have a G in their alphabet.

Additionally, as the Jews apparently had too many rules in the first edition of their book, the Torah, the Christians, in their new and improved edition of the Jews' old book, now renamed Theoldtest, streamlined the rules down to ten, renamed their rule book Thenewtest, and decided in the rewrite to recast God into an all-loving and forgiving god.

Not so the Arab god.

According to the Arabs their god is apparently pissed off at mankind for passing him around like an unwanted Christmas fruit cake over the centuries and so went back to being the earlier angry, vengeful Jewish god smiting people down, laying waste to entire populations for minor infractions of the rules like exposing woman's ankles to public view and turning people into pillars of salt. Which was kind of a favor because when you live in a desert salt is kind of hard to come by. Also, apparently to save time, the Arabs edited the Jews ten original rules and whittled them down to five.

But in all editions of all the dozens of holy books floating around, one thing never changed. Yahweh, God and Allah all seemed overly concerned with what people did when they were naked. Especially in the dark.

However, despite all these bad things, the gods mentioned in all these books still kept promising to come back some day to straighten things out.

Oddly, in light of these facts, political candidates in America still found it virtually impossible to get elected to higher office in the United States without associating themselves with one or more of the all but antiquated superstitions such as Christianity, Judaism or Islam. This in spite of the fact that the theoretical premise of the foundation of their government was separation of church and state.

Because it was essential to have all bases covered to launch a successful attack on the White House, faith-wise that is, the *Cathedral Church of St. Paul* in Boston was selected for the East coast FUBAR HQ and *The Crystal Cathedral* in Garden Grove, Orange County, California would serve as the West coast headquarters for the party.

Additionally this would guarantee exposure to thousands of tourists as well as the holy 'chosen' on a weekly basis. To help insure adequate donations to church and party, promotional booths complete with interns, posters, bumper stickers and informational brochures were set up in the lobbies of each of the two church-headquarters. For appearance sake it was agreed that these areas would still be referred to as 'vestibules'.

Because of its ties and access to old Boston money which had conduits to New York money, St Paul's was widely considered old school. Also being the most established religious group on the east coast gave tremendous PR leverage in a time when most Americans had forgotten, lost track of or forlorned their roots, both ethnic and moral.

There was one further advantage to establishing in the Boston area. The FUBAR's would court and reap the imaginary but still rumored-to-exist Irish vote.

The Crystal Cathedral, site of the new west coast headquarters, also offered cultural advantages. Access to Disneyland, Hollywood and the *Good Night Show, Not So Late Night Live!* and *The Ellen Degenerate Show* in Pasadena where herds of perpetually screaming females would attract a plethora of voters.

The Reformed Church in America, primary tenants of *The Crystal Cathedral*, a branch of the *Reformed Church of Canada* which came from *the North American*

Branch of the Dutch Reformed Church which was an off shoot of *the Reformed Protestant Dutch Church*, was not only well reformed, but well established.

Not to be out done by the Boston religious constituency, The Orange County location would afford the FUBAR's candidate access to the oldest established religious constituencies on that coast. That of the completely off the rails, wacko religions such as *the Cult of Prince Phillip Movement*, who advocate the dead prince for god-like status, *The Church of the Latter-Day Dude* or *The Church of Euthanasia* which advocates killing yourself in the name of their god. A religion which unfortunately seems to lack enough orthodox followers.

In one stroke of genius Snodgrass had checked off the holy box, the location box and most importantly access to the politico-financial cash box.

Then came the all-important decision, which state/district would Thaddeus claim to be from?

Bloodbank-Leech and his promoters were retained to help manage the campaign and so did some more research.

They found that with ten presidents and vice presidents including Teddy Roosevelt, FDR, Martin Van Buren, Grover Cleveland Thomas Jefferson and George Washington himself from New York, the Big Apple state seemed like the safe bet to claim as a home.

They also found that back over a century ago a relatively forgotten candidate, sometimes mistaken for a real estate agent due to her fashion sense, named Hillary Clinton, although from Illinois claimed New York as her home state. Additionally, the man who started the U.S. on the downhill financial spiral that eventually led to the ECOLI crisis, George Bush, grew up and was educated in New England but claimed Texas as his home state. Which would explain why, they reasoned, that according to the historical record, the rest of his family had mastered intelligent speech and spoke without a speech impediment.

So, as there was an historical precedent for candidates altering their states of residence for political advantage it was at one of the daily meetings Sydney and Thaddeus were presented with the choice of Ohio or New York to claim for Thad's new home state.

"Sydney how many Electoral College votes does Ohio get?" Thad asked sitting across from Sydney and several 'advisors'.

"Eighteen, why?"

"New York gets twenty-nine, no?"

"Yep! You're getting sharper all the time!" Sydney congratulated. "That settles it! New York is your new home town, candidate Pervers."

With that settled it was time to tackle the relatively minor problem of the political issues.

As the incumbency protection racket established by pay offs and promises, was so well entrenched in the electoral system and as most politicians who had successfully seceded from society to higher politics had done so by starting off in either Old New York or New New York, 47% of former presidents had claimed NY and or NYC as their home domicile, so this seemed like a sound strategy.

So, it was decided that Team Thaddeus would launch their campaign in the most corrupt, disorderly crime -ridden state in the union. Home of the pay day loan industry, the payday loan scam, also known as legal loan sharking and the base of predatory lending as their basis for their corporate lobbying and the place they would launch their bid to buy/win the presidential campaign.

The state of Texas.

Ж

Thaddeus had always been having serious doubts about not only winning but what he was doing in the upper echelon of political circles altogether. It was after their first strategy meeting that Thaddeus and Sydney were left alone in the upstairs lounge of the club that his mounting doubt overflowed.

"I . . . I'm not qualified!" He confessed to Snodgrass coddling his drink as they sat across from one another.

"Qualified, smal-a-fied! Don't be stupid! People don't vote for candidates based on their political or strategically demonstrated prowess! They vote for them based on what they have in common. Whites vote for whites, blacks vote for blacks and Hispanics will vote for Hispanics, even when nobody else does. Presbyterians will vote for Presbyterians, Catholics will vote for Catholics and Jews will vote for Jews, or gays. Or whoever has the most hands-off policy towards private business and will pledge to support Israel. And gays will vote for gays, they don't care if the guy has to call in sick once a month. They vote him in because he's gay. It's an instinctual, tribal thing."

He refilled Thaddeus' wine glass.

"Look, when non-landholders got the vote in this country nothing really changed, the polling numbers just got bigger. When women got the vote there were all manner of dire predictions. Within one election cycle the averages of the outcomes were exactly the same as they were before emancipation, there was no overall effect on the results. The guys with the highest financial backing still won. When the blacks demonstrated for the vote, nothing happened. Then when they petitioned for the vote, still nothing happened. But when it finally became legal for blacks to vote . . . well, because of Jim Crow, still nothing happened. Then, when the laws were enforced, and the gun totting rednecks were chased away from the polling stations so the blacks were allowed to vote, they voted. And nothing changed."

"Yeah, Hurley talked about that." Thaddeus remained uneasy.

"These facts are particularly true of Presidential elections. We've had Christian presidents, mostly Presbyterians and Episcopalians, some Baptists. One female by accident, one Jew and one and a half blacks. But they all had one thing in common, they were all dedicated liars, cheats and thieves who feather their own nest first and who would sell their mother for a vote!" He sipped at his scotch. "It defines the species."

Thaddeus, though still riddled with self-doubt, seemed temporarily appeased.

"What do we do about a running mate?"

"You mean a Vice Presidential candidate?"

"Exactly. It would have to be someone who agrees with our political views, or strategies, our values and morals."

"Not an issue! There's always plenty of hangers-on around to choose from. People looking to get ahead and who are 'flexible' in terms of the things they 'absolutely' believe in, politics, morality and so forth. You know, ambitious fuckers!"

"I see."

"Don't worry, we'll find somebody." Sydney encouraged. "It's gonna be fine! Trust me. I'm from the government!"

Ж

Due to control of the media, the thousands of lobbyists and the fact that he had J.J. Hurley to lean on, the Senate was now, comparatively speaking, a walk-through gig for Thaddeus but voter manipulation was completely outside his pervue.

With virtually nothing to do for the last twenty years but plan his surrogate assault on number 1600 Pennsylvania Avenue, Sydney attacked this wholly predictable obstacle of voter predictability head-on.

In as much as it was technically illegal to pay money and buy votes for office, other incentives were offered in exchange for support.

With Bloodbank-Leech's For Office Use Only P.R. firm heading up a massive media campaign, brochures were handed out advertising the unlimited accomplishments and added benefits of having a FUBAR candidate for 'Leader of the Free World'. In as much as most Americans believed that most of the rest of the world to not be free, this sold well.

With registration numbers, cleverly printed in the lower left hand corner in small print, the flyers could also act as vouchers for non-financial incentives at well-known shops and other private businesses owned by participating members. Once the vote was verified by a lipstick camera handed to the voter just before he entered the voting booth, he recorded his vote, returned the camera and, proving he voted correctly, received a 'floucher'. A flyer-voucher for free or discount merchandise in his or her city

Cosco, J.C. Penny's and the majority of Sixth Avenue stores in the greater New New York area were quick to sign up for the scheme.

The government program, under the auspices of motivating voters, had instantly become a 'anybody who's anybody', 'jump on the bandwagon' situation for the major retailers. The hook to induce businesses to sign on? If you didn't join in and offer incentives for folks to get out and vote, you were unpatriotic.

Patriotism became one of the a major themes Sydney built the campaign on.

The Chicago branch of Macy's led the Monroe Street, Adams Street and the Pacific Street stores and boutiques, while the Shops at North Bridge all pitched in to contribute to the Mid-west effort.

With all the east coast entrepreneurs solidly behind

the effort and now the Mid-west businesses as well, the Rodeo Drive, Melrose and Hollywood Boulevard shops were not to be left out and so jumped on board.

'The Pervers Challenge', as it was touted, registered seventy million hits on You Tube, 36 million on Facebook and broke one hundred million Tweets in the first two weeks alone.

Within six weeks 'TPC' evolved in the vernacular as a synonym for hope and change in the future of America. Pins, Tee shirts, buttons and bumper stickers abounded. Ads, posters and billboards sprang up across the landscape. Taxis, trains and planes brandished the garishly loud red, white and black notices and bulletins with three simple letters in an attractive Old English font could be seen in cities and across highways:

"𝕿.𝕻.𝕰.!"

Wisely giving credit to candidate Pervers for conception and institution of the plan, Sydney Snodgrass and the FUBARS hit home run after home run in the media polls. Thaddeus Enoch Pervers had risen to the forefront of American pop culture.

The Pervers Challenge plan was a resounding success. The competition as well as the issues, not for the first time in a presidential race, became secondary.

More importantly, for the first time in U.S. history polls showed both established parties uniting in opposition to the Johnny-come-lately candidate of the new party.

𝕶

The multi-million dollar P.R. blitzkrieg launched by Snodgrass and the FUBARS was only one of a three pronged attack launched to achieve their goal.

Through a friend in Texas, who he helped out with a

divorce case a few years back, another governor friend who he went to high school with and a third governor he bribed, Sydney was able to have the three governors as well as four State Attorneys General strike tens of thousands of blacks and Hispanics from the voting registers in fear they might go for the opposition. They excuse? Unpaid parking tickets.

For obvious reasons this little tactic was kept from Thaddeus.

This action was immediately attacked by the A.C.L.U. and other citizen's rights groups, but the reality of the situation was that any counter suit launched would take years to reach the Supreme Court's three judges in Washedupton, would cost the litigants millions and be upheld until a final decision was announced years after the election.

Most importantly, using the *Citizen's United v. Federal Elections Commission* decision rendered decades ago, Sydney was able to solicit unlimited contributions towards advertising, promotion and celebrity appearances. For the larger corporations he was able to re-funnel large sums of money from the contributors directly to the unions and corporations for 'charitable upgrades' of their facilities across the country in exchange for an under the table deal whereby a corporation would cajole, urge, and in some cases quietly offer promotions to their employees who voted for the FUBAR candidate.

The major networks, newspapers and talk shows, particularly the president and corporate CEO of NewsCorps, Lush Limburger, featured daily anti-Pervers comments, interviewees and editorials lambasting the Johnny-come-lately with little or no political record.

NewsCorps actually allotted 100 million in an all-out anti-Pervers campaign timed to eliminate him before election day.

It was no surprise then when the political pundits

were shocked beyond words by the exit poll numbers; astronomically in favor of Thaddeus.

With the campaign slogan; "Yes we do!", even the GOP, Government of the Corporate Presidents, was impressed with his numbers particularly due to the fact that Pervers hadn't done anything aside climb the political ladder to the dizzying heights of potential presidential candidate.

Ж

The U-Need-A-RestTavern was originally opened to garner the lower class, the lower-middle class and the middle- middle class drinking crowds of the city. However, since the cities of America had fallen on hard times the lower-middle and middle-middle class crowds had all but evaporated.

The two working class bums sat silently in front of their near empty beer glasses at the end of the bar.

It was the first Tuesday of November, just past ten in the morning, Election Day and although selling alcohol on this day before five o'clock was technically illegal, it was the day most Americans felt they needed a drink. Particularly in light of the fact that a complete unknown had seemed to hijack what most Americans believed to be a near as perfect a system as possible.

This kind of thing was not supposed to happen.

In the dark, sparsely occupied Downtown Manhattan bar room, one bum was giving a running commentary between drinks as they looked up at the wide screen television at the end of the bar. They were watching the election results being broadcast live on TV.

Apparently unable to speak without a full glass in front of them, at that moment they sat quietly awaiting their refills. The 'on' switch of the remote was reactivated when two pints of Budweiser Extra Light appeared in front of them

"But he's rating higher than anyone in the last three election cycles! How do we account for those numbers? Despite **all** the polls!" Bum #1 enquired.

"Easy! Truth is 99% perception. His guy Snodgrass focused all his money on the angle that his man can do the job." Bum #2 informed.

"What job, exactly?"

"What job?! What job do they always promise? Save America! Save the American people! The people are buying into it, now they think he can save them."

"Can he, save them I mean?"

"Hell no! Nobody can save us." Bum #2 insisted.

"What makes you so sure?"

"Simple! They don't get that it's not the politicians, or the system or some clandestine conspiracy of Illuminati hold up on a secret mountain top somewhere in Switzerland or some god damned place!"

"What the hell is it then?"

"It's them! The people, they're stupid! It's supposed to be their government but they let the rich cats steal it from them! Wake up Satch, school's out! Something like 400 people control fifty percent of the vote! 3% control 95% of the wealth!" Bum #2 lectured with the prowess of Columbia Sociology Professor, which he used to be. "Talk about political systems? Take the French."

"No thanks."

"People in this country are always quick to piss all over other countries like the French. Shootin' their mouths off about how America 'saved' the French back during WWII but in the same breath they forget how the French saved our ass in the revolution against the Brits! All the while ignoring the fact that the French are one of the few people who haven't let their politicians hijack their government!"

"Oh yeah? Educate me professor!"

"Simple! Government fucks sumthin' up, the people

go on strike! The Frogs know the one thing that's kryptonite to a politician."

"Yeah, what's that?"

"Bad press!"

The news report turned their attention to re-runs of candidate Pervers speeches over the last year as he stood at podia, on stages and in various public locations around the country.

The picture switched to candidate Pervers on stage in a massive hall, smothered in microphones and addressing the multitude gathered therein.

I will repeal the law forbidding U.S. History be taught in schools! I will require the Bureau of BFM, Books, Film and Media reverse this terrible decision made by the present administration. I will push to reverse the requiring that all educational media be scanned prior to permission to publish licence and be released to the public.

The bartender, wiping a beer glass, stepped closer to the telly and they all listened attentively as the station switched to another of Pervers' Town Hall speeches.

Most believe that the days of verifiable truths and falsehoods seem to be over. That we now live a world where truth and falsehoods are no longer verifiable. I happen to agree with this but believe it can be changed. Through the continued negligence of our leaders and the gradual decline and eventual failure of the press we have arrived at the dawn and continued propagation of what I call the Age of the Tralse! I will eliminate all tralshoods in our government!

Massive applause filled the air.

1600 PENN AVE

CHAPTER EIGHTEEN

Ж

The weather was clear and chilly but sunny that Tuesday morning in Washedupton P.C. The chosen 200 were quickly herding into their seats on the western front of the U.S. Capital Building. In the cordoned off areas down at street level the throng had started to gather three hours earlier and stragglers were now quickly filling the few empty pockets along the main avenue. The mob huddled together to keep warm.

On foot, in patrol vehicles and high above in choppers Capital Police, Secret Service Guys and city cops diligently patrolled in and around the entire area reinforced by FBI, CIA, DEA, ONSI, National Guard, Homeland Security and volunteer Boy Scouts to tend the gates in the fenced off areas. If some no goodnick was planning anything nefarious that morning his chances of getting caught were calculated at 89.927%.

His chances of escape zero!

High up in the news platform atop the 75 foot crane the two main announcers for the day, a fifty-something trying to look thirty-something with a slicked back, Fonzie, D.A. haircut and a bleached blond bouffant with enough starch to stand a queen-sized bed sheet on end, were ready to kick off the celebrations with their unique brand of tag team commentary.

"Good morning Mr. and Mrs. America we are coming to you live from high over the steps of the Capitol Building in beautiful downtown Washedupton P.C. It's Inauguration Day and, as has been the tradition for over two centuries since it was first established by FDR back in nineteen hundred and thirty-two, festivities will commence at 12:00, noon sharp on this the 20th of January!"

"I think it was 1933 Dick."

"No Sheryl, it was 1932. But thank you for your input. Hi folks, I'm Dick Hard."

"And I'm Sheryl Swallows, welcome to the festivities where Dick and I will be putting it to you along with Dixie Enormous who will be trolling along the parade route down on the street interviewing working people and minor dignitaries not important enough to have made it up into the stands."

"And let's don't forget the disgruntled celebrities with sagging careers who have suddenly turned political."

"Thank you Dick. Besides the inauguration there are many forms of entertainment here today. For the Metal Heads tuning in we have Burnt Beyond Recognition with their cover version of *Death Kills* and for the Pop enthusiasts -"

"And the tone deaf."

"We have Lady GooGoo who will sing her new touching and poignant love song, *I Wanna Fuck You.*" Sheryl shook her head. "Taking the stage now are The New New York City Rockettes! You know Dick, some objected to their skimpy outfits, labelling it offensive to women-"

"Yeah, especially fat women!"

"So today they will appear fully clothed in head to toe wet suits. And because there have been complaints-"

"Mostly by ugly women." Dick again interjected.

"They will be wearing masks of former . . ." Sheryl paused in disbelief to re-read the copy on her cheat sheet. "Former presidents. Starting on the sixth of this month, that's two weeks ago, crews have been setting up barriers, flags and banners all along the parade route, down Independence Avenue and all across the steps of the Capitol Building, President Elect Pervers' daily place of work for the last three years."

"Yes, they started just after New Year's Day!"

"The sixth **is** after News Year's Day, Dick."

"That's why I said **just after** New Year's Day'. Sheryl."

The sophomoric banter was suddenly interrupted by a loud and distinct 'HARUMPF!' over the headsets of the two commentators.

"And that would be our woman-"

"PERSON on the street, Sheryl! Let's not get sexist on air."

"Thank you, DICK! **Person** on the street, Dixie Enormous. Dixie can you give us a feel for what's going on down there?"

The TV frame switched to street level to reveal a thirty-something, petite woman wrapped in an array of heavy winter clothing.

"Yes Sheryl, thank you. I'm standing here with Bob Rachet who's in charge of crowd control here at the inauguration. Bob what can you tell us?"

The fifty-something, grey haired man in coveralls and red baseball cap, standing next to her responded in a heavy New England accent.

"Well Dixie," He quickly assumed an air of supreme authority and he spoke with a heavy Boston dialect. "Ahh . . . crowd control, which is ahh . . . always an issue, has become more so of ahh . . . problem in recent elections. Few people realize although the official guest list, those souls fortunate enough to have garnered the actual privilege of sitting front row center, so-to-speak, is fixed at 200. However, it has become ahh . . . quite impossible to guestimate the number of spectators which might show up. Guesstimates can vary widely depending on if you go by the mass media or by the President Elect's own Press Secretaries and PR people."

"That has come up in the past, hasn't it Mr. Rachet?"

"Yes, it has Miss Enormous."

"So Bob, what happens if the pundits, who have often been wrong before, miss their guess?"

"Well, we are ah . . . well prepared for just such an eventuality. If, say, the number of spectators falls far short of what we expected, we have crews standing by to simply move the barriers in closer to the Capitol steps and we will ahh . . . simultaneously at the same time broadcast a secret code word over the air."

"A secret code word Bob?"

"Ah . . . yes. A secret code word; 'Fake News', that's all we gotta say and the crews will slip into action and move the barriers in closer to make it look like there are more people. Also on issuance of the secret code word the crews from the NewsCorps cameras have strict orders to fly in closer and only broadcast tight shots and slow, low pans of the crowd."

"I see."

"On the other hand however, should we be, inundated as it were, we would simply close off the ah . . . entrances, call in the National Guard and not allow anyone else into the ceremony."

"But these people have travelled hundreds if not thousands of miles to witness this historic day! Some with families and elderly in tow! It wouldn't be fair to block them! What would you say to them?"

"Oh, ah . . . we would simply tell them that there is a bomb threat, imminent danger of radioactive contamination or that a bio-contaminate has been ahh . . . accidently released into the air and we had to seal off the area."

"Well it's good to see you and your team are so well prepared Bob. Back to you in the booth Sheryl."

"Thank you Dixie Enormous." Sheryl signed back on. "Now we turn to the President's schedule for today.

You want to run us through that, Dick?" Sheryl passed the baton while struggling with a flask of vodka she fished out from under the news desk.

"Thank you Miss Swallows. First up this morning the Big Guy is having breakfast at the Abbey Hotel with business leaders from across the district and then following the swearing in ceremony he is scheduled to walk the parade route then it's off for lunch with business leaders from up and down the coast. This evening is the Inaugural Ball where he is slated to have dinner with Wall Street executives and business leaders from across the country."

"So it's safe to say for today at least, he's going to make a meal of it?" Sheryl quipped as she threw back another shot of Stoley's.

"Ah! Biting humor there from my extinguished colleague, Miss Swallows! Good one Sheryl! Why don't you tell the folks about the swearing in ceremony?"

"Good call Dick. Especially since I see the players are already gathering around the podium. There's the President Elect, Thaddeus Enoch Pervers the Vice President Elect, what's-his-name, several official witnesses, Mr. Pervers' son Taranjello-"

"You know, there's an interesting anecdote about his son's name –" Dick started.

"I'm sure there is Dick, and perhaps you could tell us about it. At the next inauguration. As I was saying to the folks at home, I can see the records custodian stepping up
to the podium now and he is wheeling in the specially designed hand truck stacked with the mandatory stack of holy books for the swearing in. The Bibles, one orthodox, one Roman Catholic and one King James. Also the Book of Mormon, a copy of the Torah, the Hindu Shruti, the Dao de jing as well as the Buddhist Tripitaka and on the very bottom is an illustrated copy of the Qur'an."

"And if you notice Sheryl there's a small group of protesters off to the side demonstrating because the White House has decided that the Book of Satan, first added to the pile during the first Lump administration, will not be included today."

"That's right and thank you for that expert commentary, **Dick**."

"You're welcome. **Sheryl!**"

"And in an apparent gesture of good will, the White House Press Secretary's office has asked the P.C. Police to hold off on beating and arresting any demonstrators until **after** the ceremony is complete."

"So we are making progress?" Swallows quipped.

"As some of you know, those of you who still tune in to the major media outlet, The New New York Stock Exchange, the NASDAQ, the New York Board of Trade and the American Stock Exchange all merged back during the Justin Bieber Administration and so the actual swearing in which will take place in about one minute, will be administered by Chief Head of the New York Stock Exchange Conglomerate, Norman Hershfeld Rothschild."

"You know Dick, years ago they used to use the Head of the Supreme Court to swear in the president."

"That's right Sheryl, back before scientists discovered the bribery gene which affects seven out ten judges."

"Hey Dick! How can you tell which one is the Head Judge when they're all wearing the same black robes?" Sheryl was getting a little tipsy.

"I'm not sure Sheryl. How?"

"He's the one wearing the knee pads! GET IT?!" She elbowed him, cackling uncontrollably as he tried rescuing the broadcast

"As a footnote, this ceremony is actually being broadcast live with a dozen 50 foot television screens set up all along Wall Street." Dick added.

Following the swearing in, from which Prudence was noticeably absent due to her inability to get out of bed, Thaddeus stepped away from the stack of bibles and prepared to address the American people. He was greeted with near dead silence by the mob.

"I'm not much at making speeches, but I guess I can't slip out of this one." Sporadic laughter wafted across the audience. "First I wanna thank you all for your votes of confidence." There was a spattering of applause which boosted Thaddeus's confidence, but only slightly. "Our nation has faced many difficult times in the past. Times that have put our ideals and ideas to the test. I get the sense that we can all agree that they're being tested again right about now." A slightly stronger round of applause accompanied by a few people. Loud but indiscernibly garbled hollering answered this statement.

"But I want to talk about the people who are supposed to fix this country's problems. The people **you** the voter put in office. The people you gave the cushy, high paying, low-hours-at-the-office jobs to, The Congress." Several 'boos' rang out. "Now I'm not gonna stand up here and claim all the problems in this country are because of the Senate not investigating all the crooked people they should be investigating. Or that the House is not doing its job of coming up with the right bills or at least bills that are benefiting anybody. No." As rehearsed, he inserted a dramatic pause. "Top of my list is the stagnation of Congress which is crippling growth, atrophying the job market and leaving the country open to yet more foreign cannibalization of our great nation."

Behind him the House Whip leaned into the V.P. and whispered.

"How to win friends and influence people!"

"What do you mean?" V.P. What's-his-name asked.

"He's gonna make a lot of enemies on the Hill with those comments!"

"It's just talk, good old American rhetoric. Standard procedure for new cancidates." The V.P. assured.

"I don't want to stand up here and make a bunch of fool promises, promises I have no way of keeping. But I will promise you one thing. I will devote 100% of my energies to getting the job you elected me for done! But most of all I promise the people of this country that I will, no matter what it takes, get things moving again!"

Starting in the balcony behind him and then spreading out across the plaza, wild applause broke out across the crowd.

"Well, I'd say that about sums it up Sheryl!" Dick up in the booth stated.

Thaddeus enjoyed his day in the sun knowing that early the next morning he would awake to face an intense staff briefing on the most recent polls, various orientations to include security, terrorism, the current state of the economy and defence, more polls and the usual array of diplomatic greetings from around the world. Or at least the most important countries. And of course, yet more polls and the future predictions of the polls which would, as soon as released, inundate and dominate the press.

Ж

Just as Snodgrass wasn't foolish enough to risk destruction and loss of his meat puppet when he first got Thaddeus into the senate, so too did he take precautions to avoid allowing Pervers to go chaperoned for his transition from presidential candidate to Commander-in-Chief.

Although he was never without a guardian, minder or mentor of some kind during his stay in the congress, he would now be constantly in the public eye and under the proverbial microscope so he would also have a babysitter of some description.

To this end his first week in the top executive position would be spent at Camp David attending the P.C. PL&IC program.

The PC Political Life and Image Coaching program was first established by the Bill Clinton administration who became known for keeping a half dozen 'personal advisors', then called interns, on the payroll, all female. They were known as the 'etiquette brigade' and were charged with advising the president on how to walk, talk, act, eat and . . . anything else he had to do so as not to offend anyone. It was later permanently established at tax payer expense, as the P.C. PL&IC Program.

Recommended by Bloodbank-Leech of the FOUO ad agency Thaddeus was provided with and would be monitored by a Politically Correct agent, permanently assigned to the White House staff compliments of the Department of Political Correctness under the Secretary of State.

Ursala Mary Uttley, a six foot one, grey haired and bespecled rail of a spinster with a slight hunch, who everyone believed to be a sad war widow, was assigned by the Department to be Thaddeus' PC advisor.

Once, sometimes twice a year, Uttley would take a two week vacation and scour the Asian country side where she believed her husband, a hero fighter pilot, had been shot down by the enemy during the war and was still being held prisoner.

The widow Uttley, who in reality was left at the altar by her boyfriend of three and half months and never psychologically recovered, had never had a fighter pilot husband. The facts that the Fourth Afghanistan War ended fifty years ago, long before the fifth war in Iraq, and that Uttley was never married didn't seem to deter her from her annual mission..

She was just another nutter who by virtue of the fact that she had a screw loose qualified for government employment.

She wound up at the PC Department thanks to the Cambodian secretary at the government personnel office who couldn't pronounce the adverb 'utterly' when being told by her boss to get someone over to the Politically Correct office to fill in a vacancy and so she sent an order down to the assignments clerk to send someone named 'Uttley' over immediately. Ursula Mary was the only Uttley on the government payroll.

Even before the standard week long orientation of the requisite job skills and responsibilities Thaddeus would be informed of, he would be subjected to an intense one day course of training administered by a P.C. PL&IC coach permanently assigned to the White House staff.

Early that morning, following a short walk through a secret tunnel under the Rose Garden, Thaddeus and his eight man Secret Service Guy detail came to and entered a one man steel door.

The room was more of a chamber, circular in design, extending five meters from the center with a vaulted ceiling. There were only two chairs, a small desk and a bookshelf with only one, very thick book behind the desk, so the rest of the entourage spread out, evenly spaced around the wall and stood at parade rest.

"Good morning. Nice to meet you." Thaddeus warmly greeted. Uttley ignored his overt attempt at what she interpreted as sexual advances.

"Welcome Mr. President. I'll be your coach guide for the next week." Uttley introduced herself.

"Coach guide?"

"Yes sir. Over the decades since our inception we've developed so many specialities that it no longer became practical for one PC Technician to handle the teaching of all the behaviors required of a Tier Two professional politician."

"Tier Two? I'm the President! What constitutes a Tier One politician?"

"Tier One is reserved for the people with the real power, the folks who grant the politicians their right to power and control it through monitoring their public imagery."

"Exactly who would that be?"

"Well, the top corporate CEO's of course! GE, Shell, BP, IBM, DuPont. Those guys."

"I see."

"That's what makes our brand of capitalism unique, it's diversity!" She informed.

"Uh huh." He grunted. Even as a young man Thaddeus knew when he was out argued.

"Shall we start?" She asked and Thad nodded. "Through polls & pollsters we have developed a firm profile of how the new president or party candidate should dress, eat, use the toilet, point, scratch how long to pause when speaking and most importantly what vocabulary is allowed and what words are forbidden."

"Forbidden?! What happened to free speech? I thought democracy was supposed to champion free speech?"

"Democracy? Don't be silly, this is America Mr. President. We determine what democracy is. Besides, it's modern times sir, things have changed. We have to keep up with the latest trends and that includes how to communicate."

"I see."

"Okay Mr. President, pauses are extremely indicative of what you are trying to say in the speeches you will be required to make. For instance -"

"Why don't I just use the words I'm saying to indicate what I mean? Wouldn't that be a lot more clear?"

Uttley fought back a smirk at Thaddeus' blatant naiveté.

"Mr. President, it is a long standing tradition that no one on The Hill, least of all presidents of the nation, speak like a commoner. Like a lowly factory worker-"

"What's wrong with factory workers?!" He demanded.

"Oh! Nothing, nothing really. It's just that . . . this technique is designed to avoid just spewing out what's on your mind by being open, direct and to the point. I mean, if we went that route next thing you know we'd have Presidents Tweeting for god's sake! The point is if you don't learn to speak cryptically how else could you send cryptic messages to the opposition, much less other nations? You see my point?"

"I'm not sure. Are you being direct or speaking to me cryptically?"

"Let's proceed, shall we? We have your normal standard pause or NSP pause, whose recommended time is between 1.1 and 1.3 seconds. Your normal emphatic pause, otherwise known as the NEP, recommended time frame between 2 and 2.1 seconds and the hard emphasis, or HE pause designated by a 2.7 second break in speech."

"What about if I'm really angry like if somebody is trying to feed me a line of bullshit?" The Head Secret Service Guy behind them fought back a laugh. Uttley was unphased.

"A full 3 seconds is considered appropriate for an angry emphasis."

"What about an indignant emphasis?" He asked.

"Same. Also never use your index finger to call attention to something."

"How do I use my cell phone?"

"All your calls will be placed by an aide." As she spoke she lifted a three inch thick, hard bound tome from the book shelf next to her and plopped it down on the desk in front of him.

"What's this?" He challenged.

"It's the new issue of the PC Handbook from the Bureau of Political Correctness. It's updated quarterly. I have it memorized."

"Huh, how efficient."

"Now most importantly is your vocabulary. Choose a word."

"Which word?"

"Any word."

"How about . . . caveman?"

"No, can't say that."

"Why not?"

"It's sexist and specieist. They are best referred to as Pre-petroleum Persons."

"What about Orientals? What are they, Asians?"

"We say Asianentals. Also we no longer use Negroes, Blacks or African Americans."

"What do we call them then?"

"The current accepted term is Blams."

"Blams?!"

"That's right, Black Americans. Blams."

"What about white people? What does your book say to call us?"

"Well, as black people for so many years were referred to by color, the commission feels it's only fair to rename Caucasians as Clear people."

"Clear people?!" He affirmed.

"Yes sir, clear people."

"How about sick people or cripples?"

"Oh no! We have none of those in this country. They are Physically Challenged."

"Sick people, physically challenged?!"

"Yes."

"What about really sick people? People with serious diseases like . . . lepers?"

"Assembly Challenged."

"What if they're already dead?

"Those would be Living Impaired."

"And what do we call just good old fashioned Americans? Culturally challenged?"

"The U.S. is not the only America and Amerigo Vespucci has been declared a racist, a chauvinist and a xenophobic colonialist. So democratic elements of the Bureau have decided to enter a bill in Congress to change the name of the country."

"TO WHAT?!"

"The Board has decided because we are all from the U.S.A. that instead of Americans we shall be called Usians."

Thad's face was turning red. The Head SS Guy stepped forward and whispered into the President's ear.

"Mr. President, we have a ten o'clock with the pollster psychology people." He reminded. Thaddeus nodded. It was the break he was waiting for.

"Lesson over, send me a manual!" He snapped. "Let's go!" The POTUS ordered. He signalled his body guard as he made for the door.

"I'll let you go now, but remember, always smile, never point and practice that improved lexicon!" Uttley haughtily reminded him.

Once back out in the long, narrow corridor Thad was compelled to comment.

"Makes me sick to my stomach what a tiny minority of boneheads can do to this country!" He picked up his pace as they approached the exit. "Huh! What the hell's vomiting called?" Thad queried out loud. "A God damned unplanned review of recent food choices?" He swore as they left the building and climbed into the limos. "Truth; the new hate speech!" He slammed the rear door as he sat.

The Executive Limo drove off, whisking them away to their next stop on the morning's itinerary.

Ж

Time passed and the days and nights began to run together. At first Pervers was taken off guard by the tremendous level of attention paid to the office of the President. With over 3,000 staff not counting the additional 3,000 armed troops assigned to the White House alone, there always seemed to be someone there to perform the most menial of day-to-day tasks. If he so much as dropped a pen, there was someone there to pick it up or with a new one in hand.

He was paid so much attention to that when shown the toilet in the Oval Office he reassured the staff that he would manage all business therein on his own.

With the help of his advisors Thaddeus developed an appreciable knack for the job. He issued orders when necessary, a veto when he thought prudent and advice when he could.

Prudence, with no skills, no education to her name and no ambition, spent her days at their eight room house watching TV and growing fatter. With a car and driver at her beck and call she would venture on occasional trips out and about as the mood suited her but they were few and far between so Thaddeus eventually convinced her to move into a room in the White House so he could keep an eye on her.

Taranjello on the other hand surprised the family when he announced he would like to try his hand at some kind of school.

University wasn't even discussed and the distinction between uni and college had to be explained by one of the President's aides. Junior College was presented as an option but the word 'college' spooked him, so the career councillor/aide provided by the White House suggested a trade school. After a few more hours of deliberation, with frequent trips to the dictionary for lexical references, a potential future career was decided upon.

Thaddeus was informed, money allotted, transport and lodgings arranged. In one short year Taranjello, sole offspring of the President of the United States was on track to rise to the dizzying heights of Cemetery Plot Salesman.

For Thaddeus, another, more pleasant part of the job was attending and officiating dedications such as the one at the local university's research school.

The Washedupton University Graduate School boasted a sprawling campus and was rated as one of the most prestigious universities in the nation. Not so much because of an outstanding curriculum or accomplished staff but because so many, now high ranking politicians and people with the right 'connections' graduated the place. It was, in reality one of the primary conduits to the upper echelons of power in Washedupton P.C.

When President Pervers was asked to officiate at the dedication of the new Behavioral Research wing, never having attended university himself, he was very reluctant, but was convinced it would boost his all-important poll numbers and so he agreed.

The ceremony itself was a run-of-the-mill affair. There was a crowd, neatly arranged rows of folding chairs, a podium, a microphone and several hypnosis inducing speeches.

Finally when the dust had settled, the university president insisted on giving the President a tour of the facilities. Thaddeus' Press Secretary insisted it be an abbreviated tour.

The building was a five story rectangle with each floor dedicated to a given endeavor of advanced scientific study and research.

In the first hall of the wing there was a series of rooms with grad students recording data from the conversations of focus groups being asked general political questions while being observed through one way mirrors, by small groups of yet more grad students.

In the first room there were about two dozen elderly from Florida, mostly Cuban and Jewish, who were asked about the popularity of a socialist agenda. They unanimously agreed that Medi-Care, Medicaid & Social Security were good things and that America was a great nation and would remain so as long as there' was no socialism.

"Because Socialism was only one step away from communism!" The eldest of the group declared.

A short way down the corridor was a second room where young people from New England dressed in pastel tones of Lacoste and Ralph Lauren polo shirts, chinos and Dockers, were gathered. They were essentially rich idealistic brats with no clue about real life that is to say primarily democrats. As it was being explained to Thaddeus that this was an experiment in social adaptation, air sickness bags were being handed out.

The subjects were having a wicked bad time because, as a behavioural experiment to test their moxie, they were being served Manhattan clam chowder which of course was made with tomatoes as opposed to milk and cream.

Next, the entourage wandered over to a room across the hall where young and middle-aged were mixed. This group were from the former state of California.

The test the researchers were attempting there wasn't going so good. Ever since the complete reform of marijuana laws the whole western area of the country had all but ceased being productive. Whether from Alzheimer's or the effects of long term cannabis toxicity, the reason for their difficulty in following instructions could not immediately be determined.

"Please fill in your papers now." The head grad tech instructed. A hand in the back immediately shot into the air. It was a young, long-haired, blond gentlemen.

"Yes?" The researcher asked.

"What was the question man?"

The tech looked at the Presidential entourage through the large glass window, pointed at his watch and shrugged. Their escort explained.

"We started late because we were missing one of the test subjects, a volunteer from San Diego. Apparently he was arrested when the temperature outside dropped below 65 degrees and it began to drizzle."

"Why was he arrested?" Thaddeus asked.

"He thought the weather shift was a sign of supernatural intervention so he sacrificed his neighbor's dog to the weather gods."

It was down in the basement, nearly an hour later, as they were coming to the end if the torturously detailed tour that they came to a lab funded by the For Office Use Only Corporation and Thaddeus, recognising the name, insisted they have a peek inside.

It was in the cavernous lab that an experiment against the back wall caught his eye so he wandered over.

Thaddeus was introduced to the team, the requisite homage was paid to the Commander-in-Chief by the three lab rats in lab coats and Thaddeus stepped up to the large glass aquarium sitting on the lab table.

One of the lab geeks was speaking to a collection of gerbils through a rigged speaker system.

The half dozen gerbils inside casually milled about in the saw dust, going about the daily business of gerbiling, sniffing each other and the immediate area around themselves. Thin insulated wires trailed from their cranial cavities and led up to the aquarium cover and were attached to some sort of electrical modulating unit on top of the aquarium.

Toby, the Head Lab Guy according to his black plastic name tag, adjusted the mic on his boy band headset, hugged his clip board and leaned in next to the aquarium. An assistant leaned in and explained to Thadeus.

"Mr. President, we're concluding data collection on a series of tests with an experimental drug." He volunteered without being prodded.

"I see. What's it for?"

"Watch!" The tech instructed and Thaddeus looked back towards the glass.

"Taxes!" The Tech declared into his Madonna mic and there was no reaction from the gerbils. "Senate Overwatch Committee!" Save for the fat brown one in the corner who lifted his leg and pee'd, there was, again, no real reaction.

"Family values." The small gang of gerbils looked up and seemed to pay more attention.

"America!" He announced in a commanding voice.

In response the rodents all stopped sniffing and began nodding their heads vigorously in unison.

"America first!" Without warning the little fur balls all stood up on their hind legs and clapped wildly while enthusiastically nodding.

Lab assistants & grad students furiously scribbled away on their clip boards.

"That's pretty impressive! What is it?" Thad queried.

"The drug is called Automatonamine. We plan to put it in the complimentary drinks at political rallies." He explained with the enthusiasm of a school child telling his mom he'd just ace'd a math quiz at school. "We anticipate it will have profound effects on the less educated of the populace." The tech added.

Behind them Thaddeus' entourage of Presidential aides vigorously nodded and clapped in approval.

LIKE A SOUP SANDWICH IN THE RAIN

CHAPTER NINETEEN

Ж

Thaddeus could hardly discern the hydrangea bushes lining the front garden. The rain drenched the massive windows of the Oval Office and obscured much of the grey sunlight.

"This country is so polarized! It's not even a country anymore! It's an autonomous collection of ill-defined provinces!" Thaddeus declared as he slumped down in his seat.

"Well Mr. President, things have been worse in the past." The destitute-of-personality aide lamely offered as solace.

Pervers had done very well climbing the ladder, developing all the requisite skills of a politician such as learning how to eloquently introduce alternative facts to just the right degree so as to cast doubt. He became adept at the finer points of injecting so much double speak into a bill that it would be rendered ineffective even if passed. He did this, but there was a price.

Now, nearing the third month of his first year as POTUS it dawned on him that he had been slowly getting fed up with the overall state of things along the way. He realized that he had become fully invested in the responsibility of making things better.

As he sank deeper into the world of politics he had been blithely unaware of the fact that it had, deep in his unconscious, become more than a game. Much more.

Now he realized a hole in his inner ambitions remained.

Sitting there, staring out the large picture window behind his desk, his mind drifting, a nebulous concept began to take form. The more he concentrated on seeing the hydrangea bush, the more he was able to focus.

Suddenly, like Lamont Cranston's epiphany given him by the Tibetan Tolku, he could see the world more clearly than ever before. The question he asked Prudence when Snodgrass first contacted him so long ago had been answered.

He did have a bigger purpose in life. And he just realized what it was.

"Johnson!" The kid nearly fell off the couch as Thaddeus yelled as he spun his high backed leather chair around to his desk and scribbled across a legal pad with the ferocity of a woman sprinting towards a shoe sale.

"The name's Jameson, sir."

"Whatever. Get me a home contact number for this guy!" He tore the page from the pad and thrust it at the aide who quickly scanned it.

"Is that all I have to go on? The name Joe?"

"He works in Brubaker. It's in Ohio. The Brubaker Ball Bearing Corporation, in Brubaker, Ohio. Recycling Division."

The aide sprang to action and darted out of the room.

"And Jamestown, arrange transportation for him to get out here as soon as he can!" He called after the aide.

Thaddeus felt he was in a position to move on something he'd been batting around in his head for the last six months, even before taking office. Phase One of Perver's plan was in place.

Out in the corridor the young aide quietly cursed to himself.

"IT'S JAMESON!!"

Ж

Having become increasingly suspicious and thus

disenchanted with the career politicians who surrounded him, Thaddeus had a brief phone conversation with Joe and then, running his plan through the plethora of legal people
in the White House Legal Annex, decided to call in the BB Stackers as part of his new brain trust.

Joe, arriving in P.C. a week later, was the first to show up and after catching up on old times, he and Thaddeus solidified 'the plan'.

Following their arrival President Pervers arranged personal assistants for all three of the BB Stackers, five days of orientations and finally their own offices. Daily briefings in their respective areas were also scheduled.

Bob, because he had a semester of high school economics, was appointed head of the General Accounting Office to keep an eye on the books. Joe, with two and a half months of ROTC training before dropping out of college, was appointed Special Pentagon Liaison and Head of the Secret Service Guys while Fred, because he was the least qualified, was made Secretary of State.

Now sixteen weeks into the presidency, with his brain trust established, a full administrative staff was yet to be decided.

It was 08:30 that morning that a small army of aides, Joe, Bob and Fred along with Thaddeus and Vice President what's-his-name, shuffled into the White House conference room and convened their first, all-hands meeting.

As they gathered around the twenty foot long, oval mahogany table, food was being served by the staff for what was scheduled to be a three to four hour working breakfast.

They were served Freedom Croissants with All-American butter and jam along with Freedom waffles freshly made on the kitchen's Freedom press to start the meal.

According to the menu lunch would be plates of

salads and sandwiches with Freedom onion soup and Freedom fries on the side. However, there would be no Freedom dressing as it had been banned from the White House kitchen by the previous administration.

After everyone had eaten the table was cleared, coffee served and the itinerary attended to.

The first item on the day's 'to-do' list was to round out the administrative staff.

"We have to keep the church people happy." Someone suggested after perusing the potential personnel list provided.

"Why?" Bob challenged. "Nobody goes to church anymore. Ever since we cured cancer and made all those advancements in sex therapy most of the population is atheist or agnostic! Besides, there was no more reason to keep giving the churches those huge tax breaks."

"Because if we don't put some church people on staff people will be offended! The Churches have always had special consideration. Why do you think no priests went to jail for abusing kids!?" A senior staff member argued.

"They didn't get jailed because, you go putting holy people in jail and everybody starts doubting their beliefs then the whole thing falls apart!" Another chimed in.

"Yeah and next thing you know," Bob poignantly interjected. ". . .the people stop believing in God and stop going to . . . oh . . . ah, never mind."

Someone on the other side of the table took up the challenge.

"My point is small businesses, workers and big businesses pay taxes **and** don't get any subsidiaries! They needed to lose their tax free status and now we don't need none of them churchies on staff."

Thaddeus scratched his head looking for a solution when Joe came up with a suggestion.

"Thad, tell the PR boys to find someone, a special saint, they can make the patron saint of the White House or something or other, then have a ceremony in front of the press and appoint someone the official White House Chaplin. Someone we can call when we need him. That way they'll be no need for someone on staff all the time and we'll always have a Chaplin to pay homage to all the religious folks still out there. Whoever we decide on doesn't even have to be alive, its only ceremonial anyway! Two burning bushes with one squirt of the fire extinguisher, know-what-I-mean?"

"Like who fer instance?" Fred challenged.

"I dunno! Maybe like that old pope from way back when who championed homosexuality, or Mother Teresa or Saint Justin."

"Saint Justin?" Fred challenged.

"Yeah, saint Justin, Justin Bieber. Remember they canonized him late in the first half of the century."

"Fer what? You gotta do a miracle to be a saint!"

"They said it was a miracle he got so far so fast and so rich with absolutely no talent! So they canonized him." Joe argued.

"So let it be written, so let it be said." Thaddeus decreed. "What's next?"

"Sir, the agenda calls for addressing the problem of 90% of all the judges in the state districts running unopposed." The senior aide informed.

"Have we determined a reason as to why that is?" The President inquired.

"According to studies from UCLA, Harvard, Princeton and Yale as bad as things have gotten, most Americans are still basically honest, so there's no one to run against the incumbents so the same dishonest people always wind up on the ballots and so get re-elected."

"Run it by legal, see if we can't somehow impose term limits. What's next?"

"The Treasury has submitted a report that nuisance suits instigated by people are taking a toll on the national budget. According to the report the GNP last year was down a full point which they traced directly to court fees associated with these types of suits."

"Do we have a clue as to who these people are, cramming up the court system with these types of actions?" Thaddeus asked.

"Well sir, according to the report . . ." He flipped through the sheaf of papers in his hand. ". . . the demographic seems to be dominated by the lower income, lower intellect and less educated portion of the population."

"You mean stupid people?" Joe summarized.

"Well sir I wouldn't put it exactly like-"

"Get the House to introduce a bill so we can pass a law." Joe insisted.

"A law for what?"

"To remove all the warning labels from dangerous products! That should help clear out some of the stupid bastards." Joe declared.

"How do you figure?" An aide asked.

"The major networks ran a story last year that warning labels cost this country in excess of a half billion a year in manufacturing and distribution, that's not counting the lawyers people have to pay to research and advise on the laws about them. There are warning labels on some household cleaning products warning people that if they can't read don't use the product. Veterinarians have put warning labels on dog and cat medicine warning the animals not to drive after taking the pills!" Everyone stared at him. "It's a fact! I'm saying remove all the warning labels from dangerous products, that's my solution!"

"Really? Can we do that?" The aide challenged.

"Only one way to find out. Got'a do something to clean out the shallow end of the gene pool." Joe pushed.

"Might that result in more law suits, sir?"

"Maybe, but if it does we'll just have it declared a nuisance suit!" Fred added.

The aide glanced over at Thaddeus who nodded his approval. Just then the intercom rang. It was the President's secretary.

Sir, we have the final employment forms for the new staff.

"Bring them in please Julie." He ordered.

A moment later she came in and presented him with a stack of papers to be signed for approval of the hiring of various new White House staff positions.

"What happened to the old staff?" Thad questioned.

"The old staff members sir, by law, are dismissed with each new change of administration."

"So we change our entire executive staff every four years like what . . . like a high school student body?"

"Afraid so sir." She informed him.

"Well, okay. Start setting up interviews and get back to me, let me know who's going to be working for me."

"It's all been done sir, they've all been selected. We just need your John Hancock on the approval forms." She slid the forms across the table.

"Well, wait a minute. How do you know who to pick, I mean what's our hiring criteria if interviews haven't been conducted?" The POTUS asked.

"Oh that's a no brainer sir. We don't do interviews anymore, too time consuming. We just go by the old Al Sharpton/Jesse Jackson hiring scale. Its federal regulation."

"What the hell is that?" Joe demanded.

"A scale passed by the congress years ago whereby points are awarded for each of seven categories on the applicants' resume." The senior aide said.

"How's that work?" Thaddeus asked.

"Well sir, let's say we have a vacancy in reception."

"Okay."

"The applicant gets 1 point for education, 2 points for experience, 3 points for typing skills, 4 points for references, 10 points for ethnicity, 12 points for sexual orientation and 25 points for gender."

"Gender and Ethnicity?!"

"Got'a check all the boxes sir."

"What if they can't type, file or organize?"

"That's why we have to hire back-ups and standbys sir."

"I see, got it all figured out do ya? Okay, hire somebody for reception."

"One's not enough sir. We have to have at least two of everyone."

"Did you compile a list for me?"

"Yes sir. But according to Human Resources we have two of each –"

"Lemme see that!" He grabbed the list and read through it. "Two Blams, two Chicanos, two Asians . . ."

"Problem is sir, the Asians aren't too good at massive administrative organization and the Germans are."

"Then switch them out!"

"We can't."

"Why not?"

"It would be considered stereotyping which is racist which is -"

"What she's trying to say Mr. President is, since the Roman Empire was broken up by decedents of the Celtic tribes the Germans got the organization gene. The Brits got the conquering gene and the Asians got the reproductive gene."

"Asiaentals!" Someone corrected.

"What?"

"Asiaentals! They like to be called Asiaentals. It's more general." The aide explained.

"Oh yeah, okay. Two of everything!? Why is that sound so familiar?" Thaddeus asked.

"Dunno. Probably read it somewhere." Joe shrugged.

The White House, through the preceding

administrations, indeed the entire Executive branch had essentially been reduced to a storage container akin to Noah's Ark. Instead of animals there were at least two of each sex, religion and ethnicity.

"What about women? Have we got enough women yet?" Thaddeus queried.

"Gyno-Americans, sir!" She corrected "We are told that we no longer prefer that other word." Julie corrected. "Not women. The National Organization of Women says using the word 'woman' is sexist!"

"What's the plural for bitch?" Joe mumbled to himself a he massaged is brow. The secretary left and they resumed.

"Next –" The aide was cut off.

"Let's take a break. Will everyone except Joe, Fred and Bob excuse us for a few minutes?"

"Yes sir." The senior aide said and rounded up his people. The VP informed the president that he had a meeting with the ambassador of Swaziland in an hour and had to prepare and so too excused himself.

When the room was cleared Thaddeus went to the secret liquor cabinet everyone knew about, under the bust of Benjamin Franklin, and prepared four scotches.

"This place is a fucking zoo!" Joe declared.

"When you called us I thought you were joking around about this stuff!" Bob added.

"Well you can see, I wasn't. I mean look at this slush pile I'm supposed to wade through!" He lifted then dropped a handful of papers on the table in front of him. "This is just to be done today! These are complaints against some of the congressional members." He selected some at random. "Unsolicited sexual advancements to an undercover officer in the men's room at Dulles International. 'Sexts' from a nom de penis we've traced to several different representatives and a senior congresswoman. Tweeting the pages obscene messages in congress! Some of those pages aren't even in high school fer crying out loud!"

"What the hell ever happened to just getting caught in strip clubs or with a mistress in a shady motel god damn it!?"

Ж

Gradually the Perver's marriage began suffering more and more. But only from Thaddeus' standpoint. A perfectly content Prudence, now too fat to get out of bed without the aid of a mechanical device, hadn't had sexual relations with her husband since . . . since the early factory days back in Brubaker.

The reality of his situation hit Pervers one evening as dinner was announced while he was in the study reviewing a proposed house bill.

"Will my wife be joining us for dinner?" He inquired of the man servant.

"I'm afraid not Mr. President. The First Lady is otherwise engaged. In addition to which the Presidential pneumatic pallet jack is out for repairs. Back on Friday."

By now Prudence had her own suit in the White House. Actually she had the entire East Wing. She had become so large that a full time staff were required to attend to her. She required constant attention, cleaning and worst of all, feeding.

The woman had not only evolved the requirement to be fed three to four times the normal daily consumption of a human being of her age, but had also developed the ability to consume a pound of cooked animal flesh, (mostly cooked), a pound and a half of potatoes, two pounds of vegetables and a loaf of bread at a sitting.

A typical evening meal would consist of Consommé soup, poached salmon or bass with cucumber sauce, a plate of chicken Kiev, several stalks each of celery, Romaine lettuce, asparagus and fiddlehead fern, a 24 oz. filet Mignon, with side order of peas and carrots, a pound and a half of boiled potatoes followed by roast squab with water cress, and an entire pepperoni pizza, which she would eat whole. A large cherry cheesecake Danish topped with a pound of Neapolitan ice cream for dessert to follow.

With a diet Coke.

It was no surprise therefore to staff or family when she was the first person in history to receive a blanket ban from the All You Can Eat Buffet Restaurant Association of America which resulted in a law suit.

The case was referred to their long time lawyers, the esteemed Sixth Avenue law firm of Due, Wee, Cheatem & Howe but it was eventually realized that, rather than fight the case, it would save John Doe Taxpayer tens of thousands if they built the First Lady her own All You Can Eat franchise.

There was only one outlet, located on the back of the White House lawn, and the decision was made that it should be a themed restaurant.

Because her family had always been Nixon supporters from years back, chronicling from the time leading up to his election to the presidency - the single outlet franchise would be called Big Dick's Halfway Inn.

Ж

Though things were undeniably hectic in the first quarter, it was now at the six month mark that the Presidency seemed to be running on greased grooves and the possibility of marginal political progress lay on the horizon.

Lessons learned in the senate proved their worth as Thaddeus now understood more clearly what was expected of the Chief Executive and his staff regarding local, domestic and foreign issues.

He fulfilled his cultural obligations and maintained his public profile by attending the Asianentals' celebrations in January, the Blams history month functions in February and the Irish dance and drink-a-thon functions in March.

Fully briefed beforehand by the appropriate cabinet members he met with diplomats, dignitaries and directors.

Most importantly Pervers was comforted by the fact that both Prudence and Taranjello had settled into their new lives and routines.

However as his head hit the pillow one night, mistakenly under the belief that his mind was clear and he was at peace with himself that he was doing all he could to heal a broken country, one last nagging thought bounced around in his head.

Congress still stalled on a national budget compromise.

A VISIT TO LEFTY

CHAPTER TWENTY

Ж

Now approaching the Christmas recess and nearly a full year as the Chief Executive, Thaddeus had become increasingly dismayed at the plethora of pet projects which seemed to be clogging up the senate. He particularly felt many were political, self-serving and essentially non-productive.

Most importantly they were noncontributing to the welfare of the general public.

There were farming, industrial and the least contributory, special interest projects cleverly labeled as 'humanitarian'. To aggravate matters there were the usual housing scandals, construction contracts not being put out for open bid and covert, gay and straight, sex crimes being committed in the senate.

But by far the most damaging scandal currently shrouding the apparently constantly cloud ridden congress was the fact that the two sides refused to agree on a budget.

The Balanced Budget Amendment, which had been lingering in Congress for the last 12-13 administrations had become a particular pet peeve of The President's primarily due to its contribution to the present dilapidated state of the economy. New funding for medical research, rebuilding of the infrastructure and most importantly for education, was all log jammed in either the House or the Senate due to party politics.

Never before had the limitations, restraints and narrowness of the two party system been more emphasized then when each time the BBA came up for vote.

Both party heads would attempt to alter language, insert 'what ifs' or add riders to the bill and the other side would, according to dogma, like an auction at a used car lot, dutifully counter with bright ideas of their own.

And so, just as the two parties, for over 165 years, claimed falsely to have reached peace in the Middle East, so too would press releases be issued that a balanced budget was near at hand only to later disappoint the public, shut down the government at the end of the fiscal year and it would all blow up in everybody's face. The bill would inevitably be shelved patiently gathering dust awaiting the paper armies to regroup and launch the next attack.

The leaders of the two parties had negotiated peace in the Middle East so many times with the fighting re-erupting anew each time with increased intensity that eventually Israel and Palestine had eliminated each from the map and the territories were taken over by Saudi Arabia who rented the desert land out to Russia's newest satellite state Syria which now waged constant war with the new Jewish state, renamed again as Canaan.

And now, in the late Fall, budget points of contention once again put the government in danger of shutting down for an indefinite period of time and bringing the country's gargantuan administrative nerve center to a grinding halt.

Ж

It was late one Friday evening in the smaller of the two dining rooms that Thaddeus, Joe, Fred and Bob sat sharing an after dinner brandy.

Down the hall in the southwest corner, tucked away in the garishly decorated Beyoncé Bedroom, Prudence sat, happily propped up in her king sized bed, a plethora of remote controls scattered about, watching *As The World Turns Through The Days Of Our Lives* on the newly installed eight foot neutrino screen T.V.

She was particularly engrossed because it was the episode where Brad finds out that his wife Shelia cheated on him and that their baby girl, Madison was illegitimate, but it was okay because Shelia, an adopted orphan when she was three, actually turned out to be Brad's sister by another mother so, no harm done.

"All's well that ends well!" Prudence comforted herself with a smile as she popped another Twinkie in her mouth.

Back in the dining room, as the table was being cleared, one by one the guests looked up then sat perfectly still as a deep rumbling slowly began swelling in intensity as it emanated from somewhere unknown inside the house.

Out in the Rose Garden birds launched from trees and bushes as squirrels fled for cover and Lyndon, the pet hound dog howled loudly.

The paintings on the wall vibrated, the table shook and the silver ware shimmied across the partially cleared table top. Everyone froze.

A few seconds of dead calm was followed by a tremendous explosion which shook the whole White House and blew out several windows.

Secret Service Guys scrambled to the dining room as the diners, led by Joe, dashed from the room and headed down the long hallway to where it appeared the detonation had originated.

The agents and the guests arrived simultaneously outside the bedroom where parts and pieces of Prudence Pervers dripped from the formerly white ceiling, powder blue walls, and carped floor and used-to-be expensive drapery.

They glanced down and in synchronization realized what happened. Fred kicked the empty, industrial sized 36 pack of Twinkies across the floor.

The official Coroner's report would record that, through indirect but profuse amounts evidence, Prudence's mouth had pushed her body to critical mass.

Bob held up a vacated cellophane Twinkie wrapper pouring out the few remaining crumbs.

"Must'a been that last Twinkie that done it!" He quietly theorized.

Ж

By order of the President the First Lady's room was permanently sealed and cordoned off and, at the suggestion of the BB Stackers, renamed in solemn memorium from the Beyoncé Bedroom to the Prudence Pervers Pantry.

It was three days later, after the furore and press of the funeral died down, Bob quietly knocked on the door to the Oval Office but there was no answer. He knocked again and waited. Nothing. Finally he quietly pushed open the door and gingerly stepped into the room followed by Joe and Fred.

Thaddeus sat quietly at his desk, facing the large picture window, back to the room, slowly nursing his Budweiser longneck. Bob was the first to speak.

"You okay Thad?"

"I'm worried." He despondently whispered.

"Perfectly understandable old buddy!" Bob said.

"But don't worry, we got your back!" Fred added.

"Well I can't worry about it too much longer." Thad replied.

"You go ahead and worry just as long as you want to, Big T!" Joe encouraged. "Don't matter what people say about her, she was a good woman."

"At least she died doing what she liked!" Bob mumbled.

"No, no! I'm talking about this stalemate in the Congress. They've got a vote soon."

The three exchanged glances.

"Thad, it's been less than a week since the funeral! Shouldn't you be thinking about Prudence? Taranjello?"

"We talked, he's okay. He's back at school."

"Well take some time off, maybe take Marine One up to Camp David?" Joe suggested.

"Maybe just take her up for a spin, you know fly around a little!"

"Yeah, yeah, I hear ya, thanks. But this thing in Congress . . ." Thaddeus pushed.

"What'a you care?! Now that you're in, you can do what you want!" Joe prodded. "You know like all those movie stars that make all those shitty movies and TV shows just to get paid, break into the biz and get a foot up. Then they go off and do what they want, like make their own shitty movies only they get to direct. Hell you got the country behind you now!" Fred heartened.

"They bought the gas leak explosion story! For the next few weeks you can do anything you want and the public will stand behind you!"

"Yeah, I'm not too comfortable with that story but I get ya Joe. It's just that . . ."

"Just what?! You got a great paying job, your nice new big house! What else you after?" Joe queried. Thaddeus shrugged and chugged his beer. "What is it then?"

"It's just that. . ." As Thaddeus was not a particularly educated man and even with all the coaching and formal lessons he had been given, the words came hard because there was no pre-thought, preparation or rehearsal. No professionally composed script. But he formed the words in his mind as he spoke. "It's just that I got involved in this thing, gave up my job at the factory,

Prudence, Taranjello, all semblance of a normal life to make a difference. To make things better. And . . ."

"And?"

"And IT AIN'T HAPPENING!" The others were taken off guard by his outburst.

"What did you expect? Did you really think in your heart-of-hearts that the President of the United States was going to make any difference? Just because you got a big shiny, white house, a big spacious, funny shaped office and a 4,000 person staff with 3,000 military and a shit load of volunteers at your beck and call it was gonna make you somebody special!?"

"Well, yeah, kind of!"

"Well wake up Satch, school's out! It don't! It just makes you the biggest politician, not even that. It just makes you the most well-known politician. There's an old Italian saying; The Golden Rule: He who has the gold makes the rules'. The only thing you control now days is one big shiny white house, a big jet and a helicopter!"

"And a big spacious, funny shaped office and a nice shiny limousine at your beck and call." Bob added.

"Hell, any two term senator with a handful of lobbyists in his back pocket has more real pull than you do!" Joe added.

"There's got'a be something about presidential powers somewhere that I can use to get these assholes moving!"

"What about it Fred?" Joe probed. At that Fred resumed his presidential counselor role as legal advisor and spoke up.

"In Article II, Section 2, clause 2 of the Appointments Clause the President has an array of different powers. Commander-in-Chief, treaties, appointing ambassadors, but not much regarding the budget. That's pretty much the purview of the Congress."

"Very impressive! When'd you learn all that shit?" Joe inquired.

"Googled it." He shrugged.

"What about vetoes?" Thad asked.

"Basically, if Congress is not in session, the POTUS can pocket the bill and after ten days it's automatically vetoed. If they are in session he has ten days to veto it outright. Otherwise it's law!" Fred explained. Bob suddenly broke into song.

"I fought the law and the law won! I fought the law and the law -"

"BOB, SHUT IT!" Joe snapped. Bob shrank in his chair.

"Well, they're in session." Thad said.

"Yeah, for another week. If you ask me they're just stalling for time until the recess so they don't have to come to a damn decision! Besides if you do veto anything they pass they can just turn around and vote a two thirds majority and override you."

"I'm starting to see Joe's point."

"In essence . . . veto your veto!" Bob declared. Fred and Joe shot him a dirty look.

"You're not helping here!" Joe chastised.

"You think they'd do that?" Thaddeus asked.

"Well given the present climate . . . I mean could be, but again, what'a you care?" Joe reiterated.

"At the very least think of all those people." Thaddeus quietly pleaded with his empty beer bottle.

"What fucking people?" Fred was genuinely confused.

"Five million homeless despite there being over fifteen million abandoned homes in this country! Ten million in prison or on probation, with more than two dozen private firms profiting off them! Fourteen and a half percent unemployment! How the fuck can I fix all that, especially without money which I can't get without a budget?!"

"You can't, so don't waste your time!" Joe laughed it off and chugged his beer. "Besides, even if you could as soon as the next guy came along after you, he'd undo everything anyway!"

"I feel so helpless, like a god damned lost child in the woods!" Thad vented.

"We all reach that point sometimes Thad!" Fred consoled as he passed another Budweiser from the Styrofoam cooler sitting on the $17,000 18th Century Hepplewhite, mahogany table.

"Yeah, but I'm the God damned president of the United States and this is a United States problem! So how come I can't do anything about it?! How can they not care that these types of delays translate to jobs, which translate to financial hardships for American families! Every day those blockheads dick around banging heads over the new budget it means another 10,000 jobs and more people screwed! In the three and a half days they been at it so far that's the entire former population of Vrindaban, North and South Vrindaban!"

"Where the fuck is Vrindaban?" Joe challenged.

"Not important." Thad defended.

"Sounds to me like one of them vivacious circles." Bob took a turn at consoling his good buddy.

"Yeah, that's what it is, Webster!" Joe teased.

"Point is they do this shit every year!" Fred said.

"Well not every year!" Joe corrected.

"How do you mean, 'not every year'?"

"Only at the end of every physical year!"

"You go Noah Webster!" Fred interjected.

Thaddeus finished his beer and called it a night.

Ж

It was just past ten in the morning when Ernie and Bert, a pair of senior reps from the east coast G.O.P., Government Of the corporate Presidents, stepped out of their rent-a-car and into the parking lot of the Martha J. Stewart Memorial State Correctional Facility in Virginia.

They had been dispatched by their party chief to investigate a request from the prison's warden which they had received more than a week ago but set on the back burner as they were occupied with their fervent effort to regain control of the senate which had been steadily slipping away since this unknown Pervers guy had appeared on the scene and rested control of Washedupton politics.

After presenting their credentials they were escorted to the main office. There they stated their purpose and the warden filled them in as they, the warden and a platoon of heavily armed guards made their way through the long, winding warren of cinder block corridors.

"All I know is this guy says he's got important information that will affect the security of the country. So with all these wild-eyed Islamists, anti-abortionists, gun control freaks, militiamen and anti-pet licensing fanatics running around I figure it's a lead we can't be ignorin'." The warden explained.

"If you're so worried about terrorism why didn't you call the CIA?!" Bert questioned.

"Or the FBI?" Ernie likewise inquired.

"Or the Department of Homeland Security?" Bert queried.

"Or the NSA?" Ernie queried further.

"Or the Federal Department of Anti-terrorism?" Bert added.

"Or the local police?" Ernie tagged.

"Local police? What'a you stupid? What the hell they gonna do, arrest him?" Was the warden's rejoinder.

"You could'a called the I.I.S." Bert pushed.

"What the hell's the I.I.S.?" The warden challenged.

"Islamic Investigative Services."

"Never heard of it!"

"It's a new department. They just passed the funding

last week." Ernie informed.

"By the way Warden, our current alert condition is Mauve One." Bert added.

"I thought it was chartreuse?"

"You're thinking of light mauve. That was last week."

"Oh."

Finally they arrived at the private interview room where their supposed stoolie was being held.

"This guy dangerous?" Burt nervously asked as he perused the small room through the tiny window in the steel door from the corridor.

"Plenty!"

"What'd he do to get himself in here?" Bert asked.

"Multiple parking violations." The Warden declared with pride as if he himself had captured Charles Manson and had him right there in the room.

"Multiple parking violations?" Ernie questioned.

"Yeah! Not just meter violations either! We're talking about blocking fire hydrants, handicap spaces-"

"Multiple parking violations?" Ernie reiterated.

"Law says all multiple offenders to be treated the same." The warden mumbled.

The ten by ten foot room sported a four seat table, adjoining chairs and a one way mirror on the left hand wall.

The heavily chained, muzzled and hooded prisoner was seated on the other side of the table. Two white eyeballs peeked out from between the thick cocoon of chrome chain which only roughly formed the shape of a man.

Tall, pugnacious guards in full body armor, with 12 gauge, pump shotguns at the ready, .357 Magnums slung on their hips and knives in their boots straddled the anonymous prisoner on either side.

Bert noted the plastic, biodegradable can of Diet Coke with a two foot bendy straw, a pack of artificial cigarettes, (valuable currency in prison), and a note pad with pen in front of their man, although how he was supposed to communicate mummified in chains, gagged and hooded was not clear.

The warden and his body guard left them in the care of the two guards in the interrogation room and marched off back up the corridor. The two politicians took their seats at the table in front of the iron encased human.

"Hello Lefty." Bert greeted. One of the guards pulled the hood from the short little prisoner.

"MMMMMFFF." The garbled response emanated from the pile of chains in front of them.

"He says, 'hello'!" The guard on the left translated.

"How's this supposed to work?" Bert asked.

As the GOP were primarily responsible for the ever increasing abuse of prisoners in U.S. jails, on the platform of "Tougher on Crime", every time they had no intelligent or legitimate solutions to offer they sponsored a bill to increase penalties for convictions and 'tighten' security of the guys and gals already caged up. Consequently neither of the emissaries were phased in the least by the prisoner's bondaged situation. In fact Both Bert and Ernie, as did many of the capitol's politicians, had major stock holdings in commercial prison companies which now exclusively controlled the U.S. prison industry, one of the fastest growing portfolios on Wall Street. Not surprising in a country with the largest prison/conviction population in the 'Free World'.

"Youse talk, I'll translate." The guard instructed.

"So what's you got for us Lefty?" Bert kicked things off.

"AMMMF, AAMMFF WTTHHH AA GGGGYY, HHHIIIOOO SSTTATE."

"I once done time with a guy from Ohio State -" The guard translated.

"Oh, a college man! Me and Bernie here went to

Alabama State!"

"NNN AA CLLLGGG SSAAPPP!"

"Not college ya sap!"

"OOOHHHH SSTATA PPPRRRRNN! HHHEE SSS DDDNN FFF TT TTEEN FF RR RRR LLLGGGHHTTSSS."

"Ohio State Prison! He was doin' five to ten for running red lights."

"Dangerous profession crime!"

"NNTT FF UUURR PPOOLLLTTTNN!"

"Not if you're a politician!"

"Go on." Ernie prodded.

"NNNHH . . ."

"As I was saying . . ."

"FFRRRMM MMMAANN CCRRRTTIIAL."

"He transferred in from Mansfield Correctional."

"In Mansfield, Ohio!" Bert proudly boasted.

The head on the chains shook slightly as he spoke.

"NNNAAHH, IINN JJJEERRRSSIIIEEYYY! OOODFFF OOOHHHIIII, WWHHHHRR UU TTHHIIKKK, MMMBB SSHHIIITT?"

"No, in Jersey! Of course Ohio, where the hell you think, dumb shit?!" They both glared at the guard.

"Don't look at me, I'm just telling you what the guy's saying!" The guard defended. Ernie started jotting down notes.

"HHHH MMMNN SSS NNNN TRRESSS BBB JJJJJ DDDMMMVVV!"

"His sister's husband's best friend's cousin used to work in the state DMV."

"Hey Lefty, this story got a fairy tale ending or is it a re-write of Scheherazade?" Bert pushed.

"UUU DDD WWWNANA III EEE RRR SSSMMMB EEESSLLALE!! UUKK OOOOFF!"

"Okay, you don't want the information I got for you? Somebody else'll pay for it! Fuck off!"

"How do we know your story's not all bullshit, just

something to get you more time knocked off your sentence?"

"WWTTT SSS UUU IINNKK BBLLIINNGG UUU?"

"What makes you think I'm bullshitting you?!"

"Because so far things ain't jiving the way they're supposed to!"

"LLLIIKK WWHHATT?"

"What part don't you believe?"

"Well, anybody doing any work at the DMV for starters. Secondly-"

"II GGGOOTTT SSSMMMTTHINGGG UU KKINN USSS AAGAGINST PPPERVERSS!! UU WWNNT IIT NNOOT?!"

"I got something you can use against Pervers. You want it or not?"

Both politicians stared open mouthed.

"WWWLLL? AAKKKE AAA DDECCISSIOON! II GGGTTA GGEEETT BBBKK TTOOO RRREECC RROOMM, PPPRROGGRAMMAM CCNMMMINNNG OOONN!"

"Well? Make a decision, I got'a get back to the rec room before my program comes on."

"What program?!" Ernie demanded. The guard answered before Lefty was able to mumble his reply.

"*As The World Turns Through The Days Of Our Lives*! What's-a-matter, don't you guys keep up on current events?!" The incensed guard challenged.

Not believing if Lefty was on the level or not the two politicians reserved judgement.

"Spill it!" Ernie demanded.

"NNNEEEVVRRR RRRSSTSTRRDD."

"He ain't never registered."

"We know he registered! We got copies of his intent to run for office forms from the state courthouse in Columbus."

"HHHMFF?" Lefty grunted. The guard interpreted.

"How did youse two chumps ever get to a position of responsibility in the U.S. government?!"

"We were appointed! What's that got to do with anything?" Bert asked just as Ernie suffered an epiphany

"I GOT IT! You mean he never registered for military duty?"

"AAAGGHHH! WWRRRNNGG ANNSS, AANKK UU FFOR SSHHHRRLLKKK!"

"AAAGGHHH! Wrong answer! Thank you for playing. Guess again Sherlock." The guard explained. Apparently Ernie's was an inaccurate epiphany.

"You mean to vote? Tell me he's not a citizen and can't vote?" He slid to the edge of his seat.

"OO OOO! HHEESS SSITTZZNN!"

"No, no. He's a citizen okay."

"Son, you're pissing me off! Now quit wasting our time! You got something to tell us or not?!"

With that the prisoner leaned in as far as his full body chain suit would allow and whispered to Ernie. Bert overheard as well.

Understanding what Lefty relayed, the simultaneously dashed from the room and disappeared down the corridor making their way back up to the warden's office.

When it had sunk in what the Warden had just been told, he fell back into his leather, high backed chair. His face turned white and he stared off into the distance. Ernie rushed around behind the desk.

"Which phone's the hot line to the State House?" He frantically asked. "The one you use when a prisoner is about to be executed and you want to call at the last minute to see if he's pardoned?"

"Not sure. We ain't never used it." He answered. "I think maybe this one here." The Warden pointed to the red phone.

After brushing off the one inch thick layer of dust Ernie rang through to the Governor's Mansion.

"Get me the Governor!" He ordered.

Back in the interrogation room the two guards hefted Lefty up onto the chrome gurney to wheel him back to his eight and a half foot by four foot cell.

"MMMM FFFF!" He muffle-yelled.

"OH! Sorry Lefty!" The bigger guard apologized as he went back to the table to fetch Lefty's diet coke with the bendy straw and his artificial cigarettes.

THE CRIME EXPOSED

CHAPTER TWENTY-ONE

🜨

Like a stranded castaway flagging a passing ship Fred burst into the Oval Office wildly waving the morning's newspaper. Over on the couch Joe sat swigging coffee.

"You seen this?!" He asked Thaddeus as he slapped a copy of the *Washedupton Post* down on the President's desk.

"They bring me the paper before I get up." Thaddeus quietly answered. He paid the banner headline no mind but kept on with his paper work. "They want me to call a cabinet meeting at ten. What'a you think?"

"Do you **want** to call a cabinet meeting?"

"Suppose I ought'a hear what they got to say."

"They're mostly left over cronies from the other two parties. You know what they're gonna say!" Fred struggled to contain his anger. One of Thad's immutable rules was no tempers in the Big O.O. The Oval Office. Fred took a seat next to Joe and poured himself a coffee.

"Trial of the century? Thought we already had one of those?" Joe remarked as he lowered the spread out copy of the New New York Times on to the coffee table in front of him.

"What'a you think Joe?"

"Admit nothing, deny everything and make counter accusations!" Joe advised.

"Look if we drag this thing out, especially in the face of overwhelming evidence of my guilt –"

"WAIT, WAIT, WAIT A MINUTE! You're actually guilty of this shit they're accusing you of?"

"Yeah." He casually shrugged. "I was on my way out to the court house to register when the whole car accident thing happened. You know about that."

"We knew about the car accident but not about the jury duty thing." Joe explained.

"Still with all the past shit that's come outt'a the White House . . ."

Just then Bob came into the office holding a copy of the *Washedupton Journal* aloft.

"Hey, you guys seen this?" In response the other three all held up newspapers.

"Day late and a dollar short Bob!" Fred quipped.

"Oh." He perused the room. "So what'a we talking about then?" Bob inquired.

"A way out'a this!" Joe informed.

"Well, what did Nixon do way back when with Watergate?" Bob sought to rescue himself.

"He lied." Thaddeus answered.

"Well did Clinton when he got caught with his pants down?"

"He lied."

"What about Reagan when he got caught in that Iranian contradictions thing?" Bob carelessly ventured.

"You mean the Iran-Contra Affair." Joe corrected.

"Yeah, whatever!"

"He lied." Thaddeus, Fred and Joe answered in unison. "We need an example to pattern our strategy on!" Joe suggested.

"Like the Nixon Watergate thing?" Bob's mentality was hardwired for tenacity.

"More like the Reagan multi-million dollar housing rip-off thing."

"Or the Clinton sex in the White House thing."

"SEX! In the White House?!" Bob genuinely gasped.

"Right here in the Oval Office." Joe said. "On that very chair I think I read." Joe added. Bob sprang from the overstuffed chair he was planted in.

"Or the other Clinton sex scandal thing."

"You mean the husband sex thing?"

"I thought the wife was the one who had sex in the White House?!"

"No, no, no. That was the husband. Nobody cared if the wife had extra marital sex. You got'a remember, that was back when the whole gay-lesbian scene was the 'in' thing and accepted by the people."

"Oh!"

By the second day of the Pearl Harbor-like sneak attack by the press on the president the story had made national headlines.

Although what used to be considered the Left was now the Right and the Right was distinctly more left, they had both moved to be so centralist that the public was no longer able to distinguish one party from the next.

The Executive secretary rang through on the intercom.

"Yes Julie?"

Sorry to disturb you sir, but you said to keep you up to date on the Senate activities.

"Yes?"

You'll probably want to see this.

"Send it in." A small unit under his desktop buzzed, clicked and then burped out a sheet of paper across left side of his desk.

"Son-of-a-bitch!" Thaddeus swore as he read the update.

"What?"

"The Senate has just moved to break early for the Christmas recess!"

"They do that every year! Why don't they just change the calendar and call it the October break?" Joe protested.

"Bastards probably want to let the story soak into the press over the holiday so they can build capital on it and cash in after the people have been spoon fed it daily in the mainstream media for a month!" Fred observed.

"Okay, so what? They want to impeach you for breaking the law and not telling them about it during the campaign?!" Bob questioned.

"Nobody ever asked!" Thaddeus defended. "Besides, I couldn't help it! The whole-"

"The whole kidnapping thing. You have a good excuse, you were in a car accident!" Joe bolstered. "You're not gonna get impeached, even if they do vote to hold a hearing."

"Probably not, but think if the repercussions! Every time either side makes any accusations, founded, unfounded whatever, the damn press are like a mongrel dog with a soup bone! It'll be in the info-news for weeks, everything will be disrupted in the Congress and it'll be one more excuse for them not to get anything done!"

"We understand Thad, but-"

"You realize I'm in the White House eight months-"

"Nine months big guy!"

"Nine months and so far they've not passed one bill!"

"It's that damn balanced budget amendment, they won't ratify it! One excuse after the other. Now they've got this failing to register thing to lean on!" Joe joined in the rant.

"Yeah! It dominates the papers and airwaves, causes all kinds of disruptions and nobody gets any real work done!" Bob unnecessarily reinforced.

"BINGO!" Thaddeus jumped from his seat. "Exactamundo!" He pointed at Bob who was stunned.

"That's exactly why I **was** going to hold a press conference, come clean and get on with the business of running the country. Well done Bob!" Thaddeus congratulated.

"I said something good?" Bob asked.

"So when are you planning on doing this, holding the press conference?" Fred asked.

"I was planning on doing it today or tomorrow."

"What time? Don't you want the pencils to rustle you up a speech or something? Something about how you've been under a lot of stress since Prudence-"

"Past Imperfect!" Thaddeus cut him off.

"What?"

"The Past Imperfect! 'WAS' going to do that."

"He's cracking up!" Fred theorized.

"No he' not! He's cooking up! Cooking something up!" Joe observed. Thaddeus, in a fit of inspiration, began to circle the room.

"I have a plan to unplug the plumbing, drain the toilet, and get things flowing again!" He plopped into his tall back, leather chair and pulled in close to his desk. "Gather around." He flipped a toggle switch on his desk and spoke into the hidden mic. "Julie, schedule the Executive conference Room for three to four hours this afternoon."

Yes Mr. President. Shall I schedule catering?

"No, won't be necessary. Thank you Julie."

"What'a we gonna need the Exec board room for Thad?"

"We ain't! We're gonna have our Executive meeting right here right now!"

"Then what'a we need the Executive-" Bob was cut off as Joe elbowed him in the ribs.

"It's a rouse idiot!"

"They want to change the date of the Christmas break, yet again? No problem! We'll help them change the date!" Thaddeus came around from behind the desk.

"Fred, get me all the relevant regs pertaining to Executive-Legislative relations. Joe, I need the codes for domestic disasters alleviations and rescue efforts."

"Right!" Joe affirmed.

"What'a I do boss?" Bob pleaded. Thaddeus smiled and placed a hand on Bob's shoulder.

"Bob, I've saved the most important job for you!" Bob beamed at the comment. "Get a hold of the FOUO people tell them I need a conference call in one hour."

"Right Chief!" Bob rendered a sharp salute and didi maowed out of the A.O.

Ж

For the other two parties to wrest back control of the government radical measures would have to be taken. What Thaddeus Pervers did, with the help of Snodgrass and company, was tantamount to the ill-fated ventures by other groups in the past who had had the brazen temerity to attempt to establish a third political party and give the people an alternative to an either/or choice in their political elections

The unexpected phone call from the prison warden, himself a G.O.P. political appointee, revealing Thaddeus' dirty little secret was, for the party heads, like John Wayne arriving with the cavalry just as the Indians were bursting through the gates.

Now that they tipped their hand and had announced their attack, Thaddeus et al had to organize a stiff defence.

President Pervers crime? Nothing as trivial, inane or minor as breaking into the other party's hotel suite or lying about Weapons of Mass Destruction.

Nothing as insidious as getting a blow job in the White House.

Nothing as inconsequential, insignificant or frivolous as other scandals such as a multi-million dollar housing fraud, false claims of DNC bugging or election fixing by illegally striking tens of thousands of registered voters from the rolls. Nothing quite so trivial. Nothing or superficial, foolish, silly or juvenile.

President Thaddeus Enoch Pervers' transgression was far more serious.

He never reported to register for jury duty.

As he never got to register for jury duty, due to inadvertently stopping a kidnapping, Thaddeus was never called. But because he never registered and was never called to serve, his name had gone forward to the New Office of Homeland Security & Personal Affairs where his citizen registration number was red flagged as a possible dissident and, therefore a future terroristic threat.

A file was started. Worse yet, it was entered in his permanent record.

And it was this file that the semi-alert warden had happened on. With the discovery of this political goldmine, the two parties, the only legitimate parties, the only two parties worthy of serving America and controlling her people, the country and therefore the world, the question remained what to do with the information.

After double-secret meetings on both sides were held, representatives were elected, a final super top secret meeting was held and options reviewed. Finally, following an all-night, heated debate the representatives agreed on the first thing they had joined forces for in the last dozen election cycles.

To avoid having it look as though the whole thing was a political smear campaign, because the first rule of instituting a political smear campaign was to make it look like it wasn't a political smear, they would leak the information to the highest bidder.

Within 24 hours Thaddeus' dirty little secret had gone public.

The story inundated the wire services, the Lush Limburger Show, the talk news and other gossip programs. The long syndicated shows such as *Doctor Still*, *Open Window*, *Hellen* and *The Phew* all frolicked in ratings spikes unseen since the days of legitimate television and before victimhood had become a recognized disease.

Through the rumor mill, prior to releasing the story, the party heads allowed the sensational headlines to generate sympathy for the argument of the deadly dangers of violating the Vote or Die Regulations and the anti-Aiding and Abetting Terrorism laws.

Talk shows discussed the hot topic, call-ins were sponsored on radio, opinion columns featuring 'what if?' scenarios were run and documentaries aired and late night talk shows bristled with badly written monologues lampooning the Pervers' administration.

By the time the actual crime came to light, it was considered so terrible, so heinous, so treasonous that there was no recourse but to lobby for prosecution of the 'Wonder Boy President' who had so underhandedly gained and undermined the confidence of the good people of these here United States where so many had given their lives to defend. And what about the children! It had to done for the children!

Through the appropriate channels Thaddeus Enoch Pervers would be presumed innocent, prosecuted and found guilty, and sentenced. All following due process of course. He would be tried for non-registration for jury duty, conspiracy, failure to comply with a federal regulation, public disobedience and finally not doing the right thing. Should it come to trial something was sure to stick.

In the true spirit of American Politics; that is the legal means to deprive a man of what's rightfully his, the battle was launched.

The result, according to the press, would be the 'trial of the century'.

Ж

Following the public revelation things began to move quickly.

It took only a few days before debate raged in the Senate. Strangely enough, and quite unexpectedly, there was no opposing side because, upon legal advice, Thaddeus decided to wait until his detractors had fully argued themselves out and settled on a definitive course of action. No opposing side of course made debating difficult, so the 'Onhorable Gentlemen on The Hill reduced themselves to arguing the finer points of how exactly to prosecute the president.

Eventually the opportunistic feeding frenzy, after reaching new heights, settled down to a steady rhythm of motions, denials and counter motions until a vote was called for and it was voted on and approved by a two thirds majority,

After a full ten days of silence, including during the entire week of senate debates, Thaddeus realized he was duty bound to do what he could to relieve the torture the press were putting the people of America through. Like an eighteen year old virgin frat boy with a pricey call girl, the three lettered networks had ceaselessly pounded the public with all manner of inane detail and statistics from lists of the dozens of crimes committed by presidents through the years to the fact that none of them had faced any jail time. And it was high time that change! Or so the prevalent agenda steered itself.

It was at that point that Pervers decided to make an announcement, or rather have a 'spokesman for The President' make an announcement. They called a press conference to announce that, in two days' time, the president would call a press conference to make an announcement.

Thaddeus then again called his closest advisors, the BB Stackers, together in the Presidential library a few nights before the big vote by the Senate.

"You're worried about how ya gonna go down in history?" Fred challenged. "History?! Who the fuck reads history? We're Americans. We get all the history we need from the movies. Down in history!" Fred assured his friend.

"My kid went down in history! He used to get C's now he gets D's!" Bob laughed at his own joke and elbowed Pervers. "Nobody gives a fuck about grades or history, this is America!" He added, consoling his best friend.

"There have been about forty attempts at impeachment but only sixteen Federal officials have been impeached, seven have gone to trial and been convicted, surprisingly all judges. But nobody did any time." Fred informed.

"So basically the American people spent millions-"

"Billions in today's money." Joe corrected.

"Billions to get a handful of judges fired?"

"Basically, yeah."

"In over three hundred years there were only seven bad judges in our history?!" Thaddeus challenged.

"Oh hell no! There have been hundreds! At least. But only seven got caught. Slick fuckers those judges! They're like lawyers only with superpowers!"

"That's . . . that's -"

"That's the reason they call it all a game. It's not committing the crime that makes them a criminal, it's the getting caught."

"Besides, even if you're found guilty, you still have to be convicted." Fred explained.

"What?" Pervers queried.

"I told you it's not like a for real trial. If you're

found guilty they still have to vote again on whether or not to convict you then another vote on the punishment."

"Bottom line Thaddy, no matter what they come up with, unless they can produce a dead body, you're not going to jail." He informed. "Probably."

"You think?" Bob questioned.

"Well, they didn't prosecute Reagan for lying about Granada." Thaddeus encouraged himself.

"Or Clinton for lying about the Uraniumgate." Bob added.

"Or Clinton about getting a blow job in the White House and lying to Congress about it." Fred rcalled.

"Or the other Clinton for lying about Bengazi. Walked away Scott free!"

"So what you're telling me is, as long as I lie, I won't be found guilty?" Thaddeus clarified.

"That seems to be the way it works." Joe shrugged.

"Essentially history will judge you by how skilled a liar you are." Fred contributed. "Not necessarily by what you contributed.

"Or not telling the truth, to be kind about it." Bob added.

While the Senate and House floors were awash with debate Thaddeus had carried on with the duties of office.

Bills were signed, visits to factories and towns were embarked upon and previously scheduled talks and speeches were made. All engagements down played or avoided all together the disturbing topic of the unmentionable crime and possible impeachment.

Both houses were again called to convene on the premise that it was an emergency meeting visa vie the president's impeachment. Witnesses were called, the Head of the GOP, the Head of the Dems and all relevant people were summoned to include Lefty.

Thaddeus was called to testify but humiliated them by refusing to show. With no power to subpoena the President the Congress were at a loss. Again.

John Q. Public on the other hand, inundated with the proceedings of the debates broadcast 24/7 live from the Capitol as they unfolded, could have cared less. The people, by-and-large, had grown so weary of the endless petty scandals, lies and chicanery of the P.C. bureaucrats that they were virtually numb to any more bad news coming out of the nation's capital.

So essentially it came down to Thaddeus Pervers and the two, hereto warring parties. Finally, it seemed, he had united them on something.

The final Congressional decision was that Thaddeus Enoch Pervers would be prosecuted in a special hearing by the House of Representatives.

It was that afternoon, just as things seemed at their bleakest, that Thaddeus received the news that Sydney Snodgrass had checked out. The old guy's card had been punched and he was called back to that big caucus the sky.

As per Snodgrass' last will and testament, and probably to allow him the opportunity to intervene in others' political destinies in future, Sydney had been cryogenically frozen. As a consequence, and by additional request of Snodgrass himself, there would be no funeral.

THE TYPO

CHAPTER TWENTY-TWO

Ж

GUILTY! The TV and radio stations proudly announced. "Guilty!" read the headlines across the press that day. Magazines, tabloids and broadsheet newspapers, in order to ensure maximum sales, vied for the catchiest headlines.

Thaddeus Thumped by Congress!

Chief Exec Found Guilty in Violation of Federal Law JRL-HS-1234!

President Pervers Perverts Justice!

It was less than forty-eight hours after the hearings that the decision of the hastily organized Congressional Ethics Committee was announced to the press. Despite the fact that a trial had yet to be held.

This turn of events compelled Thaddeus to make a definitive move.

Ж

The skies were grey and gloomy as it appeared the sun didn't seem to want to get out of bed that morning. The temperature, though seasonally moderate, was windy and cool, what Californians used to call freezing.

It was fourteen minutes to ten in the morning as Senators shuffled up the broad, granite staircase and piled into the Capitol Building through the main entrance, some tagged with hangers-on, some with friends and a few with relatives.

No one thought to question why there was no press.

Not since those dark days following the Japanese attack on Pearl Harbor had the U.S. Congress been so well attended. Well, maybe during those dark days following the Arab's evil attack on the World Trade Center way back when. Or those gloomy days when the Wall Street Stock Market crashed back in 1929. Or again during the housing scams of the 80's. Or during the stock market scams of the 90's. And the 2000's. And so on and so forth.

Representatives and Senators spilled into the semi-circular, sacred chambers with reverence and respect to carry out their solemn duty and by five minutes after the hour the show was ready to go on. Curtain time was signalled as the Speaker of the House, ceremonial gavel of authority in hand, took his place at the podium on the stage and addressed the audience. The house fell silent.

"HEAR YE, HEAR YE, HEAR YE! This special session of the Congress of the United States shall now come to order! Mr. Sergeant-at-Arms, are all present and accounted for?!"

"Yes Mr Speaker, all present and accounted for. Save for the Esteemed Gentlemen from Arkansas." With shock the Speaker turned and looked over at the MAA.

"What?"

The MAA scurried over to the Speaker and leaned in, cupped his hand to the Speaker's ear and whispered.

"It's squirrel hunting season."

"What?!"

"Squirrel hunting season started today! State-wide tradition. How'd it look if the state representatives wasn't there to kill the ceremonial squirrel? They was caught between a rock and a hard place! If'n they didn't show up to blast the ceremonial first squirrel, ain't no way they'd'a raised enough donations to get re-elected!"

"Oh, alright then." The Speaker acknowledged. The Sergeant-at-Arms scurried back across the stage to his post.

The large oak doors in the center back of the chamber opened and Thaddeus flanked by Vice-President what's-his-name and Bob strode down the aisle towards the podium.

Bob peeled off and headed to the wings, the VP took his place to the right and behind the President and Thaddeus stepped to the podium, adjusted the floating mic and cleared his throat as he perused the room.

"Ladies and Gentlemen of the Congress of the United States, I come to you with a heavy heart. You have summoned me here today to face the very serious charges of failing to register for jury duty." From his lessons with the PC Political Life and Image Coaching program Thaddeus knew a dramatic pause was indicated and so he paused. Dramatically. For exactly 2.7 seconds. "Let me put the rumors and speculation to rest. I am guilty of the charges which have been levelled against me."

A mighty rumbling broke across the crowd forcing the Speaker to man his gavel to restore calm.

"SILENCE IN THE CHAMBERS! SILENCE IN THE CHAMBERS!" The din gradually diminished. "Decorum gentlemen, decorum!" The Speaker chastised. Thaddeus pressed on.

"Thank you Mr. Speaker. I want to tell the people of this great country. . . the members of this loyal government and the distinguished members of this chamber that, despite the fact that I was involved in thwarting a series crime –"

As he spoke three United States Senate Pages, one boy, one girl and one transgender, the girl clutching a message, appeared at the side of the stage and tugged at the coat of the Sergeant-at-Arms.

"Not now!" The MAA scolded in a loud whisper trying to shoo them away. The boy tugged again, this time harder and the girl waved the message more vigorously. "WHAT?" The MAA yelled in a loud whisper.

"FOR THE PRESIDENT!" The boy loudly whispered back. He took the message and dismissed the trio. The boy and the girl scurried away in different directions, leaving the confused transgender who didn't know which way to go.

The MAA sauntered across the stage and up to Vice President what's-his-name and handed him the message. The VP saw the red 'EYES ONLY'! boldly stamped across the front and made the decision to interrupt Thaddeus.

"Sorry sir, but it's marked 'EYES ONLY'!" Thaddeus opened the sealed envelope and read the message. A look of consternation settled on his face.

"Gentlemen, I've just been informed that our forces have invaded a suspected terrorist strong hold." A quiet but controlled pandemonium erupted. "This message has just arrived from the office of the Head of the Department of the Joint Security Forces & Secret Police Stuff. Details are sketchy however they are pursuing the matter as we speak."

Ж

At that moment, deep in the South Pacific, 2,812.32 miles west of Hawaii, on the tiny, tropical island nation of Nauru, Col. Jacob Lesley "The Hawk" Brassbottom was the Commander commanding the invasion force, which was activated only that morning when the Secretary of State was provided with the excuse he needed to green light the forces to land.

The excuse was that the U.S., a week earlier, had been asked by the President of Nauru for help due to the recent outbreak of riots by the indigenous peoples. The Hawk and his troops were sent in, and as he always wanted to but never did, insisted on leading the troops in. Finally this time the colonel was allowed to accompany the forward recon party when they hit the beach.

Brassbottom was a tall, square shouldered, square jawed, cigar chomping man of solid morale, solid principles and solid solidness all the way through.

The Hawk had been on the President's council for military advice for the last four administrations. The same president, but four terms of the same president. Twice as the Head of the Joint Chiefs of Staff. Unfortunately except in the movies, The Hawk had never seen combat and the last time the Colonel hit the beach was 27 years ago on Coney Island with his wife and kids. Brassbottom having never seen combat desperately wanted something in his record before his retirement next month, a little something to help him get that general's star before retirement.

However, at H+6 things were not going according to plan.

At that moment Col. Brassbottom, along with his adjutant and radioman, were desperately trapped, surrounded in a small thatched hut by attacking natives. The din of the attack compelled the men huddled inside the hut to shout in order to be heard.

"WELL I DON'T CARE ABOUT NO GOD DAMNED SOLAR FLARES INTERFERRING WITH YOUR RADIO TRANMISSIONS! YOU GET ME THE HEXAGON! WE NEED RE-INFORCEMENTS HERE PRONTO!" The colonel commanded into the headset.

Yelling and screaming in Nauaurian could be heard over the radio frequency by the men in the radio room back aboard the command ship. The commotion was coming from outside the thatched hut. The whole structure began to rhythmically shake as the three soldiers were under a fearsome attack by an entire company of natives.

A company of fat, sweaty, female natives all dressed in McDonalds', Taco Bell and KFC uniforms. Females who hadn't seen a man who weighed under 300 pounds in nearly a decade.

The facts were these: Under the previous Oboomboom administration, when western industry flocked to the tiny island country of Nauru twenty years ago, to exploit its sulphur deposits, the country experienced the unprecedented expansion the economists predicted, but not in the manner anticipated.

Prior to the industrial invasion the small population subsisted on a very narrow agrarian economy of bread fruit and mango with no exports, no industry and no discernable GNP.

Once contracts were signed with the chief of the Nauruans, now renamed President, it took less than a week for mining operations to settle into a comfortable rhythm of mining and shipping at which point the U.S. introduced the good natives to the extravagant pleasures of the West, specifically: name brand clothing and fast food.

Now, two and a half years later, the sulphur mines had run dry and the Dig Deep Corporation of San Luis Obispo, headquartered in sunny southern California, had pulled up stakes and left.

As a result unemployment shot to 95%. As an additional effect of this short but tragic chain of events, the only food stuffs available on the island were the fast food outlets founded when the future growth of the island was more optimistic and which had now been left behind.

With no tillable land left for indigenous farming due to the mining operations, the only remaining food sources were McDonalds, Taco Bell and Kentucky Fried Chicken.

So influential in changing the culture of the Nauruans was the Californian mining company that the national symbol of the country was now a pair of golden arches on a red field over a leg of fried chicken.

Wikipedia listed the national native food as a burrito supreme with extra sour cream. A side of chilli fries was added for holidays.

The air deliveries to the restaurants had become so important that the clocks and calendars had, in time, all been reset to begin with each resupply.

Trouble began to arise when consumption outstripped the storage capacity of the three restaurants.

Due to uncontrolled crowds rushing the airstrip, landing for the monthly resupply flights had proven too dangerous. Brave pilots were lost. Then, due to shifting weather patterns, airdrop had also become less reliable.

The Nauaurian president contacted the U.S. authorities for help and the military were put on stand-by.

Miscalculating the ferocity of hunger which had taken hold of the obese and angry natives when the fast food chains ran short of French fries one day last week, the Hexagon reacted to the ensuing riots by launching the invasion early.

The three trapped soldiers were now in deadly fear for the very lives.

Ж

There's an old adage: When it rains it pours, and back in the congress it seemed to Thaddeus that it was pouring.

Three United States House of Representative Pages, one Clear one BLAM and one Asianental, appeared next to the MAA and tapped him on the arm. They handed him another sealed message for the President. Once again the MAA walked over to the VP who leaned forward from his seat behind the Chief and handed him the message.

The cryptic communiqué announced; 'Marx Brothers have initiated *Operation Big Mac!*'

"What the hell is *Operation Big Mac*?!" The POTUS blurted out.

After a short inquiry Thaddeus was informed that *Operation Big Mac* was the invasion of the country of Nauru.

"Why in the hell was I never informed about this in my daily security briefings?" He demanded.

"It was considered SDTS." The Speaker informed him. "Besides the Joint Chiefs thought it would be a nice surprise if they conquered a country first then told you about it. Kind of like a birthday present, sir."

"Only one problem with that. IT'S NOT MY BIRTHDAY! Now will somebody please explain to me what in the hell is 'SDTS'?!"

"Super Dooper Top Secret, Mr. President." The Speaker duely informed. "It's the second highest security classification there is."

"SECOND? WHAT THE HELL IS THE FIRST?"

"Nobody knows sir. It's too secret." The Speaker explained.

Just then Joe burst on to the stage with some information.

"Okay, we got the low down on this country, Na-Na, Naru. . ."

"Come over here!" Thaddeus directed guiding Joe to the rear of the podium and out of earshot to talk. "Nauru! The country is called Nauru." Thaddeus corrected.

"Whatever! According to the CIA it's a tiny defenceless, island country, about six kilometres wide in the middle of the South Pacific, 3,000 miles south west of Hawaii."

"Six kilometers, is that big? What the hell is a kilometer? What's that in miles?" Thaddeus asked. After a calculator and a college graduate with a degree in math were sent for to calculate the conversion rate, the President was informed the island was 3.7 miles across."

"THREE POINT SEVEN MILES! Why in the hell did Oboomboom want to invade an island three and a half miles across?! Was there a shortage of coconuts somewhere?!" Thaddeus demanded.

"Apparently sir there was a typo." Joe informed.

"A typo?!"

"Yes sir. We were supposed to invade Namibia. To fight against the terrorist group, the Boko Haram."

"Procol Harum?! The *Whiter Shade of Pale* Procol Harum? I like those guys. I thought they were all dead?!"

"They are sir, all except the one guy they froze." Joe clarified further. "But it's not Procol Harum sir, it's Bo-ko Ha-ram. Terrorists. But that's not all sir."

"Oh good, there's more!"

"I'm afraid so sir, it would appear that the guys at the Hexagon-"

"You mean the Pentagon?!" Thaddeus incorrectly corrected.

"No sir, the Hexagon. When President Lump quadrupled the military budget, to fight terrorists, he authorized a new wing -"

"Yeah, yeah I forgot. What's the 'more' bad news?"

"It would appear that the Hexagon, when they gave the green light on the invasion . . . well we've received reports that the pre-landing, recon contingent has run into stiff resistance."

"Shit!" Thaddeus quietly mumbled.

Meanwhile, back on the tiny island of Nauru:

Surrounding the hut, like a pod of beached beluga, profuse mounds of panting portliness lie pronate in the sand. The obese native attackers had temporarily run out of steam and collapsed.

While the mini-diaspora of uniformed women lie gasping, half unconscious, General Brassbottom, his trusty radio operator and adjutant huddled in the far corner of the battered hut, a mere hundred yards from the beach and within sight of the massive fleet anchored two miles off shore, planned, panted and prayed. The trapped trio were enjoying a welcomed respite from the off-again, on-again, vicious attacks they had been enduring over the last couple of hours.

Fortunately the two dozen native women, who initiated the attack shortly after the Americans landed to reconnoitre the beach, due to their immense rotundness, could only sustain their attacks for five to ten minutes at a time before collapsing into the sand exhausted. Years of fast food aggravated by their sedentary life style had rendered every member of the island incapable of climbing a standard flight of stairs without a ten minute break topped off by a Big Gulp of Coca-Cola or Fanta.

Unbeknownst to the trapped beleaguered soldiers, back on the command ship a plan for their rescue was underway.

Assigned to the fleet were a team of the elite U.S. Navy Walruses and in conjunction with the U.S. Army Mauve Berets a daring commando mission was getting underway.

Ж

As dusk settled across the island two, black rubber rafts silently paddled through the night. The fearless raiding party silently rowed the full two miles ashore then quietly crept onto the beach, their secret commando gear confidently stowed in the rafts with them.

Back at the hut containing the Americans, designated "Point Pizza", two dozen native men had replaced the two dozen native women attempting to breech the abode but they too were only good for about ten minutes before they became exhausted and collapsed in the sand.

Meanwhile, while the rescue party silently crept up the beach and into the jungle, the leader of the Mauve Berets had split his squad into two teams. Alpha Team would act as a rear guard contingent safeguarding the rafts and maintaining radio contact with the fleet's flag ship while Bravo Team would function as a decoy group, laying the trap cleverly contrived by the Intel people back aboard the command ship. Large, open bags of cheese burgers, chicken wings and French fries were strategically scattered along the main trail and up wind from the trapped Americans. A trooper quietly strung large signs sporting red arrows pointing to the other side of the island which read; "FREE Coke and Pepperoni Pizza" on palm trees.

That night, under cover of darkness, reaching the hut by navigating towards the sound of snoring, several of the naval commandos took up strategic firing positions with tranquilizer guns while the lead element carefully but silently breached the front door. Their leader moved swiftly to the sleeping soldiers and stirred the shocked colonel.

"Sir, I'm a U.S. Navy Walrus! I'm here to get you out!"

Through his fatigue induced haze Brassbottom looked
hard at the subdued shoulder crest embroidered on the sailor's collar which depicted a Pacific walrus eating a seal.

The colonel hugged him. The three soldiers were led out the door of the hut and quietly tip toed past the snoring sea of sleeping natives.

With only yards to go to clear the area one of

soldiers carelessly stepped on a dried palm frond. At the crack of the frond the Americans all froze but the tactic failed. A big native, whose dream of a double Big Mac with cheese meal was interrupted, woke and spotted them in the moonlight. He began yelling.

The footrace to the beach was on. The special forces walruses, nearly dragging the colonel and his men along, were greatly relieved when, halfway to the rubber boats at the beach staging area, the stampeding natives suddenly stopped and, like a pack of bloodhounds, sniffed the air around them before running off at ninety degrees to the right and disappearing off into the jungle. The trap worked.

The Mauve Berets had accomplished their mission.

A half an hour later the raiding party along with the three soldiers were safely back aboard the command vessel being hailed as heroes.

Ж

Now, nearly two hours into what was to be his resignation speech, and still not having announced his resignation, Thaddeus was having second thoughts about stepping down and leaving such a mess behind. Even though it wasn't his mess.

While he was collecting himself to launch back into his speech he looked over to see the weary Sergeant-at-Arms once again approaching the podium with a message in hand.

The VP declined to take it and instead just pointed to the President. Thaddeus, with no small amount of apprehension, broke the seal on the envelope, read it and stepped back to the podium.

"Gentlemen, I have just received word that the situation in Nauru has been temporarily stabilized."

A great cheer filled the chambers but quickly died down at the ominous sound of the gavel of truth when, as if the Speaker of the House were playing a game of one man Whack-A-Mole, he attacked the gavel block with his gavel.

"GENTLEMEN, GENTLEMEN, GENTLEMEN! MAY I REMIND YOU THIS IS A HOUSE OF GOVERNMENT, NOT AN NFL FOOTBAL GAME!" The naughty elderly school boys quieted down and took their seats. "May we resume?!" Silence prevailed. "Thank you." He sternly perused the chambers. "Mr. President, the floor, once again, is yours." The Headmaster sternly announced.

Thaddeus stepped back to the podium.

"Thank you Mr. Speaker. I-" Pervers began to speak but was immediately interrupted.

"Mr. Speaker!" It was the GOP Whip who stood up and yelled across the floor. "How long must we be made to suffer President Pervers' improvised filibuster?"

Others quickly followed initiating a ground swell of objections aggravated by the fact that the senators and representatives mistakenly believed the hearing, now moving into its third hour, would be brief.

Although having kept the Chamber appraised of the rapidly developing Nauru situation, the natives were getting restless and teetered on the edge of a full scale revolt.

But then again Congressmen always were the biggest problem in Washedupton.

CONTINGENCY 12

CHAPTER TWENTY-THREE

Ж

A few short weeks ago, right after the GOP dropped their bombshell concerning Thaddeus' criminal past, a meeting was held.

Anticipating the unanticipatable by the opposition parties in Congress and to add stability and credence to the administration as well as to garner more public support for Pervers himself, the For Office Use Only people were paid by Moss & O'Shea to come up with that most time honoured technique of boosting a politician's public image.

The staged gimmick.

Bloodbank-Leech's people deduced the best idea to boost a President's standing in the public eye was to show him handling himself well in time of crisis.

Initially they suggested starting a war with a third world country on a trumped up premise, invading the country, and afterwards converting it to American styled Capitalism, building factories and putting the populace to work producing commodities for export to the U.S.

This however had been done so many times throughout history that an alternate route was decided upon. They would stage a fake terrorist attack.

They quickly found the ideal location; an old, abandoned munitions factory outside of Okefenokee, Florida. It would draw headlines being a former government installation and best of all no one would be hurt. But it still left room for the mainstream media to wildly exaggerate damage and a non-factual death toll.

As the congressmen in the chambers shouted, debated and hurled insults at each other Thaddeus glanced at his wrist watch. It was ten and a half minutes before the FOUO plan was scheduled to launch.

Up in the balcony one of the pages jumped up when he felt his Apple Wrist Pod vibrating and read the incoming message from a friend back home.

Terrified he scrambled to the rail of the balcony and yelled out.

"OH MY GOD! THEY JUST ATTACKED OHIO!"

The entire gallery turned to look up at him as the security guards ran to their emergency posts.

Thaddeus was puzzled by the early launch and apparent change of location but reasoned Leech and company were the professionals so they must know what they were doing. He had no way to know the truth. It wasn't Bloodbank-Leech and his people.

In an unexpected twist a real world terrorist attack had occurred.

Seconds after the page's alert a Secret Service Guy quickly approached the podium and presented President Pervers with details of the attack. To avoid a replay of the earlier scene of panic the SSG took the president off to the side to brief him.

"Sir, it appears a Girl Scout cookie factory in Lima, Ohio has been bombed."

"Jesus! Anyone hurt?!"

"The girls were outside gathering in preparation for the delivery of their new batch of cookies. As far as we know at this time there were some cuts from flying debris, a pregnant den mother's water broke and their pet mascot, a black and white Jack Russell named Oreo is missing."

"That's it?! I mean, what the hell was their purpose?"

"Well sir, the terrorists sent a message, but it's a little difficult to understand."

"Is it in secret code, encrypted somehow? Should we send it over to the NSA?"

"No sir, not in code, it's worse. It's written in British English."

"Damn it man, even at that we must have somebody can understand it! What's the gist of it?!"

"Near as we can figure sir it says that the new Girl Scout cookies', the flavor they call 'Rah-Rah Raisin'-"

"I've heard of those. I hear they're really good!"

"Yes sir. The flavor has been misinterpreted in some of the advertisements in newspapers and magazines as 'Allah Raisin'. And there's a stamped surface on the top of the cookie which . . . well . . ."

"For god's sake man, spit it out! What is it?!" The President demanded. In response the Secret Service Guy reached into his jacket pocket and produced his phone. He slowly flipped through the photos, stopped and showed one to the president. It was a close-up of a Rah-Rah Raisin Girl Scout cookie.

"Sir, as you can see the stamp on the face of the cookie vaguely appears to be an image of the Prophet Mohammed."

"WHAT?!"

"Yes sir and . . ." He flipped further and showed Thaddeus a second photo, this one half frosted. ". . . when they cover this half with the vanilla icing, it looks like a turban."

"SHIT!"

"On top of that sir-"

"Oh good, I was hoping there'd be more!"

"When the Girl Scouts took out the nation-wide ads to advertise the new cookie, they included the phrase, our new cookies have been **'christened'** Rah-Rah Raisin. The Muslims have no sense of humor about this sir."

"Well, notify your Ohio office they have our full support. Get them anything they need and keep me appraised."

"Yes sir. Anything else sir?"

"No, not for the moment. Thank you." The agent turned to leave." As he did Thaddeus had an afterthought.

"WAIT!" He grabbed the agent's arm.

"Yes sir?" The agent asked as Thad pulled him off to the side and spoke discreetly.

"If anybody asks about the terrorists, we know where their base of operations is."

"Who's base sir?"

"The terrorists, the Procol Harum-"

"Boko Haram sir!"

"Yeah, those guys, we know where they are."

"We do, sir?!"

"Yes. We do."

"Well, where is it sir?"

"We have traced the terrorists' hideout to the tiny island nation by the name of Nauru."

"Yes sir, Nauru. I see!" The penny dropped. "Shall I order air strikes sir?"

"No, no that won't be necessary. I'm told we have some forces in the area. Pass the word to keep the carrier fleet there and on standby."

"Very good sir."

"And keep me informed of your progress."

"Yes sir." The agent took his leave.

Pervers intended to use the Islamist's ridiculous and cowardly attack as an excuse for the Army's ridiculous and ill planned attack on Nauru. He was quick to realize of course that timing was critical.

Sometimes two wrongs can make a right! He told himself.

Mentally perusing through the predicament the government was in, President Pervers precipitated a plot through the plight. That is, the man made a plan.

Thaddeus pulled the Speaker of the House aside and asked him to call a thirty minute recess after which time he would return and bring things to a conclusion.

Reluctantly the Speaker agreed and announced there would be a thirty minute recess but asked that no one leave the chamber as upon return of President Pervers the Congress would adjourn to the Senate and the House chambers respectively and hold separate votes on the issue at hand. Namely, the impeachment of the president.

Thaddeus and his advisers, AKA the BB Stackers, had already left the chambers and retired to a meeting room at the rear of the Capitol Building.

Ж

Minutes later, they were all gathered round the small conference table in back office. Cognizant of having only thirty minutes to untangle this mess, Thaddeus, with the help of Fred, Bob and Joe got straight to it.

"Okay, the way I see it this terrorist thing has to take front seat." Thaddeus launched into the meeting.

"Yeah, why in hell would they attack a cookie factory in Ohio?" Bob inquired.

"You'd think they'd attack a more strategic target, like a military base or a munitions factory or something."

"They never attack a location where people can shoot back."

"Never mind that now! Joe, write this down. First, get a hold of the guys at the Hexagon tell them to send a message to the flagship on station off the coast of Nauru. Tell the admiral to re-order the forward invading party to tell the natives we want to negotiate, send somebody in with a white flag and tell them negotiate only with the chief."

"Got it."

"Next, get me an emergency conference call to the King of Namibia. What time is it in Namibia, anybody know?"

Fred, after going to work for Thaddeus was never without his 90 gigabyte, 1000 RAM, Xeon Phi chip handheld computer. He had the answer in 2.5 seconds.

"Five hours ahead of us, sir. Making it 17:35 in the capital."

"Nice one Fred." Thad commented.

Bob returned with a portable, palm top sat phone and, through the switch board Thaddeus rang the presidential palace in Windhoek.

"Sir, it's Ndeshipanda Geinagob on the line." The operator announced.

"Quick, somebody tell me how do you say hello in Namibian?" Pervers asked.

Fred's fingers again frantically danced across his key board and found the answer. He brandished the screen for Thaddeus to see.

"Wa lalapo Mr. President!" Pervers greeted.

"Wa lalapo to you Thaddeus!"

"You know my name?!"

"The whole world knows your name Mr. Thaddeus Enoch Pervers! The man who rose from a lowly factory position to become leader of his country! A Disney Tale Fairy story, no?"

"Something like that. Mr. Geinagob-"

"Please, we are both Heads of State! Call me Ndeshipanda Aiseku Pentubie Jojo!"

"Okay, N-des-hipanda. The reason I'm calling is I'd like to talk to you about these Boko Haram guys. Can we do that?"

"What about them?!" Anger quickly seized his voice.

"They're sort of an international embarrassment aren't they?"

"EMBARRESMENT?! They are blow up things, are setting fires, are kidnapping people and then they are like a bunch of baby chickens running over the border to Batswana!"

"Well now that's exactly what I'd like to talk to you about Ndeshipanda. Chickens."

"I like chicken!" He yelped like a child.

"Yeah, me too! How would you like to get those guys out of your hair once and for all?"

"Yes Thaddeus, we would love to buy nuclear weapons from you, but it will have to be on a lend-lease sort of arrangement, can you do that?"

"No, no, no we're not offering you nuclear weapons Mr. President."

"Ndeshipanda! Please."

"Okay, Ndeshipanda. I'm not talking about nuclear weapons. What is your relationship with the government of your bordering nation Botswana, Mr. President?"

"TERRIBLE! They are always refusing to chase the Boko's after they attack us and retreat over the border!"

Fred, standing next to him, followed the conversation with great aplomb ready with his computer typing away for any info that might be required on short notice.

"I see. Let me ask you this, how would it be if Namibia got a 175 million dollars relief package over the next seven years and all you had to do was to give the Chief of the Bokos their own plot of land to farm?"

"Farm?! What would they farm exactly? The land out there is terrible!"

"Chickens! They're going to farm chickens."

"Your terms sound generous Thaddeus but I would much prefer I-pads!"

"I-pads?"

"I-pads! Preferably Sony! The new model Xperia Z 16's with voice activated screens and touch control with voice recognition."

"How many people in your country Ndeshipanda?"

"I'm not sure Thaddeus, it keeps changing. Sometimes the people along the border lands are

Namibian sometimes they are Botswanian and other times they are Angolan."

"Why the fluctuation in loyalties Ndeshipanda?"

"Depends who is winning the football and who is shooting at them."

"Can we say a population of about three million?" Thaddeus switched the speakerphone to hold and turned to his advisors. "Can we do I-pads guys?"

Fred banged away on his key board as Joe and Bob huddled up.

"Yes. And the current population of Namibia is 3.4 million." Fred informed.

"What do you say Ndeshipanda to I-pads and some cash?"

"Thaddeus, 200 million in aid over the next five years and 1,000 Sony Xperias, and you supply the chickens." Ndeshipanda counter offered.

"How about 5,000 Xperias, 250 million in aid over the next three years and the Bokos get their chicken operation? Plus you can tell the leader of the Bokos the chicken farm comes with a minimum twenty year export contract so they can sell their chickens!"

"But who will buy so many chickens for so long time?"

"Leave it to me."

"It's a deal Mr. Thaddeus Enoch Pervers of the U.S.A.!"

"Thank you, eh. . ." He quickly turned to Fred who had already called up the word for thank you in Namibian and pointed to the screen. "Dankie, Ndeshipanda! You're a gentleman and a scholar!" They both signed off.

"Bob find VP what's-his-name and tell him to pack his bags. He's going to Namibia to broker a deal."

"Will do boss!" Bob made a note of it.

It was inundated with a deeper sense of cause and a renewed sense of energy and enthusiasm that Thaddeus began attacking this latest set of problems.

"Joe, cancel the invasion of Namibia. Get the guys in legal to draw up a treaty and send it over to the Namibian embassy then send a message to the fleet commander off the coast of Nauru. Hold off the invasion there and when they get a hold of the chief tell them to tell him that the President of the United States is willing to guarantee the people of Nauru twenty years, no a life time supply of chicken for their KFC outlet."

"Will do Boss." Joe added the instruction to his trusty pad.

"Next, get a hold of McDonalds' CEO and tell him if he can guarantee me enough Big Macs, fries and drinks—"

"What about the kids?" Bob interrupted.

"And Happy Meals for . . ." He leaned over to Fred, ". . . how many people on Nauru?"

"13,521 including sheep." Fred blurted out reading from his computer screen.

"Tell him if he can guarantee me enough Big Macs, fries and drinks for 13,521 people for ten years the White House will cut McDonalds' tax bill by 15, no 20% for the same period of time. Get back to me as soon as you get an answer."

Bob scurried from the room with his notes. Thaddeus pushed back in his chair and smiled.

"That's Nauru, Namibia and the Procol Harum all done in one the stroke of pen!" Thaddeus gleefully declared.

"That's great boss. But what about your resignation and the senate . . . Mr. President?" Fred asked.

"What are you going to do about the Senate's stalemate on the balanced budget as well?" Joe pushed.

"I'm working on that one, Joe." He answered, staring off into the distance. There was a knock at the conference room door. Joe answered it. It was a set of conjoined triplets, pages from the senate floor.

"Sir, they're ready for you." The three pages announced in unison.

"Thank you guys, we'll be right there." Joe responded.

Suddenly Thaddeus jumped out of his chair.

"THE WAR! THAT'S IT, WAR!" He shouted.

"What?" Fred and Bob simultaneously blurted.

"Joe, activate the National Guard!!"

"What?!"

"The P.C. National Guard! Call over to Arlington and activate two companies and have them report to the Capitol Building on the double!"

"What do I give them for a reason?"

"Anti-terrorist measures. Let me know when they're enroute. Bob, Fred you guys come back out with me. Fred bring your computer."

Ж

The absence of press covering the special session of congress wasn't accidental, in fact it was carefully planned.

Having attempted to establish a good working relationship with the press when first elected, and having failed, miserably, Thaddeus adopted another approach. Through covert liaisons he sent word to the half dozen most prominent journalists in P.C. and invited them to a press conference with a twist, a first-of-its-kind in recent memory. Free food, an in depth Q&A and the big draw – an open bar.

Knowing full well the seed planted with the handful of prominent reporters would grow like a congressional bribery investigation, Thaddeus rented the Grand Ballroom in the Hyatt Regency in downtown P.C. and promised a 'revealing' press brief complete with a 'surprise' scoop.

A short two hours after the hotel manager opened the ball room doors, while Thaddeus was putting out fires over at the Capitol Building, the entire Fourth Estate were getting tipsy and waiting to hear 'a big announcement' concerning the president's pending impeachment.

Meanwhile, as the 7th Fleet floated in the South Pacific, the National Guard raced towards the Capitol Building, the entire U.S. Senate sat writhing in their seats and the whole of the P.C. Press Corps were re-enacting the feast scene from *Caligula*, stuffing their faces and swilling booze over at the hotel, the majority of the nation's population was glued to the NewsCorp broadcasts emanating from their vapor screen television sets. The entire nation was now following the most exciting thing to happen in American politics since John Lincoln McKinley-Garfield had been assassinated by a radical environmentalist for not approving the *Cat & Dog Excrement Recycling Bill*.

Wendy Chimes here with Brady Brinkwater coming to you live from our WKRB studios here in Oshkosh. It would appear that President Pervers, the man that has been branded as unhinged, unbalanced, unstable and bat-shit crazy by the majority of the info-mercial media, even in the face of the worst crises to hit the congress in –"

"Well, not exactly the worst, Wendy. If you'll recall back in 19-" Her male co-anchor interrupted.

"OKAY, maybe the second worst." Wendy conceded.

"Well, let's not forget the time -" He persisted.

"One of the worst!"

"I think you're also forgetting the Forty-"

"BRADY, SHUT THE FUCK UP!"

Ж

"Ladies and Gentlemen," Pervers, again back at the podium, opened his third attempt at his speech to the Congressional Chambers. "Regarding the situation in Nauru which, it saddens me to tell you, is far from stable. As you well know the War Resolutions Act requires me to inform you within forty-eight hours of committing troops to a foreign situation. I am now officially informing you, that in view of the fact that the enemy have attacked several of our troops I am declaring that a state of war now exists between our two countries." Audible mumbling crept across crowd.

Indicative of the general atmosphere, one senator in the back whispered to another and quipped. "Probably some kind of ploy!"

Thaddeus heard but ignored the challenge.

"You are well aware that we now have a carrier group from the Seventh Fleet standing by off the coast of the nation of Nauru. As you also know, by law I have sixty days to secure a declaration of war from you the Congress, or for you to order me to bring the troops home in which case I have thirty days to withdraw them."

"What about your resignation sir?! You've admitted guilt now let's-" It was the disgruntled senator from Alabama who sprang to his feet and sounded off but was promptly cut short by Pervers.

"Thank you for calling attention to that fact Congressman Stump however, pending the possibility of an increase in hostilities, that matter is temporarily on hold." Thaddeus declared, much to the delight of the BB Stackers seated off to his left.

The noise level in the chamber immediately peaked to a crescendo as uncontrolled chatter broke out. One voice rose above the rest and yelled.

"WELL MR. PRESIDENT, YOU CAN BET YOUR BOTTOM DOLLAR BOY WE GONNA VOTE TO BRING THEM TROOPS HOME, AND RIGHT NOW!" Shouted the senator from Colorado.

"That is the legal right of this body senator. However, following your demands that I withdraw the troops, I still have 30 days to complete that withdrawal so all-in-all that gives me 90 days!"

During the ensuing exchange the Speaker of the House stood, leaned in, caught Thaddeus' attention and whispered to him. "Just how many troops did you land on that island, Mr. President?" Thaddeus winked back.

"All together? None. Yet." He whispered. The Speaker smiled and sat back down.

"WHAT EXACTLY DO YOU WANT FROM US?!" Another senator yelled as the din worsened.

Pervers stood tall, collected himself, placed both hands on the podium and slowly perused the chaos that had gripped the Congressional chambers.

The entire collection of senators and representatives was on its feet yelling and screaming at each other, each attempting to out shout the other, fists waving only moments from an all-out Donnybrook.

Thaddeus looked over at Fred, pointed to his watch and shrugged. Fred, sitting off to the side glanced down at his screen, smiled and signalled Thaddeus.

"They're here!" He mouthed over to Pervers who shot Fred a thumbs up.

It was at that moment that Thaddeus Enoch Pervers carpied the diem he had been preparing for.

He nodded back to the Speaker who, reached over, turned his microphone up to '10' and like Thor about to strike a foe with mighty Mjolnir, manned his all-powerful gavel, slowly stood and attacked his gavel block several times in rapid succession.

"GENTLEMEN! GENTLEMEN!! WE WILL HAVE ORDER IN THE CHAMBERS OR I WILL

ORDER THE SERGEANT-AT-ARMS TO CLEAR THE ROOM AND DECLARE A DEFAULT OF SESSION!"

As if he cast a magic spell on the room the unruly reps stopped, settled down and one by one took their seats.

"What the hell did you say?!" Thaddeus whispered.

"If a default is declared due to bad behavior in the chambers they all get fined $50,000!"

"Nice one! Well done Mr. Speaker!"

The chambers now back in order Thaddeus resumed.

"Before we get to the matter of my resignation we will take up a seperate matter. Due to your childish, petty, self-centered and inconsiderate budget dispute, which got us all in this mess in the first place and which has halted the effective operation of this government, we are all going to stay here until you have reached a compromise! And to make sure it is a fair and equitable compromise, which benefits the people of this country, I am extending my power of veto! I am declaring an invocation of Contingency 12!"

Loud murmurs now swept the room.

"What the hell is Contingency 12?"

"Contingency what?"

The Speaker smiled a knowing smile as he overheard several senators in the front row query.

"ARE YOU THREATENING US WITH SOME SORT OF SEQUESTER, SIR?!"

"No I think sequester isn't the right word here, senator." Thaddeus replied.

"Then what word would you use, MISTA PRESIDENT?!"

"I'm giving the Congress a time out!"

"YOU CAN'T DO THAT! IT'S ILLEGAL!"

"Actually it is quite legal, under Contingency 12!" The Speaker responded from behind The President.

"WHAT THE HELL IS CONTINGENCY 12?!"

Contingency 12 was a little known emergency contingency which gave and the president extra executive powers in times of national crisis. Aside from complete command of all the armed forces and military operations without running it through Congress first, these powers also restricted Congressional review and veto for the first ninety days of activation of said forces. The president alone had the power to invoke the law. However, there was a limitation. Contingency 12 only granted these powers for 90 days. Thaddeus' presidential term was to end in two months. It did however temporarily suspend habeas corpus and extend presidential authority to send troops where ever he pleased.

"Well you can always hire a lawyer and take it to the Supreme Court, Senator. Oh, wait a minute! Most of you guys are lawyers! So you should be able to prepare a pretty good case! That is if you all work together. Of course, let's don't forget, if you want to take me to court these things take up to a year or more to respond, at which time I'll be out of office, there-by passing the headache onto the next guy." Silence slowly crept through the room. "Is this a great system or what?" Thaddeus jibbed.

The rumblings, protest and cursing again rose to the level of Times Square at rush hour.

Ж

As the leaders of the Free World's formerly most powerful country sat and argued in the royal chambers, people along Independence Avenue to the south of the Capitol stopped and stared.

A mile long convoy of troop trucks approached and turned onto 1st Street. The officer in the Humvee at the head of the speeding column lead the troop trucks around the ovoid road until they'd gone full circle and came back around to Southwest Drive where they merged with more deuce and a half's, jeeps and caissons still pouring into the area. The immaculately clean Humvee adorned with a red flag sporting two white stars, shut down its engine, two rifle wielding soldiers scampered up alongside and the passenger door slowly opened.

With the Capitol completely surrounded Major General Quagmire's spit shined, brown leather riding boot, stepped majestically from his vehicle, and make no mistake about it. It was HIS immaculately clean, O.D. green Humvee adorned with a red flag sporting two white stars in the same manner those were HIS deuce and half's, HIS caissons and HIS men.

He had been given this mission directly from the Commander-in-Chief and would die with flag-in-hand if it came to that. No one was going in or out of that Capitol Building without expressed permission, checked and double checked, from the President himself. Not man, woman, child or stray garden cat. Not without a verified hall pass from the man himself.

Before his left foot hit the ground the General was giving orders to evacuate all civilians from the visitor's area, to halt the afternoon tours of the landmark building and to seal off the perimeter. Next he directed that civilians were to be kept back at least three hundred feet and that a command area should be established behind the Capitol in the Visitors' Center Park.

Soldiers scurried about, as officers drank coffee, NCO's supervised and privates did all the work.

Twenty-two minutes later nothing short of a low crawling gnat was going to penetrate the perimeter of the Capitol Building grounds and just as had been the case for so many years, nothing was coming out of the congressional chambers either.

The P.C. P.D., because they were told it was an emergency, arrived about forty-five minutes later and were informed it was a Federal matter and the boys in blue were relegated to forming a cordon outside the Capitol circle to keep the civilians at a safe distance should the shooting start.

As soon as Quagmire had received reports from his company commanders that all was secure, he was flanked by the customary armed guard, and it was with purpose and dignity that he made his way up the Capitol steps towards the entrance.

With Thaddeus still at the podium the back doors burst open and the general marched up the aisle, stood before the podium and saluted President Pervers.

"Sir, Major General Quagmire, Commanding Officer P.C. National Guard reporting as ordered sir!" His salute to the president was so sharp that the breeze it generated caused several sheets of paper to gently float from a nearby desk and onto the floor. "Sir, I wish to report that Companies Alpha and Bravo are in position and your perimeter is secure, as ordered Mr. President!"

"Thank you general." Thaddeus returned the salute while a page hastened to gather up the errant papers. "Maintain all posts until further notice, and no one is allowed in or out of the building without my expressed permission. Is that clear?"

"Yes Mr. President."

"Thank you general, you're dismissed." It was to dead silence that the general marched back out of the chambers and vanished into the corridor.

The Senator from Texas was the first to spring to his feet. "Why is the National Guard reporting to you in the middle of a session?" He demanded and stamped one of his $1,850 hand-awled, snake skin cowboy boots on the floor.

"I have ordered the Capitol Building surrounded and placed under 24 hour guard until further notice. We have reports that there may be other pending terrorist attacks.

Possibly even in the greater P.C. area. Simply a precaution, senator."

"Son do realize how many laws you've broken here today?"

"Yes senator. Under Contingency 12, exactly none."

"You can't just take the U.S. Senate hostage and expect to get away with it! Especially for the purposes of blackmail and extortion!"

"Oh, it's not for blackmail and extortion! It's for your own protection. This is merely a precaution. We can't have the most important government body in the country at risk in these troubled times."

"Bullshit son! Now I'm from Dallas and if there's two things we know about in Dallas it's guns, steers and bullshit!"

"But as long as we're all here –" Thaddeus began.

"SO IT IS A HOSTAGE SIT-CHI-ATION!" Another senator demanded.

"Okay, let's call it a hostage situation. In that case every hostage situation, if it is truly a hostage situation, has demands. Ergo I have come prepared to negotiate!" Thaddeus confidently recited into the microphone as he produced a folded sheet of paper from his breast pocket. The bickering and arguing across the floor gradually died down.

"My Special Assistant will now read the terms I have drafted." Joe stepped up to the mic, took the single sheet of loose leaf paper and cleared his throat and perused the room.

"Hey guys. Thrill to be here today. Like to give a quick shout out to the guys back at the bowling alley! Brubaker! Yo guys!"

Thaddeus reached over and smacked Joe on the shoulder.

"Oh sorry." Joe assumed his best authoritative voice. "I Thaddeus Enoch Pervers, duly elected President of the United States, do herby propose to you, the Congress, the following items;

Item #1- A binding, balanced budget voted upon and approved before Halloween of each year that is, 60 days prior to the start of the New Year.

Item #2 - A third party, voted in by the people, which by law is protected from being frozen out of the electoral process and is to be included in all advertising and public debates afforded the other two parties. Additionally the third party, which shall be duly named, will have equal funding to come from equal contributions of the other two parties and tax dollars until it can raise its own funds, and voluntary contributions.

Item #3 - There are to be mandatory caps on campaign fund raising, presidential and senatorial, spending across the board so as to insure equity of public profile of each of the parties. The aim of which is to afford the American public a fair opportunity to evaluate all candidates. The cap shall be five million dollars and shall be eligible for review every four years and in accordance with inflation, be considered for a limit raise every two years. As such the amount of the raise, which must be proposed and voted on by both parties, shall not exceed 1/2 % above that year's inflation. Said raise must be approved by a two thirds majority of the senate. That is all."

Joe stepped down and it was among a dumbfound crowd that Thaddeus took the floor.

"Now, to make it perfectly clear and to avoid any lawyerly tactics such as the manipulation of semantics, I'll spell it for you. Under the Pervers' system there shall be a point system for all three parties. Any screw-ups or scandals such as sex, drugs or vote rigging gets you and your party a yellow flag and moves that party back to the line of scrimmage. That is your campaign spending limit is lowered and you get a three point fine. If a member of your party is caught embezzling funds this earns a free kick for the other two parties, that is they get ½% raise in campaign funding. False statements to the press earns your party a five yard penalty and a loss of down. At the end of the campaign season, the day before people go to the poles, the penalties are assed and assigned. Each penalty point will be worth 10,000 points."

"And just how is this ree-dick-u-lous system o' yours supposed to get us positive points?" The senator from New York challenged.

"Very good question Senator Firefly! By constructing, voting for and passing a bill which contains a major good thing for the American people your party scores a touchdown, that is 6 points. For example, any politician who constructs a bill which raises employment, improves housing or transportation or educational opportunities."

"Sounds like a load'a hogwash to me Pervers!"

"Careful Jubile! I'm liable to find your li'l ol' ass in contempt!" Thaddeus threatened.

"Contempt o' what?! This ain't no damn court room!"

"That's right, but it is the U.S. Senate, and this is an official hearing called by you lot. That means ANY misbehavior in the course of this session is punishable by law."

"I object!" The senator from Arkansas called out.

In response Thaddeus slammed the Speaker's gavel twice on the block. "Objection over ruled senator." Billy Bob Joe Cleatus Jackson plopped back down in his seat.

Thaddeus slowly perused the befuddled mess the chambers had become and smiled.

"Copies of my demands are being passed out by the pages. Any you boys got any plans for the holidays? I got 89 days left. I'll be in the Presidential study. Send word when you get your heads out of your collective asses!"

As he waltzed off stage Thaddeus looked over in the

wings and spied Fred in one wing and Bob in the other.

A junior senator in the very back row defiantly waltzed over to a rear door and attempted to leave the chambers. He was greeted with a wave from a heavily armed private smiling back at him. The senator quickly slammed the door shut and returned to his seat.

Ж

At that moment the one hundred strong press corps, those that were still nearly sober, had been gathered standing in the Grand Ballroom of the Hyatt Regency Hotel for the better part of three hours and were starting to wonder when this 'surprise speech' was going to take place.

An off duty CIA agent wandered in from the lobby and stepped up to the bar.

"What can I get for you sir?"

"Lemme have a martini, extra dry, stirred not shaken." The agent ordered and as the bartender was preparing his drink he glanced over to the end of the bar where he spied a young reporter on his phone apparently talking with a loved one.

"I'm certain! There's a revolution or something going on as we speak!" He babbled into his wrist phone. The voice on the other end was indiscernible.

"I dunno! Must be one'a those coup da villes or something!" He declared.

The voice on the other end of the line posed a question and the reporter repeated his message.

"Yeah man! Words all over the street! A bunch of army guys got the Capitol Building surrounded and they got the President and the whole Congress locked inside!"

The agent dashed down the bar to the reporter and grabbed him by the elbow.

"I'm with the government. Are you serious about the Capitol being surrounded?!"

"Hell yeah! Seen it with my own eyes!"

The secret agent, unaware there were ninety-nine other reporters in the room, became deadly serious and made direct eye contact with the reporter.

"Whatever you do, **do not** run that story until you get clearance, you understand?!"

"Whatever you say Mac! You're from the government." The reporter shrugged.

The bartender returned with the agent's martini and was greeted by an empty bar stool as the door back out to the lobby swung closed.

The dumbfounded reporter quickly hit speed dial on his wrist phone and was greeted with his editor's voice.

"Chet? Pete. Have I got a scoop for you!"

Now with the scoop of the century Peter P. Peabody, former junior reporter, confidently informed his editor that the United States government had been taken over by foreign agents.

He was asked by the editor of he could have a twelve hundred word story done up in the next half hour.

Which he did for a negotiated price of course.

A BATTLE OF WILLS

CHAPTER TWENTY-FOUR

𝕂

As news of the hostage situation in the capitol first leaked out the general public were horrified, but as underground news sources gradually released the facts of the situation, something the infomercial stations had forgotten how to do, the fact that the Congress were being forced to work together for the good of the nation for the first time in more than a century, the American population rallied.

That morning in the WNPC T.V. Studios in Washedupton P.C.:

"Good morning Mr. and Mrs. America Cheryl Swallows here with my co-host Dick Hard who..."

She looked over at an empty seat. *"Appears to have gone to the little boys' room."* She carried on. *"We're coming to you live from our WNPC studio just blocks away from the Capitol Building right where this adventure started not so long ago here in beautiful downtown Washedupton.*

Our lead story The Senate Held Hostage; Day Two, continues. We have a new twist to report, President Pervers, has apparently made demands of the congress explaining in a telephone interview late last night that he promised the people of America he would break the deadlocks which have plagued the Senate and the House for so long and, as in his own words, '... make them do the job they were hired for.'

We go now live down to the streets of the city where our on the spot reporter Dixie Enormous is gauging public reaction to this unprecedented development."

"Thank you Cheryl. We've seen Presidents declare war on other countries without informing the Congress, we've seen them sell cocaine from Afghanistan and Iran to finance war in Central America and we've even seen them get a B.J. in the Lincoln bedroom. Allegedly. But we've never had a Commander-in-Chief take a congressional body hostage!"

"Much less the entire Congress Dixie!" Cheryl added.

"Exactly Cheryl, and with diplomats and politicians all over the world glued to events here in Washedupton, here's the ringer! At the onset of events here nearly forty-eight hours ago, Infotainment networks and affiliates across the country conducted poll after poll and have seen the American people condemn President Pervers' hijacking of the government with comparisons to third world nations, communist dominated countries and dictatorships in the East with some even going so far as to draw comparisons to principles and headmasters of Catholic schools.

Now however, it seems that since our last street poll only a few hours ago, public opinion regarding President Pervers has shifted dramatically. Shock and anger, which dissipated to indifference, has now given way to quite a different general consensus, a 180 degree turnaround from the onset of this unprecedented political development! People across the country are rallying to the cause. 'Pervers' Purpose', 'Thaddeus The Thrasher' and 'The Boss' are just a few of the memes, Tee shirts and bumper stickers which have appeared across the nation in the last twenty-four hours and which are declaring President Pervers a national hero!"

"We've even gotten word here in the studio that there is a movement afoot to erect a monument to him! To what do we attribute this seismic shift Dixie?" Cheryl interrupted.

"Well Cheryl, it appears, in addition to fulfilling a major campaign promise, it also seems to be the news that the President has apparently made **demands** of the **Congress** and appears to be holding their feet to the fire to do their job, something no Commander since FDR has ever done. Additionally we're getting independent reports that he has scored a triple home run as he reached an agreement with the president of Namibia over that country's domestic unrest and has located the terrorists' hideout, terrorists who, only hours ago, attacked the Girl Scouts in Ohio!"

"Can you get us any further insight into this shift in public opinion in so short a time?" Swallows gulped.

"Let's get some opinions of what the American public thinks. I'll just ask this young gentleman what he thinks."

At the street corner Dixie headed off a youth draped in a yellow Tee shirt adorned with a marijuana leaf across the front. She thrust her mini-mike at him.

"Sir, Dixie Enormous WNPC News. Do you mind if I ask you a question?"

"Ahh, you just did, man."

"I mean another question." He spotted her camera.

"WOW! Am I on TV man!" The bleary-eyed thirty-something responded.

"Yes. What is your opinion of President Pervers' recent actions?"

"President of what?"

"President of the United States, sir."

"Oh, sorry man. I don't know him. Besides, I have an alibi."

"Alibi for what?"

"For last night . . . the whole week man. Yeah, that's it, the whole week." He quickly drifted down the street away from the strange lady with the mike in her hand.

"Let's try someone who is more down here at our own altitude." She approached a heavy set middle-aged woman with a crew cut wearing sensible shoes. "Ma'am, Dixie Enormous WNPC News. Do you mind if I ask you a question?"

"Yeah, sure. What is it Sweety?"

"What is your opinion of President Pervers' recent actions?" She asked again. The big woman immediately assumed an overt expression of anger and crossed her arms.

"He's a man, I don't like men."

"Why is that ma'am?"

"Patriarchy, chauvinism, male dominance!" She vehemently spouted. "Besides, all men generalize about women!"

"Ahh, ma'am?" Dixie sought to regain control of the interview. "The question?"

"Every problem in history is directly attributable to a male dominated society, that's all I'm saying!"

"But in his time in the White House President Pervers has advanced the cause of gender equality both in signing bills and helping to originate laws aimed at helping women and families."

"He has?"

"Yes! His actions are very well documented." Dixie informed her.

"Oh." The woman was stymied. But only briefly. "That's why we have to break through the glass ceiling-"

"Ah ma'am, all jobs are required by law to provide the same pay and benefits to men and women for the same job providing they have the same skill level. The laws have been in place for more than half a century. There is no more Glass Ceiling" Dixie shrugged to the camera.

"Well then, we need to break through the glass walls and the glass floor for more support! Which is why we need more women's marches, more women in the work place and more women in women's roles!"

"Thank you ma'am." Dixie attempted to sign off.

"And don't forget - all men are pigs! Women are equal to men!"

With her cameraman Dixie slowly but steadily moved away from the frantic woman who called after her as she put more distance between them.

"Name's Francis but you can call me Frank, Frank Trebinsky. You ever get lonely honey I'm on Facebook."

"Thank you, Frank." Dixie quickly crossed the street and found another young man, this one dressed completely in black.

"Sir, Dixie Enormous WNPC News. Do you mind if I ask you a question?"

"No, go fer it."

"What's your opinion of President Pervers recent actions to hold the Congress hostage?"

"I'm glad you axed me that! I'm gonna tell you what, BLAM lives matter! America's is for the white privileged elite! Das why a brother cain't get no head! I mean get ahead! Yeah das it, get ahead! Das why the brother Martin Lother what's-his-name died fo' ow sins! What was the question?"

"The latest president, President Pervers, and his most recent actions with the congress?"

"We dun changed presidents again? DAMN! Seem like every four years somebody new in that White House!"

"Thank you for your feedback sir." Dixie stepped off to the side to give her sign off. "There you have it Cheryl, straight from the American public, in their own words. This is Dixie Enormous signing off for now."

"We're back now with my co-host reporting on the senate hostage situation. What could they be thinking locked in the chambers for nearly two days, Dick?"

"'I hope there's enough toilet paper!' That's what I'd be thinking anyway!"

"A pleasure as always Dick."

Ж

Meanwhile flowers, cards and offers of sexual favors poured in to the White House while in San Francisco the gays did what they do best, they launched a parade.

Geriatric communities all over Florida hung out clean pairs of Spanks in the trees surrounding their respective community centers as a show of support for the president and in Boston residents stopped rioting when the bars, which had been closed for the duration of the crisis, were reopened.

Texans of course dismissed all the reports of the government incident as a communist plot spawned by liberals. In all likelihood perpetrated by the same people who faked the moon landing, covered up the truth about the 9/11 WTC attacks and the JFK assassination while they continued to seek further scientific evidence the world was flat. But they got behind the president.

In essence, Pervers' Purpose pulled in the people from across the country and helped raise him to a new level of herodom.

Ж

That evening, as the sun began to set over Washedupton and tempers rose further inside the Congressional chambers, which began to smell like a football locker room, the crisis for the senators deepened.

Locked in fierce debate for the last day and a half and unable to leave the building Thaddeus, tucked away in his private office, realized that something had to be done to ease the tension.

Being informed the Capitol cafeteria had run out of food he instructed Joe to make a few phone calls and a half hour later a side door was unchained to admit a small army of McDonalds, KFC and Taco Bell delivery boys who were admitted by six heavily armed Army MP's to deliver food to the senators.

Thirty minutes later, after they attacked the food causing the delivery boys to run for the safety of the exit, the senate chambers looked like a junior high school cafeteria following lunch hour. Hamburger, taco and chicken wrappings littered the senate floor and senators lay burping and farting across senate floor chairs and desks.

As the politicians gobbled down their fast food the companies of soldiers posted outside calmly filed through the big mess tent on the Capitol lawn in an orderly fashion, listening to soothing, easy listening music as they watched cordon bleu and chicken cacciatore be heaped onto their plates, before they sat down to eat in shifts and leisurely enjoyed their meal.

Back in the senate the representative from Georgia, in between bites of a chicken leg, challenged Thaddeus.

"You think this is an appropriate way to spend the taxpayers' money Mr. President! On fast food?" A strand of chicken dangling from the corner of his mouth.

"Oh, not to worry senator, no taxpayer's money being spent here. This meal is on me!" He announced patting the older man on the shoulder. Then turned back up to the Speaker of the House and smiled. "I have connections."

"Who eats this shit?!" An ancient senator off to the side complained as he unwrapped his leather-like Big Mack and greasy fries.

"Three quarters of America, that's who! And largely because they don't make a tenth of what you do!" Fred scolded from up on the dias.

As the arguments across the floor slowly resumed a National Guard messenger poked his head in a side door, flagged down a page and passed a written message.

"That's for the Majority Whip." He informed.

The page in turn gave it to a junior senator who passed it on.

A minute later another senator approached a gaggle in the corner and passed the Majority Whip the folded over paper. The message was from the assistant party leader who was not a senator and so was at home watching reports on the news as the political events unfolded and so was compelled to quickly scribble out the note and get it over to the Capitol.

The Whip's face turned ashen as he read what was written.

"Just look at these poll numbers!" He brandished the paper to the other congressmen gathered around him. "We go against this level of popularity, these sorts of poll numbers and there ain't no chance in hell of getting' re-elected!"

"Lemme see that!" Another demanded a she grabbed the note then perused the message. "JESUS! You're right! They love him! They think he's the greatest thing since double absorbent Kotex!"

"The kind with the butterfly wings on the side!" Another added. All the men stared at him.

"We got'a do something!" The Whip declared.

"What'a you propose senator?"

"I propose we do something to get our asses outta here and home to our families, that's what I propose!"

"Like what?"

"Like sign Pervers damn agreement paper!"

"We can't just give in like that!"

"Why don't we just agree to agree and when he lets us go we get the P.C.P.D. to arrest his ass, re-appoint V.P. what's-his-name and renege on the damn bill!?"

"Because according to my sources ever since he give them that raise last year he's also got the P.C.P.D. on his side and once we agree to sign the bill he's probably gonna make us sign it while we're here and then do a news release to the whole world which means we'll look like a bunch of liars if we go back on our word!"

"Liars?! So what?!"

"We're usually so skilled at it that we can cover our tracks so they can't catch us! We try to reverse a bill after we sign the damn thing in front of the T.V. cameras and people'll have us dead to rights!"

"I can't eat another god damn hamburger!" One of the senatorial scrum declared just before he fell back into his seat.

"I think I got the shits from that fried chicken!" Another pointed out holding up a chicken bone.

"I say we take a vote. All in favor of taking a vote to take a vote on signing signify by sayin' 'aye'" The Majority Whip proposed.

Save for the Representative from New Hampshire, it was unanimous.

"The ayes have it. We vote!"

When presented to his side of the aisle, the vote to sign the president's three point, bipartisan agreement bill yielded the same results as the vote to take a vote and so the Majority Whip approached the other side of the aisle where a dozen factions spread around the chambers to inform them of his party's decision.

More votes were taken to vote on the bill and for the second time since WWII the Senate agreed to agree on something and for that brief twenty-seven and a half minutes it took to vote on what came to be known as the T-Bill, the perpetually bipartisan Congress did the job the people elected them to do.

The senatutes capitulated via the senior senator, Anadieus Dogooder, a GOP'er from Mississippi who passed the word to the Speaker of the House who then ordered the official vote put into the record.

Minutes later Fred burst through office door where Thaddeus sat, feet up on the Louis the XIV gilded table reading a comic book and drinking a Coors long neck

"THEY VOTED TO GO FOR IT!" He yelled. "YOU DID IT THAD!"

Pervers feet fell to the floor and he smiled up at Fred. "**We** did it, Fred 'ol boy! **We** did it!"

AD STATUS QUO ANTE

CHAPTER TWENTY-FIVE

Ж

The gloomy grey curtain which had previously hung over the city seemed to be slowly lifting to reveal a bright blue sky. A storm, which threatened to attack during the hostage situation bypassed the area and seemed to transition to clear weather after the law was settled and the balanced budget approved.

By the next morning the crowds on Independence Avenue disbursed and the news vans drove away while the National Guard packed up and went home to once again be consigned to eating fast food.

After a brief respite, only days later, the Senate as well as the House resumed.

"Mr. Speaker!" It was the representative from Texas, Jubile T. Firefly. "I move that the House moves to move towards impeachment hearings. "Immediately if not sooner." A dead quiet swept the room.

"Motion has been made to move on the earlier motion." The Speaker put to the floor. "Is there a second?"

After a long silence a voice rang out.

"I second!" Came a shout form the other side of the house.

Not only was there a second, but a third, fourth and fifty-sixth. Though not unanimous, the chamber was not far from it.

In two days Thaddeus Pervers was to be impeached.

Ж

The next fforty-eight hours passed without incident,

save for the press which reaped generous profits from the headlines.

On his last night in office, with Prudence gone and Taranjello away at school, Thaddeus sat alone in the main room of the Presidential suite.

The last week in the White House had taken its toll on Thaddeus as did the days of one of the most traumatic political crises in recent memory. To that end Pervers had taken the last two days off, so it was with a surge of enthusiasm that he granted the side gate security guards permission to admit his best friends when they showed up unannounced with a case of Iron City beer and two large bags of burritos.

An hour later Thaddeus, along with the BB Stackers, Joe, Bob and Fred were gathered in the main room and sat around drinking Iron City longnecks chased with Jack Daniels and congratulating themselves on their victory.

"You think I look twenty years older don't you?" Thaddeus asked Joe.

"No, not really. I was gonna say forty!"

"Fuck you!"

"You doin' okay?" Fred asked.

"Yeah. And . . . I really need to thank you guys for getting behind me."

"When I saw that old fart from Mississippi shuffling down the aisle with that piece of paper in his hand I knew it was all over and it was all worth it!" Fred bragged. They all laughed and agreed.

"You know what you call a guy that says he's gonna do something then doesn't follow through?" Thaddeus challenged staring at the floor. "A bullshitter! I made the people a promise and god damn it I kept it!"

"Yes you did Boss, yes you did!" Joe nodded.

"You know what you're gonna say to those bastards out there Thad?"

"Yeah, pretty much. I was up most of the night

throwing some things together then had one of the speech guys look it over real quick this morning."

"Nice one."

"Hey, after I take care of this bit of business, what say we go get in a coupl'a games on the lanes and down a few more beers?" Thaddeus proposed.

Joe, Fred and Bob traded looks, smiled and nodded.

"Any decent lanes in this town?"

"There's a place called Pinstripes over on Wisconsin Avenue." Soon-to-be-ex-President Pervers answered.

Ж

It was once again a full house that morning when Thaddeus stepped to the podium in front of the Speaker's dais and launched right into what he had been mulling over in his mind for the last week and a half.

Dead silence dominated the chamber.

"To the people of the United States, to the members of this Congress and to all three members of the Supreme Court, I stand before you this morning to tender my resignation as President of our country." His mood sombre and respectful Thaddeus read from no notes and, in full expectation of what was going to be said, there was no reaction by the floor.

"In his farewell address to the people in September of 1796, George Washington warned us: 'Political parties may answer popular ends however, they are likely in the course of time, to become potent engines by which cunning, ambitious and unprincipled men will be enabled to subvert the power of the people and to usurp for themselves the reins of government.'

I was hired by the people to do a job, a temporary job, but a job none-the-less. I found out, as we all know, that in real life doing the right thing isn't always easy however, it's the weak who rely on this as an excuse for not doing it.

I was also quick to learn that in this town doing what's popular nearly always trumps what's right and that's not why I, we were hired."

He nodded out to the floor. "Hired to some of the most prestigious and privileged positions in the country. Hell, in the world!" There was a mild shifting of seats.

"Something I did learn a bit more slowly was you can't fix stupid! This remark is not meant for the stupid in power. Stupid people are in reality too stupid to do any real damage even when in power. It's the clever people who have the ability to cause the most damage. The schemers, the greedy, ambitious plotters who have no limits at which they'll stop taking, taking and taking while giving little or nothing in return.

Ultimately it's not the crooked politicians, who will change for it is the core of their nature to be devious.

Not the collection of dishonest, win-at-any-cost lawyers or few trigger happy police who are to blame for the hole America has dug herself into." He turned and addressed the next part of his remarks to the main camera pointed down the center aisle.

"In the end it comes down to you! The people. The people who have decided that they are too divided into independent groups by race, color, sexual orientation, creed, religion or superficial political affiliation. It is things like gender politics or whether you wear a red, blue or rainbow tie that determines you are somehow entitled to special privileges and considerations over and above the rest simply because you see yourself as 'different' and therefore entitled. You are not different. You are not entitled. You are American.

Lulled into the blacks, the gays, the Hispanics, the democrats, the republicans, the industrialists who have never learned the meaning of the phrase, 'enough money' and the factory workers organized by crooked unions who have destroyed our once great industrial might and allowed other more united nations to wrest economic control from areas upon which the founders built this great and unique nation.

The population of this country who have complacently slept while their country, our country has disintegrated into the absurd conviction, regarding collapse, that it could never happen here."

A chain of coughs rippled across the floor and Thaddeus perused the room, undisturbed by the continued silence of the Senate chambers but all the while at a loss as to how his words were being received.

"Let us not forget that worst of all chasms which we have been cursed by. The most deadly, diverse plague of plaques propagated by ambitious politicians aided by the Yellow Journalism of a now devoid of objectivity and nearly bereft of honesty corporate press; the war between women and men. All in the name of 'equality'. A term which continually escapes definition."

"Ultimately the people are to blame. Because they must do something they have never done before. Never since 1776! And that is unite against the forces that have made a very lucrative livelihood of dividing us for more than a century. The political forces that have no more good of the people in mind than do the cancerous cells that infect the unfortunate patients of our cancer wards in our woefully and inexcusably inadequate and unnecessarily expensive hospital systems. Or our sagging schools and marginally productive factories!"

Two or three senators upped and left the chambers. Thaddeus persevered.

"I leave you with another appropriate quote. The great historian Livy in 37 B.C. wrote: 'Rome is at the dark dawning of an age in which we can neither endure our vices or face the remedies needed to cure them! I hope that history may be a cure for a sick mind at least it can remind us of what we once were and show us the depths to which we are now sinking.'"

The awkward silence which trailed him as he

stepped from the podium and headed for the wing was so disarming that Pervers nearly stumbled halfway through his exit.

However, by the time he reached the wing one senator,
J.J. Hurley, stood and clapped exaggeratedly loud, which prompted another near him to slowly rise and follow suit.

In less than a minute the catharsis of the room compelled the remainder of the audience to rise and render such loud applause that several security guards abandoned their posts out in the corridor and dash in through the chamber doors to investigate the commotion.

Outside the Capitol Building, as the ovation, accompanied by hooting and hollering, as the roar of the crowd built to fever pitch, dozens of pigeons darted from the ornate rotunda to scatter in all directions.

Thaddeus froze behind the door of the wing and a tear came to his eye.

Ж

Meanwhile, in an abandoned munitions factory warehouse in Okefenokee, Florida, a one Mohammad Abdul Kahlid Assad was occupied to the point of exhaustion alternately kicking then hammering away at a large, homemade bomb in a pointless attempt to start the timer on the detonator.

"Cheryl Swallows once again coming to you from the WBNC news desk, this just in. Police in Florida believe they are closing in on a terrorist suspect just outside of the town."

Just then a producer scurried into frame and over to the desk to hand Cheryl a report.

"Oh! This update has just been handed to me. Apparently there's been a tremendous explosion in a warehouse in the same town.

Authorities attribute it to a gas explosion caused by some old gas pipes. The warehouse was abandoned so no injuries were reported.
Police have called off the search for the terrorist."

THE COMFORT OF THE STATUS QUO

CHAPTER TWENTY-SIX

Ж

"Good morning and welcome to the Lush Limburger Show! Welcome listeners, haters, lovers and all you out there in . . ."

Pointless political punditry permeated the population via discussions broadcast by Lush Limburger on the NewsCorp stations, the WNPC team and all of the underground info-stations each morning and were followed by most of the public including the Blinders, Dweeble Heads and even the anti-Evolutionists led by the Supremists with no lack of muddled, diverse but mostly pointless opinion from many stars of the silver screen such as Sterile Meep, Bet Afflicted and Holy Cypress.

In the Congress, after Vice President what's-his-name was sworn in, attitude of the congressional members was epitomized by snatches of conversation overheard in the halls of the Capitol Building.

"Finally somebody who's not crazy!" One remarked to another of the new leadership.

"A fucking professional who can do what a fucking politician is supposed to do to this country now that it's on its knees!"

"Yeah, not just another come-from-behind guy doing what he wants while the people just lay there!"

Ж

Thaddeus Pervers had risen to power with the proper financial backing and through the twin forces of accident and chance. He made everything right, at least for a brief period and had been impeached from office two days after what became known as the Great Congressional Hostage episode.

Vice President what's–his-name assumed command for the remainder of Perver's term and the two major parties reassumed control of the Congress.

But, as is an old American tradition, the new president in his first act of office, issued a statement of exoneration to his predecessor, no doubt a prophylactic measure to institute precedent should he ever find himself in the same situation.

Following a plea bargain arrangement where-by Thaddeus and the BB Stackers would agree to an electro-chemical mind sweep to purge their memories of all the politically unsavory events of the past few months, they were able to return to Brubaker Industries and resume their old jobs at the factory recycling ball bearings that would never get used.

However, as could have been predicted, complacency won in the end and so everything went right back to exactly to the way it was before the short but spectacular administration of Thaddeus Enoch Pervers.

That November Ronald Lump the Fifth raised enough money to buy the Presidency of the United States and get appointed, eh . . . re-elected.

At the first day of the first congressional session a bill was introduced jointly by both party whips proposing the dissolution of the FUBAR Party predicated on the extra expense it cost the taxpayer. Both the Democrats and Republicans approved the bill by unanimous consent.

President Lump didn't veto it.

Just like his efforts in North and South Vrindaban Thaddeus Pervers' all-out efforts did little more than cost him his presidency. But it did sell a few news stories.

Now, months later, traveling from the White House, cruising overhead in one of the new multi-billion dollar hovercrafts, which reduced the trans-continental voyage from New New York to Lost Angeles from three and a half hours to three hours and seventeen minutes, President Ronald Lump the Fifth marvelled that he could see that most of the landscape was still dotted with two story split level, ranch homes and tasteless prefabricated houses as he flew from Washedupton P.C. to Lost Angeles to receive the Petrochemical Industry's Humanitarian Man of the Year Award for removing baby Harp seals, Snowy White owls and Blue Whales from the National Endangered Species list there-by creating untold numbers of jobs to hundreds of workers.

Ж

THE END

Also by Paddy Kelly

Operation Underworld
2009

The American Way
2011

Don't Eat to Live. Live to Eat!
(A Book of Recipes)
2011

The Wolves of Calabria
2013

Children of the Nuclear Gods
2014

Politically Erect
2015

American Rhetoric
2016

Luck & Fame Are Four Letter Words
2017

Dr. Lindsay's Christmas
2017

The Broad in the Kimono
2018

Synopsis or option information available on line at:
http//writerpaddykelly or by contacting
paddy.incanto@gmail.co

www.ingramcontent.com/pod-product-compliance
Lightning Source LLC
Chambersburg PA
CBHW060452090426
42735CB00011B/1968